FIRST PLAYS FOR CHILDREN

First Plays for Children

*A collection of little plays
for the youngest players*

by
HELEN LOUISE MILLER

Publishers   PLAYS, INC.   Boston

Copyright © 1960, 1971 by
HELEN LOUISE MILLER

All Rights Reserved

CAUTION

All material in this volume is fully protected by copyright law. All rights, including motion picture, recitation, television, public reading, radio broadcasting, and rights of translation into foreign languages are strictly reserved.

NOTICE FOR AMATEUR PRODUCTION

These plays may be produced by schools, clubs, and similar amateur groups without payment of a royalty fee.

NOTICE FOR PROFESSIONAL PRODUCTION

For any form of non-amateur presentation (professional stage, radio or television), permission must be obtained in writing from the publisher. Inquiries should be addressed to PLAYS, INC., 8 Arlington Street, Boston, Massachusetts 02116.

Library of Congress Catalog Card Number: 60-8933
ISBN: 0-8238-0122-5

MANUFACTURED IN THE UNITED STATES OF AMERICA

Foreword to the Revised Edition

The small world of childhood is not so small after all. Through their imagination, children can transport themselves out of their environment, to a land of their own making, where they can be ten feet tall or three inches high—a land where they can roar like lions or squeak like mice, hop like rabbits, or soar like eagles. They can—and do—change their identities at will, to become princes or pirates, good guys or bad guys, or even inanimate objects—an airplane, a truck, a tree, a taxi, a tractor, a bouncing ball, or a bulldozer.

It is this quality of imagination, this power to pretend, this affinity for make-believe that generates the secret ingredient of self-expression and creativity and eventually becomes the key to self-understanding. Before children can know themselves, they must learn to know others, to understand their ways, their language, their thoughts, and their emotions. The ability to identify with other characters, real or imaginary, is the basis of self-identification and self-discovery.

So playacting becomes a tool, a key, not only to such disciplines as reading, language skills and speech arts, but also to group adjustment and participation by learning to follow directions, to speak and react on cue, and to understand the interdependence of the participants in a successful group activity.

But, best of all, playacting is fun, and the dramatized versions of everyday experiences, holiday situations, and familiar storybook plots contained in FIRST PLAYS FOR CHILDREN are designed for the pleasure of actors and audience. Thus, every group that produces a play enjoys the double delight of playmaking and playgoing.

The use of simple sets, costumes, and properties, as well as short speeches, easy rhymes, and familiar songs, keep production problems at a minimum. And since the plays are written for the many, rather than the few, the teacher or director can easily adjust the cast size.

FOREWORD

Although education for the seventies is geared to a changing world, the simple, everyday experiences of young children remain much the same from decade to decade. Boys and girls still color Easter eggs, go to the library, send Valentines, celebrate Christmas, learn to tell time, go on picnics, observe traffic rules and safety regulations, and look forward to favorite holiday treats. FIRST PLAYS FOR CHILDREN endeavors to present these familiar routines in lively dramatic style, with simple settings and storylines, exciting action, and engaging characters that emphasize the spirit and pleasure of the occasion.

Children are naturally given to laughter. Their funny bones are easily tickled by the absurd in visual form—the slapstick fall of the comedian, the exaggerated walk or antics of a clown or "ham," the use of outlandish costumes. But when they learn to chuckle over the spoken word, a funny line, or a printed page, and can follow the amusing pattern of a situation comedy which reflects, in part, their own foibles, they are taking their first step toward developing a true sense of humor. It is my hope that the short comedies in FIRST PLAYS FOR CHILDREN will be a happy introduction to the wonderful world of theater.

—Helen Louise Miller
York, Pa., 1971

CONTENTS

FOREWORD	v
THE BUSY BARBERS	3
THE HALF-PINT COWBOY	14
THE BROKEN BROOMSTICK (*Halloween*)	26
SPUNKY PUNKY (*Halloween*)	35
THE WISHING STREAM	45
THE LIBRARY CIRCUS (*Book Week*)	58
THE MOTHER GOOSE BAKESHOP	69
THANKFUL'S RED BEADS (*Thanksgiving*)	80
A THANKSGIVING RIDDLE (*Thanksgiving*)	92
A VISIT TO GOLDILOCKS	102
THE LOST CHRISTMAS CARDS (*Christmas*)	112
WAKE UP, SANTA CLAUS! (*Christmas*)	123
THE REAL PRINCESS	135
THE SAFETY CLINIC	148
TEN PENNIES FOR LINCOLN (*Lincoln's Birthday*)	158
THE COUNTRY STORE CAT	167
WAIT AND SEE	181
A SHOWER OF HEARTS (*Valentine's Day*)	188
THE WEATHERMAN ON TRIAL	199
OLD GLORY GROWS UP (*Washington's Birthday*)	211
GARDEN HOLD-UP	222
THE RABBITS WHO CHANGED THEIR MINDS (*Easter*)	233
TROUBLE IN TICK-TOCK TOWN	243

CONTENTS

MAY DAY FOR MOTHER (*Mother's Day*)   255
THREE LITTLE KITTENS   266
THE TEDDY BEAR HERO (*Memorial Day*)   275

PRODUCTION NOTES   285

FIRST PLAYS FOR CHILDREN

THE BUSY BARBERS

Characters

CLIPPY
SNIPPY } *the busy barbers*
NIPPY
PRESTO, *the magic barber*
PRESTO'S HELPER
BARBER POLE

Customers:

JUDY	FRED
BETTY	BENNY
JACK	LENNY
MARY	TED
BOB	PRUE
JANE	MOLLY
BILLY	POLLY
JOE	SUE
SALLY	MOTHERS *(14)*

SETTING: *A barber shop. There are three large chairs at center stage, and chairs or benches upstage for customers.*

AT RISE: *Beside each large chair stands a* BARBER, *with a large pair of silver cardboard scissors. On each chair is a large towel or bib.* JUDY, BETTY, JACK, MARY, BOB, JANE, BILLY, JOE, *and* SALLY *are seated on the benches. The children wear name cards.*

BARBERS (*In concert*): We are three busy Barbers.
We each have a chair.
We serve little children
By cutting their hair.
CLIPPY (*Bowing*): I'm Clippy.
SNIPPY (*Bowing*): I'm Snippy.
NIPPY (*Bowing*): I'm Nippy.
CUSTOMERS (*In concert*): And we are the children,
As you will soon learn,
Who sit here in patience,
And wait for our turn
With Clippy, (CLIPPY *bows.*)
With Snippy, (SNIPPY *bows.*)
With Nippy. (NIPPY *bows.*)

We love to watch Barbers.
And see what they do,
And if you are quiet,
We'll let you look, too.
Watch Clippy, (CLIPPY *bows.*)
Watch Snippy, (SNIPPY *bows.*)
Watch Nippy. (NIPPY *bows.*)

(BARBERS *pick up towels from chairs as* JUDY, BETTY, *and* JACK *come forward and climb into the chairs.*)
CHILDREN (*Singing to tune "Did You Ever See a Lassie?"*): Did you ever see a Barber, a Barber, a Barber,

Did you ever see a Barber do this way and that?
Do this way and that way, do this way and that way,
Did you ever see a Barber do this way and that?
(*On first verse* BARBERS *shake out their towels and fasten them around the* CUSTOMERS' *necks.*)
CUSTOMERS (*Singing*): Did you ever see a Barber, a Barber, a Barber,
Did you ever see a Barber snip this way and that?
Snip this way and that way, snip this way and that way?
Did you ever see a Barber snip this way and that?
(*On second verse* BARBERS *wield their cardboard scissors in pantomime of haircutting.*)
CUSTOMERS (*Singing*): Did you ever see a Barber, a Barber, a Barber,
Did you ever see a Barber rub this way and that?
Rub this way and that way, rub this way and that way,
Did you ever see a Barber rub this way and that?
(*On third verse* BARBERS *rub* CUSTOMERS' *heads vigorously.*)
CUSTOMERS (*Singing*): Did you ever see a Barber, a Barber, a Barber,
Did you ever see a Barber comb this way and that?
Comb this way and that way, comb this way and that way,
Did you ever see a Barber comb this way and that?
(*On fourth verse* BARBERS *comb their* CUSTOMERS' *hair.*)

CUSTOMERS (*Singing*): Did you ever see a Barber, a Barber, a Barber,
Did you ever see a Barber brush this way and that?
Brush this way and that way, brush this way and that way,
Did you ever see a Barber brush this way and that?
(*On last verse* BARBERS *brush imaginary hair from necks and shoulders of* CUSTOMERS, *unpin towels, and assist them from their chairs.*)

CUSTOMERS (*In concert*): Our thanks for the haircuts.
They're really quite nice.
We reach in our pockets (*Pretend to do so*)
And pay you the price.
To Clippy, (CLIPPY *bows.*)
To Snippy, (SNIPPY *bows.*)
To Nippy. (NIPPY *bows.*)

BARBERS (*As* JUDY, BETTY, *and* JACK *exit*): Next! (*As three new* CUSTOMERS, BILLY, JOE, *and* SALLY, *come forward and climb into the chairs,* PRESTO *enters, followed by his* HELPER *and his* BARBER POLE. *He carries a folding canvas chair. His* HELPER *and* BARBER POLE *carry a folding screen on which there is a sign* "TRICKY HAIRCUTS." *They stride past the three* BARBERS, *and* PRESTO *sets up his folding chair on opposite side of the stage. The* HELPER *and* BARBER POLE *set up the screen in front of the chair and stand on either side of it.*)

HELPER (*Pointing to* PRESTO *who stands center stage*):
He's Presto, the Barber, and I am his aide.

BARBER POLE: And I am the sign of the barbering trade.

BOTH: We're ready for business.

This way, if you please.
You'll get twice the service
For double the fees!

PRESTO (*Waving his scissors, as he makes a deep bow*):
I'm Presto the Barber.
I know every trick.
I'll give you a haircut
That's shiny and slick.

CUSTOMERS: So can Clippy, and Snippy, and Nippy.

PRESTO: I use magic scissors.
I know every style.
I can give you a haircut
To make you all smile.

CUSTOMERS: So can Clippy, and Snippy, and Nippy.

PRESTO: I'll show you my haircuts
Right here on the spot.
My scissors will change you
To someone you're not.

CUSTOMERS: What do you mean?

PRESTO: I'll make our friend Billy
Have straight hair like Joe.
And give little Sally
Real curls with a bow!

CUSTOMERS: You're fooling! You're fooling!
You talk through your hat!
No one can do magic
With haircuts like that!
Not Clippy! (CLIPPY *bows*.)
Nor Snippy! (SNIPPY *bows*.)
Nor Nippy! (NIPPY *bows*.)

PRESTO: I vow I will please you.
So happy you'll be.
And if you still doubt me,
Just try me and see.
My scissors will give you
The hair you like best.
So, if you step forward,
I'll fill your request.
(*The three children already in the barber chairs stand up and are joined by* MARY, JANE *and* BOB.)
MARY: I'd like to be different.
BOB: That's right! So would I.
ALL: Well, what do you say
That we give him a try?
CLIPPY, SNIPPY, *and* NIPPY: Beware! Beware!
He'll wreck your hair!
It's a trick! It's a trick! It's a trick!
(MARY *and* JANE *approach* PRESTO. JANE *has straight hair.* MARY's *is curly.*)
JANE: I'd like to look like Mary.
MARY: I'd like to look like Jane.
JANE: I'd like to have some fancy curls.
MARY: And I would like mine plain.
HELPER *and* BARBER POLE: Right this way, little ladies.
Right this way. (*Girls go behind screen.*)
PRESTO (*Twirling his mustache and brandishing his scissors*): I'm Presto, the Barber.
Just watch what I do!
In a very few minutes
You'll see who is who!

CLIPPY, SNIPPY, NIPPY (*Sitting forlornly in their chairs*): We know they'll be sorry,
And all hate this day.
We hoped they would listen.
We hoped they would stay
With Clippy,
And Snippy,
And Nippy.
(MARY *and* JANE *appear from behind screen. They have exchanged name signs.* MARY *is now* JANE. JANE *is* MARY.)
CUSTOMERS (*Clapping their hands*): He did it! He did it! Jane looks like Mary. Mary looks like Jane!
BOB: Quick, quick, Mr. Presto. Joe and I want to be next.
CUSTOMERS: It's fun to look like someone else,
And change your eye-appeal.
Let's rush to Mr. Presto,
And get a whole new deal.
(CUSTOMERS *rush to* MR. PRESTO'S *chair, joined by eight more children, who come running on stage.* HELPER *and* BARBER POLE *try to keep order.*)
HELPER *and* BARBER POLE: Get in line! Get in line! One at a time! (*Children line up in order of their speeches.*)
MOLLY: I want to look like Polly.
PRUE: I want to look like Sue.
POLLY: I want to look like Molly.
SUE: I want to look like Prue.
LENNY: I want to look like Benny.

TED: I want to look like Fred.
BENNY: I want to look like Lenny.
FRED: I want to look like Ted.
   (PRESTO *takes each couple behind screen, where they exchange name tags. Meanwhile,* BARBER POLE *steps forward, smiling smugly at the* BARBERS.)
BARBER POLE: Ho ho! Ha ha! It makes me laugh
   To see what Presto's done!
   He's taken all your customers,
   And stolen all your fun!
   I hope you've learned your lesson,
   And henceforth will be wise.
   When you go into business,
   It pays to advertise!
CLIPPY: In advertising Presto,
   You've made a big mistake!
SNIPPY: He's nothing but a pest-o!
NIPPY: He's nothing but a fake!
BARBER POLE: You'll be sorry! (*Goes behind screen*)
SNIPPY: Just look at our shop!
NIPPY: Not a soul is in sight!
CLIPPY, SNIPPY, NIPPY: We're three lonely barbers;
   We've lost all our trade.
   We're praying for someone
   To come to our aid.
   (MOTHERS *enter, each carrying umbrella and wearing sign*—Jane's Mother, Mary's Mother, *etc.*)
MARY'S MOTHER: I've come for my daughter Mary.
JANE'S MOTHER: And I for my Jane.
MARY: Here I am, Mother. (*Walks to her mother.*)

JANE: I'm here, Mother. (*Walks to her mother.*)
MARY'S MOTHER (*Pushing* MARY *away*): But Mary has *curly* hair!
JANE'S MOTHER (*Pushing* JANE *away*): And Jane has *straight* hair!
GIRLS' MOTHERS (*Ad lib*): I want Polly. I want Sue. I want Molly. I want Prue. (*Etc.*)
PRUE, SUE, POLLY, MOLLY: Here we are, Mother. See, we have new haircuts. (MOTHERS *thrust them away.*)
GIRLS' MOTHERS (*Ad lib*): You're not my daughter! Who are you? You're not Prue! (*Etc.*)
BENNY'S MOTHER: I want my Benny.
FRED'S MOTHER: I want my Fred.
LENNY'S MOTHER: I want my Lenny.
TED'S MOTHER: I want my Ted.
BOYS: Here we are, Mother. See, we have new haircuts. (MOTHERS *thrust children from them.*)
BOYS' MOTHERS (*Ad lib*): You're not Benny. You're not Fred. You're not Lenny. You're not Ted. (*Etc.*)
CHILDREN (*Together*): Our mothers don't know us.
 They can't tell who's who.
 Oh, please, Mr. Presto,
 Oh, what can you do?
PRESTO (*Stepping forward*): Perhaps I can explain.
MOTHERS (*Pointing at him with umbrellas*): Who is he?
PRESTO: I'm Presto, the Barber.
 With my magic shears
 I gave magic haircuts
 To each of your dears.
MOTHERS: You've made our children look like somebody else! (*They shake umbrellas at him threateningly.*)

PRESTO (*Raising arms to protect himself*): Please, ladies, please! It was what the children wanted.

CHILDREN: We don't want it now. We want to look like ourselves.

MOTHERS: Undo your magic right away.

PRESTO: But, ladies! (MOTHERS *belabor him with umbrellas. He shields himself*) Stop! Stop! I will take back my magic. (MOTHERS *step back and* CHILDREN *stand in line.* PRESTO *waves his scissors over their heads.*) Presto, Presto,
Ixnay, Esto,
Northo, Southo,
Easto, Westo!
With a snip, snip here
And a snip, snip there,
I give these children back their hair.
(CHILDREN *quickly exchange name cards and run to their own* MOTHERS. NOTE: *Exchange of cards may be done behind screen.*)

MOTHERS (*To* PRESTO, *raising umbrellas*): Now, take your magic scissors and get out of here. (*They start to chase him off the stage.*)

PRESTO (*To* HELPER *and* BARBER POLE): Come on, boys. This is no place for us! (*He picks up folding chair; the other two pick up screen and run off, pursued by* MOTHERS.)

CHILDREN: Next time we get haircuts,
We'll do as we're told.
We'll stay with our barber
And be good as gold,

(CHILDREN *sing to tune of* "*Barber, Barber, Shave a Pig.*") Barber, Barber, cut my hair.
Please, Mr. Barber, do take care.
Snip, snip here and snip, snip there,
Please, let us sit in your barber chair.
(*First three children climb into the chairs of* CLIPPY, SNIPPY *and* NIPPY. BARBER POLE *enters.*)

BARBER POLE (*Wailing*): I'm out of a job!
Oh, what shall I do?

CLIPPY: Mr. Barber Pole, be gone.

SNIPPY: We don't want your tricks!

NIPPY: Good barbering and magic
Will never, never mix! (BARBER POLE *looks at them dejectedly and exits.*)

CLIPPY, SNIPPY, NIPPY (*Adjusting towels*): We're three happy Barbers;
We want you to know
That this is the ending
Of our little show.
Next time you need haircuts,
We ask every one
To steer clear of magic,
And hope you will come
To Clippy, (CLIPPY *bows.*)
To Snippy, (SNIPPY *bows.*)
And Nippy. (NIPPY *bows.*)

THE END

THE HALF-PINT COWBOY

Characters

HALF-PINT	COWBOY DAVE
LITTLE RED DOG	COWBOY SLIM
CHIEF RED DOG	COWBOY SPIKE
COWBOY JIM	COWBOY HANK
COWBOY PETE	COWBOY CHUCK
COWBOY JOE	RUSTLER
COWBOY BILL	HUSTLER
COWBOY STEVE	BUSTLER
COWBOY SAM	FIVE INDIAN BRAVES
COWBOY DAN	

TIME: *The days of the old West.*
SETTING: *The Bar-X Ranch.*
AT RISE: HALF-PINT *is sitting on a hitching post or section of the rail fence. His broomstick horse is tied to one of the rails. A big cooking kettle is hung over a small campfire, beside which is a wooden bench with a water bucket, dipper, and some tin plates and spoons.*

HALF-PINT: I'm a little cowboy
   With muscles strong and tough,
   But for everything I want to do
   I'm never big enough!

I'm a little cowboy
Pistols at my side;
Got a little pony—
You should see me ride!

Got my cowboy lasso.
I can swing it, too!
But I'm never big enough
For what I want to do!

Got my boots and saddle,
Got a lot of stuff.
But for everything I want to do,
I'm never big enough! (COWBOYS JIM, PETE, JOE, *and* BILL *enter on broomstick horses. They ride in a circle, brandishing their guns and yelling a prolonged "Yippee!"*)

HALF-PINT: Hi, pardners!
COWBOYS: Hi, pardner!
HALF-PINT: Where are you going?
COWBOY JIM: To catch the rustlers who have been stealing our cattle.
HALF-PINT: Please take me along.
COWBOY PETE: Sorry, Half-Pint. You're not big enough.
HALF-PINT: I am so! I am so big enough!
COWBOY JOE: One of those rustlers might catch you and hang you on his belt for a watch fob.
COWBOY BILL: You stay here and look after things at the ranch. We have work to do. Come on, boys, let's hit the trail!
ALL: Yippee! Yippee! (*Exit four* COWBOYS)

HALF-PINT (*To audience*): See! What did I tell you? I'm never big enough! (*Enter* COWBOYS STEVE, SAM, DAN, *and* DAVE, *also on broomstick horses. They circle the stage, yelling and swinging their lariats.*) Hi, pardners!

COWBOYS: Hi, pardner!

HALF-PINT: Where are you going?

COWBOY STEVE: Out on the range to round up our stolen cattle.

HALF-PINT: Please take me along.

COWBOY DAN: Sorry, Half-Pint! You're not big enough!

HALF-PINT: I am so! I am so big enough!

COWBOY SAM: One of those steers might take you for a blade of grass, and swallow you in one bite.

COWBOY DAVE: You stay here and look after things at the ranch. We have work to do. Come on, boys, let's hit the trail!

ALL: Yippee! Yippee! (*Exit four* COWBOYS)

HALF-PINT (*To audience*): See! This is the way it is all the time! I'm just never big enough! (COWBOYS SLIM, SPIKE, HANK, *and* CHUCK *enter. They circle the stage on their broomstick mounts, yelling and waving their hats.*) Hi, pardners!

COWBOYS: Hi, pardner!

HALF-PINT: Where are you going?

COWBOY SLIM: To head off an Indian war party at Buckaroo Pass.

HALF-PINT: Please take me along.

COWBOY HANK: Sorry, Half-Pint. You're not big enough!

HALF-PINT: I am so! I am so big enough!
COWBOY SPIKE: There may be fighting! One of those Indians might take your scalp. They have a special fancy for curly hair!
COWBOY CHUCK: You stay here and look after things at the ranch. We have work to do. Come on, boys, let's hit the trail!
ALL: Yippee! Yippee! (*Exit four* COWBOYS)
HALF-PINT (*To audience*): See! What did I tell you? I'm never big enough to have any fun! Well, I'll show them! I'll run away and ride the range all by myself. That's what I'll do. But first I'll have to pack my things. (*Exit* HALF-PINT. LITTLE RED DOG *enters. He is hurt, so he crawls in, dragging one foot, stopping every now and then for a few groans and cries of "Water! Water!" He drags himself to the bench. Sees water bucket and dipper. Tries to get a dipper of water, but drops the dipper and sinks back on stage.* HALF-PINT *enters with bundle tied in bandanna.*)
HALF-PINT: Now I have plenty of food, but I must get some water. (*Sees* LITTLE RED DOG) Who are you? How did you get here?
LITTLE RED DOG (*Moaning*): Water! Water!
HALF-PINT (*Gets him a dipper of water and raises his head so he can drink*): Here! Here you are! Take it easy or you'll choke. My goodness! You sure are thirsty. What is your name?
LITTLE RED DOG: Me Little Red Dog. Father Chief Red Dog!
HALF-PINT: Chief Red Dog!

LITTLE RED DOG (*Moaning*): My foot! It hurts!

HALF-PINT: No wonder! (*Looking at it*) You must have sprained your ankle. What happened?

LITTLE RED DOG: Wild pony—ran away. I crawled in forest since rising sun.

HALF-PINT: You must be hungry as well as thirsty. And look! There's a bump on your head. I know what to do for that! (*Opens bundle, soaks bandanna in water and ties it around* LITTLE RED DOG'S *head.*)

LITTLE RED DOG: Feels good.

HALF-PINT: That's what my mother does when I bump my head. Now, you may eat my sandwiches while I look at your ankle.

LITTLE RED DOG (*Sitting up*): Ummm! Good! (*Gobbles a sandwich*)

HALF-PINT: I was going to eat this food when I ran away, but I'm glad to give it to you. (*Pressing ankle*) Does this hurt?

LITTLE RED DOG: Ouch!

HALF-PINT: I think I can bandage it. Then maybe you can stand up. (*Takes second bandanna from his pack*) Now hold still. (*Bandages ankle*) There! Now see if you can stand up.

LITTLE RED DOG: Me try. (*Bears weight on* HALF-PINT *as he tries to stand*) Ouch!

HALF-PINT: Sit over here. (*Helps* LITTLE RED DOG *hobble to bench*) Are you still hungry?

LITTLE RED DOG: More food.

HALF-PINT: I think there's some stew. (*Dips some stew from kettle on fire*) Here. Eat this.

LITTLE RED DOG (*Eating*): Heap good stew!
HALF-PINT: Your folks will be worried about you. Where is your father, Chief Red Dog?
LITTLE RED DOG: Lead war party to Buckaroo Pass.
HALF-PINT: Buckaroo Pass!
LITTLE RED DOG: We send smoke signals. He come back for Little Red Dog.
HALF-PINT: Do you know how to send smoke signals?
LITTLE RED DOG: Me send plenty smoke signals. (*Takes blanket off shoulders*) Me got blanket—you got fire.
HALF-PINT (*Removing tripod and kettle*): Let's go. Think you can walk?
LITTLE RED DOG: Me walk. (*Hobbles to fire. He and* HALF-PINT *go through motions of sending smoke signals with blanket.*)
HALF-PINT: What does it say, Little Red Dog?
LITTLE RED DOG: Say Little Red Dog! Help! When my father see smoke signal, he come.
HALF-PINT: What about the war party?
LITTLE RED DOG: War party can wait! Little Red Dog, Chief Red Dog's only son!
HALF-PINT: I hope they come soon.
LITTLE RED DOG: They come. (*Leans over and puts ear to ground*) They come now.
HALF-PINT: How can you tell?
LITTLE RED DOG: Listen.
HALF-PINT (*Puts ear to ground*): I don't hear a thing.
LITTLE RED DOG: Paleface bad ears! Little Red Dog hear horses. They come.
HALF-PINT: Are they coming closer?

LITTLE RED DOG: No more horses. They get off. Tie horses in woods. Come on foot. (*Enter* CHIEF RED DOG *with five* INDIAN BRAVES.) My father! You have come.

CHIEF RED DOG: I come. (*Pointing to bandages*) You hurt? Paleface do this? (BRAVES *draw tomahawks and approach* HALF-PINT.)

LITTLE RED DOG: No! No! Paleface good friend. Give Little Red Dog water—food—bind up ankle.

CHIEF RED DOG: Humph! Make war on palefaces! Palefaces bad men!

LITTLE RED DOG: Not *this* paleface, Father. This paleface good friend to Little Red Dog. (*Holds up plate of food*) See—paleface shares meat with Little Red Dog.

CHIEF RED DOG (*Sniffing*): Umm! Smell good!

HALF-PINT: There's plenty here, Chief Red Dog. There's enough for you and your men.

CHIEF RED DOG: Humph! (*To* BRAVES) Sit! War party wait! (*All sit in circle as* HALF-PINT *dishes up stew*.)

ALL: Umm! Good!

CHIEF RED DOG: You, Paleface Boy, what's your name?

HALF-PINT: They call me Half-Pint.

CHIEF RED DOG: Me call you Little Chief Half-Pint. We smoke 'em peace pipe.

HALF-PINT: I don't think I know how to smoke a peace pipe.

CHIEF RED DOG: Watch. (*Takes out peace pipe, pretends to light it. Draws a puff and passes it to* HALF-PINT) Now you smoke 'em!

HALF-PINT (*Smokes peace pipe with much choking and sputtering*): What does that mean?
CHIEF RED DOG: Smoke 'em peace pipe! No more war party! (*Pointing to each boy*) Little Red Dog, little Half-Pint—brothers! Now we go. (*Rises with* BRAVES)
HALF-PINT (*To* LITTLE RED DOG): I hope you feel better.
LITTLE RED DOG: Me better, brother. Thanks.
HALF-PINT: Will you come and see me again?
CHIEF RED DOG: He come again soon. (*Exit all* INDIANS)
HALF-PINT: I guess I won't run away after all. It's a good thing I was here to take care of Little Red Dog. I'll take these things back to the bunkhouse. (*As he collects his scattered belongings, three* RUSTLERS *enter. They wear masks and carry toy guns.*)
RUSTLER: Stick 'em up, buddy.
HUSTLER: And don't make a sound.
BUSTLER: We mean business!
HALF-PINT: Help! Help! Who are you?
RUSTLER: I told you—not a sound.
HUSTLER: Reach for the sky, kid.
BUSTLER: Are you alone here?
HALF-PINT: Yes, yes, I am all alone. What do you want?
RUSTLER: You'll soon find out. Maybe you've heard of us. I'm Rustler.
HUSTLER: I'm Hustler!
BUSTLER: I'm Bustler!
HALF-PINT: You're the cattle thieves. My partners are looking for you right now.

RUSTLER: They'll never find us.
HUSTLER: Nor the cattle either. We have them in a safe place.
BUSTLER: Now we've come for the horses.
RUSTLER: Let's tie this kid up and go get them.
HALF-PINT (*Struggling as they try to tie him up*): No! No! Help! Help! (INDIANS *rush in with tomahawks. There is a scramble, but* INDIANS *grab* RUSTLERS *and hold them with their hands behind their backs.*)
CHIEF RED DOG (*To* BRAVES): Take their scalps.
RUSTLERS: No! No! Help! Help! Please save us! Save us!
HALF-PINT: No, please, Chief Red Dog. Don't scalp them. My partners will be home soon.
BRAVES (*Raising tomahawks*): Scalp 'em! Scalp 'em! Scalp 'em!
CHIEF RED DOG: Scalps belong to white warriors. Tie them up. (BRAVES *tie prisoners' hands behind their backs.*) When white brothers come home, they take scalps.
HALF-PINT: No, they will put the rustlers in jail. This is the white man's law.
CHIEF RED DOG: White man make funny law.
HALF-PINT: You came back just in time. I thought you had gone for good.
CHIEF RED DOG: Came back to make present. (*Hands* HALF-PINT *the peace pipe.*) Tell Paleface Chief to make ready for peace pow-wow. We smoke 'em peace pipe after morning sun. We sign 'em peace paper. No more war between brothers.
BRAVES (*Sadly*): No more scalps!

CHIEF RED DOG: We follow white man's law. Come, we go. (*Exit* INDIANS *leaving* RUSTLERS *tied up on the ground.*)
RUSTLER: Hey, let us go, kid.
HUSTLER: Your cattle are safe in Bloody Canyon.
BUSTLER: We'll never bother you again.
HALF-PINT: Nothing doing! (*Enter* COWBOYS JIM, PETE, JOE *and* BILL, *on foot.*) Hi, pardners. Look what I have!
COWBOYS: The rustlers!
COWBOY JIM: How did you do it, Half-Pint?
COWBOY PETE: We rode all day without a trace of them.
COWBOY JOE: We'll have these boys behind bars before sundown.
COWBOY BILL: How did you do it, Half-Pint? How did you do it?
HALF-PINT: I didn't do it. My friend, Chief Red Dog, captured them.
ALL: Chief Red Dog! (*Enter* COWBOYS STEVE, DAN, SAM *and* DAVE, *on foot.*)
HALF-PINT: Hi, pardners! Any luck with the cattle?
COWBOY STEVE: Not a trace of them.
COWBOY DAN: Look! Look! The cattle thieves!
COWBOY SAM: What have you done with our cattle, you dogs?
COWBOY DAVE: Where are they?
HALF-PINT: The cattle are safe in Bloody Canyon.
COWBOY JIM: Half-Pint captured the rustlers single-handed.
HALF-PINT: No, I didn't. It was Chief Red Dog and his

men. (*Enter* COWBOYS SLIM, HANK, SPIKE *and* CHUCK, *on foot*.)

ALL: Half-Pint, are you all right?

COWBOY SLIM: The Indians gave us the slip.

COWBOY HANK: They never showed up at Buckaroo Pass.

COWBOY SPIKE: We were afraid they were heading this way.

COWBOY CHUCK: Chief Red Dog is leading the war party.

HALF-PINT: Not any more he isn't! Chief Red Dog is our friend. (*Showing peace pipe*) Look, here is his peace pipe. He is coming tomorrow for a peace pow-wow.

COWBOYS: Well, I'll be jiggered!

COWBOY JIM: How did a "half-pint" like you manage to do all this?

COWBOY JOE: You captured the rustlers.

COWBOY SAM: You found our cattle.

COWBOY SLIM: And you made peace with Chief Red Dog.

ALL: And you're not as big as a pound of soap!

HALF-PINT: Little Red Dog was thrown from his pony. I bandaged his ankle and gave him food. Chief Red Dog was grateful.

COWBOY SLIM: But the cattle thieves? What about them?

HALF-PINT: They came here to steal our horses. Chief Red Dog and his men tied them up.

RUSTLERS: They wanted to scalp us!

HALF-PINT: But I saved them for you.
COWBOY CHUCK (*To* RUSTLERS): On your feet!
RUSTLERS: What are you going to do with us?
COWBOY HANK: Thanks to Half-Pint, you still have your hair!
COWBOY SLIM: We're going to turn you over to the sheriff!
HALF-PINT: Please! Am I big enough to go along?
JIM, PETE, JOE, BILL: You were big enough to capture these varmints.
STEVE, SAM, DAN, DAVE: You were big enough to find our cattle!
SLIM, HANK, SPIKE, CHUCK: You were big enough to stop a war!
ALL: So you're big enough for us!
COWBOY JIM: From now on, pardner, we're going to call you Big Enough instead of Half-Pint. How do you like that?
HALF-PINT: I like that fine.
COWBOY STEVE: Then come along, Big Enough, it's time to hit the trail! (HALF-PINT *covers his prisoners with his pistols as the other cowboys line up behind him singing refrain from "The Old Chisholm Trail" as the curtain falls.*)

THE END

THE BROKEN BROOMSTICK

Characters

LITTLE WITCH	THREE JACK-O-LANTERNS
THREE SMALL SKELETONS	MR. GREEN GOBLIN
BLACK CAT	MR. OWL
MR. GHOST	OLD WOMAN IN THE SHOE
MRS. GHOST	CHILDREN
SONNY GHOST	

TIME: *Halloween night.*
SETTING: *A clearing in the woods.*
AT RISE: LITTLE WITCH *is sitting on a tree stump, crying. She is holding her broomstick, which is broken in two.*

LITTLE WITCH: Boo hoo, boo hoo!
What shall I do?
My broomstick's broken
Right in two!
Oh, me! Oh, my!
It makes me cry!
With broken broom,
I cannot fly! (THREE SMALL SKELETONS *skip on stage. When they reach center stage, they stop and bow to the audience.*)

SMALL SKELETONS (*Together*): Three Small Skeletons,
On our way to scare you!
Want to come along with us?
We dee-dee-double dare you!
1ST SMALL SKELETON (*Seeing* LITTLE WITCH): Look!
There's a little witch all by herself!
2ND SMALL SKELETON: Maybe she'd like to join us.
3RD SMALL SKELETON: Let's ask her.
SMALL SKELETONS (*Together*): Hello, Little Witch,
and Happy Halloween.
LITTLE WITCH: Hello, Small Skeletons and Happy Halloween to you. Where are you going?
1ST SMALL SKELETON: We're going out to scare people.
Want to come along?
LITTLE WITCH (*Sadly*): I can't. My broomstick is
broken. I can't fly without it.
1ST SMALL SKELETON (*Looking at broomstick*): Too
bad! Too bad! It's broken in half.
LITTLE WITCH: Could you please mend it for me?
2ND SMALL SKELETON: Oh, no! We couldn't do that.
3RD SMALL SKELETON: You see, we are only bones. If
we work too hard, we might break.
1ST SMALL SKELETON: Yes, we might break in half like
your broomstick.
2ND SMALL SKELETON: Then who would put us together
again?
3RD SMALL SKELETON: Sorry. We'd like to help you, but
we can't. (*Exit* SMALL SKELETONS.)
LITTLE WITCH (*With a sigh*): Oh, well. I'll just have to
sit here until someone else comes along. (*There is a*

meowing sound offstage. LITTLE WITCH *jumps up.*)
What's that? What's that? (*Enter large* BLACK CAT *meowing and arching his back.*)

BLACK CAT: Meow! Meow! Meow!
It's Halloween, I vow.
Meow! Meow! Meow!
I'll have some fun right now!

LITTLE WITCH (*Calling*): Here, kitty, kitty, kitty! Here, pussy, pussy, pussy!

BLACK CAT (*Looking around*): Who could be calling me such silly names! "Kitty, kitty, kitty" and "pussy, pussy, pussy!" That's sissy stuff! I'm the big Black Cat that walks the fences on Halloween Night and sings to the moon! I don't have to listen to anyone!

LITTLE WITCH: Please, listen to me, Mr. Cat. I am in trouble.

BLACK CAT: Hello, Little Witch. Why aren't you flying through the air for Halloween?

LITTLE WITCH: My broomstick is broken. Will you please fix it for me?

BLACK CAT: Bless my whiskers! I'd like to do that for you, Little Witch, but I can't spare the time. I have to start walking fences right away.

LITTLE WITCH: Oh, dear! I'm so lonely here by myself on Halloween. I want to be out scaring people.

BLACK CAT: Look over there. (*Points offstage*) Here come the Ghosts. Maybe they can help you. I really must go. (*Exits reciting*)
Meow! Meow! Meow!
It's Halloween, I vow.

Meow! Meow! Meow!
I'll have some fun right now! (MR. *and* MRS. GHOST *enter with* SONNY *between them.*)
MRS. GHOST: Now remember, Sonny, whenever we meet anyone this evening, you must say *boo!*
MR. GHOST: And say it good and loud, like this: Boo! Boo! Boo!
SONNY: I'll remember. (*Practices*) Boo! Boo! Boo!
LITTLE WITCH: Good evening, Ghosts! (*All* GHOSTS *jump as if scared.*) Excuse me, I didn't mean to frighten you.
SONNY (*Trying to hide behind* MRS. GHOST): Oooh! I'm afraid!
MR. GHOST: It's only a Little Witch, Sonny. She won't hurt you.
MRS. GHOST: Remember your manners, Sonny. Say *boo* to the Little Witch.
SONNY (*Timidly*): Boo!
MR. GHOST: You seem to be in trouble. Your broomstick is broken.
LITTLE WITCH: Yes, can you help me? Do you know how to mend a broomstick?
MR. GHOST: Mend a broomstick! Dear me! No! You must remember I am only a Bed Sheet!
MRS. GHOST: And Sonny is only a Pillow Slip!
MR. GHOST: We don't know a thing about broomsticks!
MRS. GHOST: Come along, Sonny. Say *boo* to the lady and we'll be on our way.
SONNY (*As they exit*): Boo! Boo! Boo!
LITTLE WITCH (*Crossly*): Oh, boo, yourself! I guess I'll

have to stay here all night before anyone will help me. Look! There's a light! I wonder who's coming now. (*Enter* THREE JACK-O-LANTERNS. *When they reach center stage, they sing the following song to the tune of "Frère Jacques."*)

JACK-O-LANTERNS: Jack-o-Lantern, Jack-o-Lantern,
See us glow! See us glow!
See us as we glimmer,
Growing bright or dimmer,
Glow, glow, glow!
Glow, glow, glow!

LITTLE WITCH: Good evening, Jack-o-Lanterns. You look so jolly. Can you help me?

1ST JACK-O-LANTERN: What can we do for you, Little Witch?

LITTLE WITCH: Can you mend my broomstick? See, it is broken.

2ND JACK-O-LANTERN: What a pity!

3RD JACK-O-LANTERN: I'd like to help you, Little Witch. But I am only a head.

JACK-O-LANTERNS (*Together*): We can't mend your broomstick for you! We have no hands!

LITTLE WITCH: Oh, dear! I never thought of that. Well, thanks anyway.

JACK-O-LANTERNS: You're welcome.

1ST JACK-O-LANTERN: If it will cheer you up, we'll sing our little song for you again.

LITTLE WITCH: Please do.

JACK-O-LANTERNS: Jack-o-Lantern, Jack-o-Lantern, *etc.* (*They repeat song and exit.*)

LITTLE WITCH: It's getting later and later. Halloween will soon be over. (*Enter* GREEN GOBLIN *making faces at himself in a mirror.*) Here comes a Goblin. Maybe he can help me. Please, Mr. Goblin, do you know how to mend a broomstick?

GREEN GOBLIN (*Still looking in hand mirror*): Go away, don't bother me. I'm busy making faces to scare people.

LITTLE WITCH: Show me some of your faces, please. I'd like to learn how to make real scary ones.

GREEN GOBLIN: It's easy. This is all you do.
Eyebrows up!
Eyebrows down!
First a grin!
And then a frown!
Show your tongue!
Squinch your nose!
Wiggle your ears,
And hold the pose! (*Winds up with a horrible face*)

LITTLE WITCH (*Clapping her hands*): That was lovely. Do it again—please.

GREEN GOBLIN: Sorry. There isn't time. I'm in a hurry.

LITTLE WITCH: Could you take time to mend my broomstick, please, Mr. Goblin?

GREEN GOBLIN: Not tonight, Little Witch. I'm too busy. Good-bye, see you next Halloween. (*Exit* GREEN GOBLIN.)

LITTLE WITCH: Oh, dear! I'm missing all the fun just because of this broken broomstick. And who will help me? Who will mend my broomstick? (*Sound of*

Whoooo . . . Whoooo) Who's that? Who's that?

MR. OWL (*Entering with a great flap of wings*): To whit, to woo,
I'm here to help you!

LITTLE WITCH: Oh, Mr. Owl, do you really mean it? Will you mend my broomstick?

MR. OWL: I can't mend your broomstick, Little Witch. But I am very wise. I know how you can get a whole new broom.

LITTLE WITCH: How? Tell me. Please, tell me.

MR. OWL: Do you know the Old Woman in the Shoe?

LITTLE WITCH: The one who has so many children she doesn't know what to do?

MR. OWL: That's the one.

LITTLE WITCH: Yes, I know her.

MR. OWL: Tonight the Old Woman will be taking her children to see the Halloween parade. They always use this path through the forest.

LITTLE WITCH: What does that have to do with my broomstick?

MR. OWL: The Old Woman always takes her broom with her to sweep the leaves away from the path. She doesn't want the children to track them into the house.

LITTLE WITCH: What must I do?

MR. OWL: Call on your friends, the Skeletons, Mr. Cat, the Ghosts, the Jack-o-Lanterns and Mr. Green Goblin. They can hide in the woods and jump out at her. She will throw her broom at them to chase them away, and presto—you will have a new broomstick.

LITTLE WITCH: It's a lovely idea, Mr. Owl, but my friends are all too busy to help me.

MR. OWL: They might be too busy to mend a broomstick, but they won't be to busy to scare someone on Halloween. Just call them and see.

LITTLE WITCH (*Running from one side to the other and beckoning as she calls*): Skeletons! Skeletons! Mr. Cat! Mr. Cat! (SMALL SKELETONS *and* BLACK CAT *enter.*)

MR. OWL: Calling Mr. and Mrs. Ghost! Calling Mr. and Mrs. Ghost! (GHOSTS *enter.*)

LITTLE WITCH: Jack-o-Lanterns! Jack-o-Lanterns! (JACK-O-LANTERNS *enter.*)

MR. OWL: Calling Mr. Green Goblin! Calling Mr. Green Goblin! (GREEN GOBLIN *enters. When all are assembled* MR. OWL *talks to them.*) Little Witch and I want you to scare someone for us. Will you do it?

ALL: Yes, indeed. Yes, indeed. Who is it?

MR. OWL: It's the Old Woman in the Shoe. She and her children will be coming along here any minute. So hide in the bushes and jump out at her when I give the signal.

ALL: That will be fun! (*All crouch down at back and sides of stage as if hiding.* LITTLE WITCH *crouches behind tree stump and* MR. OWL *sits on tree stump. When all are in place* OLD WOMAN *enters with* CHILDREN. *She leads the way, sweeping from side to side. The* CHILDREN *follow, all singing to tune of* "*Row, Row, Row Your Boat.*")

CHILDREN: Sweep, sweep, sweep the path,
Sweep it nice and clean.
Happily, happily, happily, happily, Happy Halloween! (*As they sing song for third time, all the characters jump out, yell, wave their arms, make faces, etc.* OLD WOMAN *waves broom at them, trying to drive them off and finally throws the broom as she and the* CHILDREN *run off shrieking.*)

MR. OWL (*Picking up broom*): Here you are, Little Witch, a brand-new broom for your Halloween ride.

LITTLE WITCH: Thank you, thank you, Mr. Owl. And thanks to my friends for all your help. I do hope we didn't scare the Old Woman too badly.

SMALL SKELETONS: Everybody likes to be scared on Halloween.

BLACK CAT: It wouldn't be Halloween without a good scare.

GHOSTS: It's our duty to say Boo when we meet someone on Halloween.

ALL (*To audience*): So Boo! Boo! Boo!
To you, and you, and you!
Our story's done,
You've had your fun,
So Boo! Boo! Boo! (*All form a chain by placing hands on the shoulders of the person ahead and march around the stage.* LITTLE WITCH *on broom brings up the rear. She waves to the audience as all march offstage with a final "Boo! Boo! Boo!" Curtain.*)

THE END

SPUNKY PUNKY

Characters

SPUNKY PUNKY
CHUNKY
PLUNKY } *six little*
BUNKY   } *pumpkins*
TUNKY
KLUNKY
FOUR OTHER LITTLE PUMPKINS
SCARECROW
BLUE JAY
THREE FARMER BOYS
JACK
JILL
SUNBEAMS
THREE LITTLE WITCHES

TIME: *The afternoon of Halloween.*
SETTING: *A garden.*
AT RISE: LITTLE PUMPKINS *stand in a row. Each child wears a big orange cardboard circle suspended from his neck and concealing most of his body. Each circle has an outer covering of green crepe paper.* SPUNKY PUNKY *is last in line. His orange cardboard has been*

cut out in the form of a jack-o'-lantern, but is also concealed by the top layer of green paper. On the other side of the stage stands a SCARECROW. PUMPKINS *sing to tune of "Ten Little Indians."*

PUMPKINS: One little, two little, three little pumpkins,
Four little, five little, six little pumpkins,
Seven little, eight little, nine little pumpkins,
Ten little pumpkins we.

SCARECROW: Quiet! Quiet! You are hurting my ears! Why must you be singing all the time?

PUMPKINS: We're singing because we are pumpkins.

SCARECROW: Ha! Ha! Ha! Too bad you can't see yourselves! You don't even look like pumpkins!

PUMPKINS: Why not? We're round and fat, aren't we?

SCARECROW: Yes, but you're the wrong color. Pumpkins are golden yellow.

PUMPKINS: What color are we?

SCARECROW: You're green. You're green as grass.

SPUNKY: I think green is a pretty color.

SCARECROW: It's all right for grass, but not for pumpkins. Maybe you're not pumpkins after all.

PUMPKINS: Not pumpkins? Then what are we?

SCARECROW: Well, you could be watermelons. *They're* green. You could be cucumbers. *They're* green.

PUMPKINS: No! No! No! We're pumpkins! We know we are!

SCARECROW: Don't be too sure! Who ever heard of a green pumpkin?

PUMPKINS (*Singing sadly to tune of "Three Blind*

Mice"): Boo, hoo, hoo!
Boo, hoo, hoo!
What shall we do?
What shall we do?
Our color's wrong, we are all bright green,
We don't understand what it all can mean!
We're the saddest pumpkins you've ever seen,
Boo, hoo, hoo! (BLUE JAY *enters as* PUMPKINS *are singing and sobbing.*)
BLUE JAY: What's this? What's this? Why are my rolypoly pumpkins in tears?
SCARECROW (*Waving his arms*): Get out! Get out! No birds allowed in this garden!
BLUE JAY: Quiet, Scarecrow! You may keep those silly old crows out of the garden, but you can't scare me. Now what's wrong with my pumpkin friends?
SPUNKY (*Pointing at* SCARECROW): He says we are the wrong color.
CHUNKY (*Pointing at* SCARECROW): He says we should be yellow.
PLUNKY (*Pointing at* SCARECROW): He says maybe we're not pumpkins after all.
BLUE JAY: Don't believe a word he says. He's only trying to scare you.
SCARECROW: Just the same, no one will ever buy a green pumpkin to make a Halloween pumpkin pie!
PUMPKINS (*Except* SPUNKY): Oh, my! Oh, my! No pumpkin pie!
That makes us cry! Oh, my! Oh, my!
BLUE JAY: Cheer up! Cheer up! I know what you need.

PUMPKINS: What?
BLUE JAY: You need water and sunshine.
CHUNKY: The water will wash the green away.
PLUNKY: The sun will toast us to a golden yellow.
BUNKY: Where will we get the water? It hasn't rained for days and days.
TUNKY: It's so shady here in the garden, the sunbeams never reach us.
BLUE JAY: Cheer up! Cheer up! I will fly away for help. And don't let Mr. Scarecrow frighten you again. (*Exit*)
SCARECROW: Silly bird! You'll never see him again!
PUMPKINS: Oh, yes, we will.
CHUNKY: The Blue Jay is our friend.
BUNKY: He will bring us water to wash away our green.
KLUNKY: He will bring the sunbeams to make us golden yellow.
TUNKY: Then we will be chosen for pumpkin pies and go to a party.
SPUNKY: I don't want to be a pumpkin pie!
ALL: Why not? That's what pumpkins are for!
SPUNKY: I don't care! I want to be different!
CHUNKY: But when you grow big and round and yellow, you're sure to be chosen for a pumpkin pie.
SPUNKY: Then I'll stay the way I am. I'll be a green pumpkin forever and ever and ever.
ALL: Look! Look! Here come the farmer boys.
1ST FARMER BOY: A little bird told us to look at our pumpkins.
2ND FARMER BOY: They're still as green as grass.

SPUNKY PUNKY

3RD FARMER BOY: They'll never be ready for Halloween.

PUMPKINS (*All but* SPUNKY *sing to tune of* "*Baa, Baa, Black Sheep*"):
Farmer, farmer, we are all so dry.
Bring us water, or we'll die.
Some for the pumpkins and some for the vine—

SPUNKY: But none for the spunky one that's last in the line!

FARMER BOYS: Don't worry, little pumpkins. The water is on its way. (*Singing to tune of* "*Jack and Jill*")
Jack and Jill went up the hill to fetch a pail of water,
They'll be here to bring you cheer, and sprinkle you with water. (*As* JACK *and* JILL *enter with watering can*) Where have you been? Did you fall down the hill again?

JACK: Not this time. We were very careful.

JILL: We didn't spill a single drop.

FARMER BOYS: Then water the pumpkins right away. (JACK *and* JILL *skip in and out among the pumpkins, watering them as they go.* SPUNKY *jumps about to avoid the water.*)

SPUNKY: Not me! Not me! I'm going to stay green forever and ever.

1ST FARMER BOY: That's enough water.

2ND FARMER BOY: Now we'll get to work with our hoes.

3RD FARMER BOY: The pumpkins are just as green as ever. (FARMER BOYS *hoe around the pumpkins.*)

SCARECROW: They need the sun, but the Sunbeams will never find them.

PUMPKINS: The Blue Jay will show them where we are!
BLUE JAY (*Ushering in line of* SUNBEAMS): Cheer up! Cheer up! Here come the jolly Sunbeams!
PUMPKINS (*Singing to tune of "Baa, Baa, Black Sheep"*): Sunbeams, sunbeams, find us where we lie, Bring us sunshine, or we die!
Some for the pumpkins and some for the vine—
SPUNKY: But none for the spunky one that's last in the line. (*As song is repeated,* SUNBEAMS *dance among the* PUMPKINS, *stripping them of their green covering.* SPUNKY *manages to avoid them.*) Not me! Not me! I'm going to stay green forever and ever! (*When dance is ended,* SUNBEAMS *exit.*)
BLUE JAY: At last! At last! They're as yellow as gold!
FARMER BOYS: The pumpkins are ripe! The pumpkins are ripe!
1ST FARMER BOY: We'll let Jack and Jill choose those they want for pumpkin pies.
JACK: Jill may have first choice. (JACK *and* JILL *take turns reciting any familiar counting out rhyme, choosing a* PUMPKIN *each time. They continue until all* PUMPKINS *are chosen except* SPUNKY.)
1ST FARMER BOY (*Pointing to* SPUNKY): There's no use taking this one. He's too green.
3RD FARMER BOY: We'll help you take the pumpkins up to the farmhouse.
JACK *and* JILL: What good pies they'll make! (JACK, JILL *and* FARMER BOYS *pretend to carry off pumpkins.*)
PUMPKINS: Thank you, little Blue Jay. Goodbye, Mr.

Scarecrow. Goodbye, Spunky. (SPUNKY, BLUE JAY *and* SCARECROW *wave goodbye.*)

SPUNKY: Now I'll never have to be a pumpkin pie.

BLUE JAY: What *will* you be?

SPUNKY: Nothing. I'll just keep on being a pumpkin forever and ever and ever.

SCARECROW: A silly, green pumpkin all by yourself in this great big field.

SPUNKY: I'll have you and my friend, the Blue Jay.

SCARECROW: You won't have me. I go inside for the winter.

BLUE JAY: You won't have me. I have my business to attend to, and I'm going to start right now. Remember, it doesn't always pay to be too spunky. (*Exit* BLUE JAY)

SPUNKY: Dear me! I wonder if I made a mistake. Do you think he was right, Mr. Scarecrow? Have I been too spunky?

SCARECROW: Maybe yes, maybe no. But if you won't be a pumpkin pie, you'd better make up your mind to be something.

SPUNKY: What could I be?

SCARECROW: How would you like to scare folks?

SPUNKY: Be a scarecrow like you?

SCARECROW: No, I scare only birds. But you could scare people.

SPUNKY: How?

SCARECROW: By showing your great big yellow teeth.

SPUNKY: I don't have any teeth.

SCARECROW: I know where you can get some. I will send

for the Three Little Witches. (*Sings to tune of "Ten Little Indians"*): Come to me, come to me, Three Little Witches,
Hurry up, hurry up, fly over ditches.
Come with your brooms and all of your riches,
Hurry up, Halloween's near!
(THREE LITTLE WITCHES *enter, riding on broomsticks.*)
WITCHES: At your service, Mr. Scarecrow. What can we do for you?
SCARECROW: I'd like you to meet my friend, Spunky. He doesn't want to be a pumpkin pie, so I thought he would make a good jack-o'-lantern.
WITCHES: But jack-o'-lanterns are yellow.
SCARECROW: Isn't there some sort of magic that would make him yellow?
SPUNKY: Please! I want to be a jack-o'-lantern ever so badly.
WITCHES: Very well. We'll see what we can do. (*They ride around* SPUNKY *singing to tune of "London Bridge."*) Round and round and round we go, round we go, round we go,
Round and round and round we go, my fine fellow.
(WITCHES *reverse direction for second verse. As* WITCHES *ride,* SPUNKY *turns in a circle and when his back is toward the audience, he tears off the green paper, revealing the jack-o'-lantern.*)
Round and round and round we go, round we go, round we go,
Round and round and round we go, now turn yellow.

SCARECROW (*As* WITCHES *step back revealing* SPUNKY *as jack-o'-lantern*): Now you are a real jack-o'-lantern.
SPUNKY: When do I start scaring people?
WITCHES: Do you really want to scare people?
SPUNKY: Maybe it would be more fun to make them laugh.
WITCHES (*Sing to tune of "London Bridge"*): You will make them laugh and grin, laugh and grin, laugh and grin,
You will make them laugh and grin, my dear Spunky.
SPUNKY: But how? Where? When?
WITCHES (*As* JACK *and* JILL *enter*): Sh-h-h! Listen, and you'll find out.
JACK: A Halloween party's no fun without a jack-o'-lantern.
JILL: There are no pumpkins left except that ugly green one.
JACK: Look! There's one grinning at us right now.
JILL: How did he get here?
JACK: I don't know, but he seems glad to see us.
JILL: Let's take him along. We'll put him in the center of the table. (JACK *and* JILL *start off with* SPUNKY. *He turns and waves.*)
SPUNKY: Thank you, Little Witches. Goodbye, Mr. Scarecrow. (*Exit* JACK *and* JILL *and* SPUNKY.)
SCARECROW: Can't you stay awhile, Little Witches?
WITCHES (*Sing to tune of "London Bridge"*): We have other tricks to do, tricks to do, tricks to do,

So we say goodbye to you, goodbye, Scarecrow. (*Exit*)

SCARECROW: It's quiet here without Spunky and the Witches. Oh, well, I'll just settle down for my Halloween nap. (*Yawns, stretches and lies down.*) Good night, everyone. (*Curtain*)

THE END

THE WISHING STREAM

Characters

PROPERTY MAN
THE CHORUS
THE ORCHESTRA
TWO LITTLE MAIDS
SING HI

SING LO
SMALL BROTHER
SMALL SISTER
OLD WOMAN

SETTING: *The stage is bare except for two rows of chairs, one at right and one at left, a large chest upstage center, and a Chinese gong beside the chest.*

AT RISE: *The* CHORUS *sits at left. The* ORCHESTRA *is at right, holding kazoos, combs, or other rhythm band instruments. The* PROPERTY MAN *stands with arms folded beside the chest. All of the characters are in Chinese costumes and wear coolie hats. The* PROPERTY MAN *strikes the gong three times and then bows.*

PROPERTY MAN: Honorable Parents, Teachers and Boys and Girls, this is a Chinese Play. I am the Property Man and inside this big box are all the properties needed for our play. At my left is the Honorable Chorus. (CHORUS *rises, bows and sits down.*) At my right is the Honorable Orchestra. (ORCHESTRA *rises, bows and remains standing.*) Sometimes the Orchestra makes horrible noises, but they mean well, so please excuse them. (*Claps hands*) Music, please, music! (ORCHESTRA *plays through the music of "Fiddle-de-dee," bows and sits down.*) It is now time for the play to begin. The Honorable Chorus will give us the cue.

CHORUS (*Rises and sings the following verses to the tune of "Fiddle-de-dee"*): Fiddle-de-dee, fiddle-de-dee,
Our play is ready for you to see.
May the actors be what you want to see,
And make you happy as you can be,
Fiddle-de-dee, fiddle-de-dee,
Our play is ready for you to see.

Fiddle-de-dee, fiddle-de-dee,
Our play is ready for you to see.
May the play be good as we hoped it would,
And give you the fun that a good play should.
Fiddle-de-dee, fiddle-de-dee,
Our play is ready for you to see!

PROPERTY MAN: When I strike the gong three times, the Honorable Actors will enter. (*Strikes gong three times and then moves to one side of the stage near the curtain.* SING HI *and* SING LO *enter with* SMALL BROTHER *trailing behind.*) Our story is about the Sing family. This is Sing Hi, the eldest. (SING HI *bows.*) This is Sing Lo, the middle son, (SING LO *bows.*) and this is Small Brother. (SMALL BROTHER *bows.*) Sing Hi and Sing Lo do not want Small Brother with them today because they are going fishing and they are afraid Small Brother will fall into the stream. Small Sister wanted to come, too, but they left while she was taking her nap.

SING HI: Go back, Small Brother. You are too young to go fishing with us.

SING LO: Sing Hi is right, Small Brother. Go home before some harm comes to you.

SMALL BROTHER: Honorable Mother said I might go with you. I can take care of myself. Where is the stream?

SING HI: The stream is right here, Small Brother. We are standing on the bank.

SMALL BROTHER: But I do not see any water.

SING LO: That is because the Property Man forgot to place it here. (*Claps hands*) Property Man, the stream at once! (PROPERTY MAN *produces roll of blue cloth from property chest, unrolls it and stretches it on the stage.*)

SING HI: Here is the stream, Small Brother. Now be careful that you don't fall in.

SMALL BROTHER (*Leaning over so far he almost loses his balance*): Where are the fish? I don't see any fish.

SING LO: That is because the water is so deep.

SING HI: The fish are at the very bottom. That is why you can't see them.

SMALL BROTHER: I think it is because the Property Man didn't put any fish in the water.

PROPERTY MAN: Small Brother is right. But I will do so at once. (*Gets several colored fish from chest and places them on the blue cloth*)

SMALL BROTHER: Now I see the fish. Now I see them. What big fellows they are!
SING HI: Yes, they are too big for you. You will not be strong enough to pull them in.
SING LO: You will break your rod and the fish will get away.
SMALL BROTHER: No, no! I will catch the biggest fish of all as soon as I get my fishing pole. (PROPERTY MAN *hands each boy a fishing rod and line. They pretend to bait their hooks and cast their lines. Then they sing to the tune of "Fiddle-de-dee."*)
ALL: Fiddle-de-dee, fiddle-de-dee,
The fish are ready to bite for me.
Oh, the fish will bite when the bait is right,
And give us fishermen great delight.
Fiddle-de-dee, fiddle-de-dee,
The fish are ready to bite for me!
SING HI: A bite! A bite! I think I have a bite. (*Pulls on his line*)
SING LO: Your hook is caught on a snag, Older Brother. I will help you. (*They loosen line.*) Now try again. (*Repeat fishing song*)
PROPERTY MAN: Alas, our actors do not know much about fishing or they would not sing so loudly. They are scaring the fish away.
SMALL BROTHER: I do not think fishing is very much fun. I am getting tired.
SING LO: Then sit down and rest.
SMALL BROTHER (*Sitting down*): The sun is very hot.

SING LO: You are right, Small Brother. The sun is very hot.
SING HI: Property Man, we need a shady spot for our fishing. (PROPERTY MAN *brings Chinese umbrella from property chest. He holds it over them.*)
SING HI: Ah, that is much better. Thank you, Property Man.
SING LO: Pretty soon the fish will bite and we will take a fine catch home for dinner.
SMALL BROTHER: I am hungry now. I do not want to wait for dinner.
SING LO: I am hungry, too. Property Man, where is our lunch basket?
PROPERTY MAN (*Consulting scroll tucked in his sleeve*): There is no lunch basket on my list, so there is no lunch basket in the property chest.
SMALL SISTER (*Off-stage*): Yoo-hoo! Yoo-hoo! Where are you? Where are you?
SING LO: That is Small Sister.
SING HI: She must have followed us. (SMALL SISTER *enters with lunch basket.*)
SMALL SISTER: Oh, there you are! How many fish have you caught?
ALL: Sh! You will frighten the fish!
SING LO: What are you doing here? You know we will not let you fish with us.
SMALL SISTER: Honorable Mother thought you might be hungry. I have brought your lunch. But if you order me to go away, I will go.

ALL: Lunch?

SMALL SISTER: A fine lunch, my brothers, with rice cakes and fortune cookies.

SING HI: Since you have come so far, you might as well stay.

SING LO: I will take your heavy basket. (*Sets it on the stage*)

SMALL BROTHER (*Peering into basket*): Honorable Mother has put in everything we like. (*All sit down and unpack food.*)

PROPERTY MAN: It is not polite for some to eat while others watch, so we will all have tea.

CHORUS (*Standing and singing to tune of "Polly, Put The Kettle On"*): Suki, bring the kettle on,
Suki, bring the kettle on,
Suki, bring the kettle on,
We'll all have tea. (ORCHESTRA *repeats music as two little* MAIDS *bring in tea tray and serve the* CHORUS.)

SMALL BROTHER: This lunch is very good, but now I am thirsty.

SING HI: The Property Man will see that we get our tea. (PROPERTY MAN *signals* MAIDS *to serve actors. Then they serve the* ORCHESTRA, *and finally the* PROPERTY MAN, *who drinks his tea at the edge of the curtain.*)

PROPERTY MAN: While we are having our tea, I will tell you what is going to happen next. Pretty soon, an old woman will enter. She looks like a beggar, but if you watch her closely you may be surprised. Well, I see everyone has finished his tea, and the actors are

THE WISHING STREAM

eating their dessert. It's time to clear away the tea things.

CHORUS (*Singing to tune of "Polly, Put The Kettle On"*): Suki, take the cups away,
Suki, take the cups away,
Suki, take the cups away,
We've all had tea. (MAIDS *remove tea things but leave the lunch basket.* PROPERTY MAN *strikes gong three times.*)

PROPERTY MAN: That is the signal for the second act to begin and the old woman will enter. (OLD WOMAN *enters. She leans on a cane and carries a few pieces of firewood. She is almost completely covered by a long cloak and hood.*)

OLD WOMAN: Oh me, oh my! Oh me, oh my!
A very old woman am I, am I!

SMALL SISTER: Good morning, Old One.

OLD WOMAN: Good day to you, Small One. Are these your brothers?

SMALL SISTER: Yes, Old One. This is Sing Hi. This is Sing Lo, and this is Small Brother. (*Boys rise, bow, and sit down again.*)

OLD WOMAN: I see you are eating rice cakes and fortune cookies. It has been a long time since I have tasted rice cakes and fortune cookies.

SING HI: I am sorry, Old One, but we have eaten most of them.

SING LO: There weren't very many.

SMALL BROTHER (*Cramming the last one into his mouth*): And we were very hungry.

OLD WOMAN: I am hungry, too.

SMALL SISTER (*About to eat her last cake*): Take my cookie, Old One. It is not much, but it is all I have.

OLD WOMAN (*Taking it*): Thank you, child. (*Eating*) Umm. It is good. I used to eat rice cakes every day, but now I have no money to buy them. All I can do is gather firewood and try to sell it. If I had a strong, young back, and swift, young legs, I could gather a big pile of wood in no time.

SMALL SISTER: My brothers have strong backs and swift legs. They could help you.

SING HI: Quiet, Small Sister. (*As they resume fishing*) You can see we are fishing.

SMALL SISTER: But you haven't caught any fish.

SING LO: We will if you let us alone. (OLD WOMAN *gives loud, cackling laugh.*)

SMALL BROTHER: Why are you laughing, Old One?

OLD WOMAN: I am laughing to see you trying to catch fish in this stream.

SING HI: What is so funny about that? The stream is full of fish. See them.

OLD WOMAN (*Laughing again*): Those are not fish, young masters. This is the Wishing Stream.

SMALL BROTHER: What do you mean?

OLD WOMAN: I mean you should be fishing for wishes instead of sitting there trying to catch a carp or a mackerel.

ALL: Fishing for wishes!

OLD WOMAN: Of course. The lucky ones who come here really make a haul.

SMALL SISTER: And do the wishes come true?
OLD WOMAN: You have to catch them first.
SING HI: If wishes are fishes in this little brook,
  I'll throw in my line after baiting my hook.
  I'll then feel a tug in a minute or two,
  And pull out a wish that I know will come true. (*Pretends to bait hook. Actually he ties a small magnet on the end of his line which will naturally pull out a metal fish or a cardboard fish to which metal has already been attached.*)
OLD WOMAN: Make your wish carefully, young master.
SING HI: I've made my wish. (*Pause*) I've got it! I've got it! I feel a bite. (*Pulls fish out of stream*) I have it! I have it! I have my wish.
SING LO: But will it come true?
OLD WOMAN: Listen! Listen carefully! And you will know the answer.
CHORUS (*Rising and singing dolefully to the tune of "Little Bo-Peep"*): Little Sing Hi has made his wish,
  Alas, it will not come true.
  Little Sing Hi is very sad,
  Crying boo-hoo, boo-hoo!
SING HI: Won't my wish really come true, Old One?
OLD WOMAN: I am sorry, Sing Hi, but you heard the magic music. Perhaps your brother will have better luck.
SING LO: Yes, yes. Let me try!
  If wishes are fishes in this little stream,
  I'll stand in a spot where the sunbeams gleam.
  I'll bait up my hook and throw in my line,

And pull out a wish that I know will be mine.
OLD WOMAN: Wish carefully, young master. (SING LO *baits hook*.)
SING LO: Here it comes! Here it comes! I've got it! I've got it! But will it come true?
CHORUS (*Singing sadly to the tune of* "*Little Bo-Peep*"):
Little Sing Lo has made his wish,
Alas, it will not come true.
Little Sing Lo is very sad,
Crying boo-hoo, boo-hoo!
OLD WOMAN: I am sorry, Sing Lo. But let's give Small Brother a turn.
SMALL BROTHER (*Baiting hook*): I know a wonderful, wonderful wish.
If wishes are fishes in this water blue,
I know where to look and I know what to do.
I'll put on the bait that I know is just right
And pull out a wish that will bring me delight.
OLD WOMAN: Wish carefully, young master.
SMALL BROTHER: I've made my wish, and here it comes! Oh, what a big one. I know it will come true.
CHORUS (*Same song*): Small Brother Sing has made his wish,
Alas, it will not come true,
Small Brother Sing is very sad,
Crying boo-hoo, boo-hoo!
SMALL SISTER: I'm so sorry, Small Brother. I know you tried very hard.
SING HI: I don't believe in the Wishing Stream.

SING LO: It's all a trick.
SMALL BROTHER: Nobody's wish will ever come true.
SMALL SISTER: Let me try. Let me try!
ALL: Fishing is not for girls.
OLD WOMAN: Give her a chance, young masters. It won't do any harm.
SING HI: Oh, very well. After all, she did bring us our lunch. (*Hands her a rod*)
SMALL SISTER (*Clutching rod, eyes shut*): If wishes are fishes in this magic pool,
I'll stand in a spot where it's shady and cool. (PROPERTY MAN *rushes over with umbrella.*)
I'll throw in my line where I'm standing—right here,
And pull out a wish for someone who's near!
CHORUS (*Singing to same tune*): Small Sister Sing has made her wish,
Hoo-ray, it will come true!
Small Sister Sing is very glad,
And we are all happy, too!
SMALL SISTER (*Jumping up and down*): I've got it! I've got it! My wish is coming true! I can hardly believe it. (*As* SMALL SISTER *has been making wish,* OLD WOMAN *has removed cloak.* OLD WOMAN *now stands young and beautiful in a dazzling costume.*)
SING HI: What did you wish, Small Sister?
SMALL SISTER: I wished that the poor old woman would be young and well and strong, and rich enough to have all the rice cakes she could eat. And look! Look at her!

OLD WOMAN: Thank you, Small Sister, thank you very much. You have learned the true secret of the Wishing Stream.
SING HI: What is it? What is it?
SING LO: Why didn't the rest of our wishes come true?
OLD WOMAN: What did you wish for, young masters?
SING HI: I wished for a jeweled sword like the Emperor's.
SING LO: I wished for a golden kite that would fly to the moon.
SMALL BROTHER: I wished for a white pony with a golden saddle.
OLD WOMAN: But Small Sister made a wish for someone else. That is why her wish came true.
SING HI: I guess we don't know so much about fishing after all.
SING LO: Or about wishing either.
SMALL BROTHER: I'm glad Small Sister's wish came true, Fair One, for you are very beautiful.
OLD WOMAN: Thank you, young master, and now let me try my luck in the Wishing Stream. (*Takes rod*)
Since wishes are fishes in this magic lake,
I have only one simple wish I can make.
I wish that each fish may be turned into gold
For each of my friends to have and to hold.
ALL: Look! Look, the fish are turning to gold.
OLD WOMAN: Property Man, bring a basket and a net so my little friends may help themselves. (PROPERTY MAN *brings basket and net and children scoop up the*

fish. OLD WOMAN *speaks to audience.*) And always
   remember, when making a wish
The very true story of these little fish.
The wish that will oftentimes come to be true
Is a wish for another—and not just for you!
CHORUS (*To tune of "Fiddle-de-dee"*): Fiddle-de-dee,
   fiddle-de-dee,
Our play is ended as you can see.
And we know your wishes will all come true
If you do just as we told you to,
Fiddle-de-dee, fiddle-de-dee,
Our play is ended as you can see! (*As the* PROPERTY
MAN *strikes the gong three times, the actors bow to the audience, then to each other, and then to the audience, as the curtains close.*)

THE END

THE LIBRARY CIRCUS

Characters

THE BARKER	THE FOX
THE RINGMASTER	THE TIGER
FOUR CLOWNS	COWARDLY LION
FIVE SINGING DOGS	LIMPING LION
FOUR WALTZING BEARS	MR. MOUSE
ANIMAL TRAINER	THREE SKATING ELEPHANTS
THE WOLF	CHILDREN (*any number*)

SETTING: *Inside the circus tent.*

AT RISE: *The circus* BARKER, *with megaphone, is drumming up trade. Two* CLOWNS *stand on either side of him.*

BARKER: Right this way, boys and girls! Right this way for the biggest show on earth! Hurry! Hurry! Hurry! Come one! Come all! Come big! Come small! The greatest show on earth! Right here under the big top! Hurry! Hurry! Hurry!

FIRST CLOWN: Hark, hark, the dogs do bark,
The circus is coming to town!
Bears will dance,
And ponies prance,
And clowns turn upside down! (CLOWNS *do a cartwheel or somersault.*)

SECOND CLOWN: Zoom! Zoom! The drums go boom!
  The circus is coming today!
  Take your seat,
  And have a treat,
  And let your hearts be gay!
THIRD CLOWN: Hi-Ho! Come, let's go!
  Be sure you're not left out!
  The animals fair
  Will all be there,
  That you have read about!
FOURTH CLOWN: The big giraffe with the delicate laugh,
  The monks and kangaroo,
  The little pig,
  And a wolf in a wig
  May all perform for you!
BARKER: We've big baboons and toy balloons,
  And lots of lemonade.
  We now begin
  So come right in
  And see the big parade! (*To the recording of a circus march, the characters in the circus enter and parade in a circle around the stage, making their exit at the same side from which they entered. As the parade leaves the stage, the* BARKER *moves center, and three* CHILDREN *come from audience.*)
BARKER: Hurry! Hurry! Hurry! The big show is about to begin! Hurry! Hurry! Hurry!
FIRST CHILD: Please, Mister, I'd like a ticket.
BARKER: Ticket? Ticket? Who said anything about tickets?

THE LIBRARY CIRCUS

SECOND CHILD: Don't we need a ticket to get in?

BARKER: Of course not! You don't need a ticket. You need a *library card!*

CHILDREN: A library card!

BARKER: Certainly. This is a *Library Circus.* Once a year the animals of Bookland get together and put on a circus. And today's the day!

FIRST CLOWN: It happens every year!

SECOND CLOWN: They open the pages,
That make up their cages
And all come scurrying out!

CHILDREN: Who?

THIRD CLOWN: The pigs and the donkeys,
The foxes and monkeys
That you have been reading about.

THIRD CHILD: We want to see them. Won't you please let us in?

BARKER: Not without your library cards!

CHILDREN: But we don't have any library cards!

BARKER: Then get them right away! Hurry! Hurry! Hurry!

FIRST CHILD (*Pulling at his sleeve*): Please, Mister, have a heart!

SECOND CHILD: The library's closed today!

BARKER: Of course it's closed—because of the circus!

THIRD CHILD: Won't you please let us in?

BARKER: I'll tell you what I'll do! It's really against the rules, but you look like good children who do a lot of reading and love books.

CHILDREN: Oh, we do! We do!

BARKER: Very well, then. I'll let you have a peek. You go out there and sit down, and I'll give you these magic glasses. (*Hands large pair of cardboard eyeglasses to* FIRST CHILD.) As soon as you can tell me the book or story in which the animals appear, I'll let you in.

CHILDREN: Oh, thank you! Thank you!

FIRST CHILD: But what about our friends? They'll want to see the circus, too.

BARKER: Pass the glasses around and let them all have a peek. If they know the books and stories, they may come, too. (CHILDREN *return to audience.*)

BARKER: And now, ladies and gentlemen—the Ringmaster! (*To a roll of drums, the* RINGMASTER *enters and bows.* BARKER *and* CLOWNS *take their places at edge of stage.*)

RINGMASTER: Ladies and gentlemen, for your entertainment, we proudly present the one and only trained troupe of singing dogs. (*Fanfare of music off-stage.*) Ladies and gentlemen—The Bow Wow Chorus! (*Five* DOGS *enter. They appear to be walking on their hind legs, forepaws extended. One* DOG *is the director. They line up and the director gives the pitch with a long, drawn-out howl. They sing to the tune of* "Bow, Wow, Wow," *substituting* "bow-wow" *for the words of the song. After the song, the* DOGS *all bow.* RINGMASTER *leads applause. Five* CHILDREN *run up from audience to speak to the* BARKER.)

FIRST CHILD: We know! We know! That's Little Tommy Tinker's dog from Mother Goose.

CHILDREN (*Repeat song using words of the nursery rhyme.*): Bow, wow, wow, whose dog art thou? I'm little Tommy Tinker's dog, Bow! Wow! Wow!

RINGMASTER (*Indicating one of the* DOGS): *This* is little Tommy Tinker's dog. But can you name the others?

SECOND CHILD (*Pointing*): I think *that* is Old Mother Hubbard's dog. (DOG *barks and hops up and down.*)

THIRD CHILD: And *that* (*Pointing*) is Dr. Dolittle's dog, Jip, in the wonderful stories about the doctor who could understand animal talk. (*Third* DOG *barks and bows.*)

FOURTH CHILD: I think *this* one is the Pokey Little Puppy, because he was the very last to arrive. (*Fourth* DOG *barks and bows.*)

FIFTH CHILD: There are so many wonderful dogs in Bookland. Maybe *this* one (*Pointing to the director*) is Angus in the story about Angus and the Ducks. Or maybe he is Dorothy's dog, Toby, in "The Wizard of Oz." Our teacher read it to us.

BARKER: You may all come in, and I hope your teacher comes to the circus, too. (*As the five* CHILDREN *take places on the bleachers*) And now, Mr. Ringmaster—on with the show!

RINGMASTER: Ladies and gentlemen, for your very special delight—the Waltzing Bears! (*To the recorded music of "The Blue Danube," four* BEARS *enter and do a clumsy waltz routine ending with an elaborate bow.* RINGMASTER *leads applause as two* CHILDREN *run up on stage.*)

CHILDREN: We know! We know! The Three Bears!

They are the three bears that Goldilocks went to visit. (*Three of the* BEARS *bow*.)

FOURTH CLOWN: But there are *four* bears. Can you name the other one?

CHILDREN: That must be Pooh! We love to hear our teacher read "Winnie the Pooh" and "The House at Pooh Corner." (POOH *bows*.)

BARKER: In you go, and I hope you enjoy yourselves. (CHILDREN *take places on the bleachers*.) Next time you go to the library, look for more stories about bears. They're lots of fun to know. Now, Mr. Ringmaster, what's next?

RINGMASTER: We next present the daring and exciting wild animal act! (CLOWNS *set up stools or blocks on which animals may sit*.) Sit tight! Hold on to your chairs! Here they come! (*Recorded circus music should be played throughout the wild animal act. The* TRAINER *enters first with a whip and a small chair. He supervises the entrance of the* WOLF, FOX, TIGER, *and two* LIONS. *One* LION *is limping. The animals run around briskly in a circle until the* TRAINER *says,* "Up!" *Then they mount their stools. The* TRAINER *bows and the* RINGMASTER *leads applause*. TRAINER *flicks his whip at the* WOLF *and the* FOX *who come down off their stools*. RINGMASTER *hands* TRAINER *two skipping ropes which he gives to the* FOX *and the* WOLF. *They skip rope until the* RINGMASTER *signals for applause*. WOLF *and* FOX *return to their stools as* TRAINER *bows*. TRAINER *next signals the* TIGER *to get off stool*. RINGMASTER *hands* TRAINER *a wire hoop*.

With much cracking of the whip and brandishing of the chair, the TRAINER *persuades the* TIGER *to jump through it two or three times.* RINGMASTER *signals for applause,* TIGER *returns to stool,* TRAINER *bows and signals* LIONS *to perform. With commands of* "Down, Roll over, Sit up, *and* Bow," *the* TRAINER *puts them through a routine. At the end of the act, the* RINGMASTER *leads applause, and* TRAINER *signals the* LIONS *to return to their places. The* LIMPING LION *does not go.*)

TRAINER (*Cracking whip*): Back! Back!

LIMPING LION: Grrrrr! (*Comes closer to* TRAINER, *holding up paw*) Grrrrr!

TRAINER: Back! Back! Back, I say! (*Threatens* LION *with chair.* LION *growls more fiercely and chases* TRAINER *around the ring.*)

TRAINER: Help! Help!

RINGMASTER (*To audience*): Keep your seats. Don't panic! Oh, dear, something must be done! (MR. MOUSE *enters.*)

MR. MOUSE (*To* RINGMASTER): What goes on here? What's happening to my friend? He needs help!

RINGMASTER: Who can help him now? The Lion will surely eat him.

MR. MOUSE: I'm not worried about the Trainer. It is the lion who is my friend. Here, Leo, here! Let me help you! (LION *looks around, sees* MR. MOUSE, *and leaps at him joyfully, still holding up one paw.*)

MR. MOUSE (*Taking paw between his hands*): Why,

you poor fellow! You have a thorn in your foot, haven't you?

LIMPING LION: Grrrr! (*Nodding head vigorously*)

MR. MOUSE: And that cowardly Trainer was afraid to take it out. Now hold still and I'll have it out in a jiffy! (*Gives a quick pull*) There! There it is! (LION *capers about in gratitude.*)

TRAINER: You are a very brave mouse. Thank you for saving my life.

MR. MOUSE: Leo wouldn't hurt you. He only wanted you to pull out that thorn, didn't you, old fellow? (LION *growls softly and nods head.*) Leo and I are very old friends. He once saved my life, and later I helped him to escape from a band of hunters.

TRAINER: Would you like to join the circus and sleep in Leo's cage?

MR. MOUSE: I am afraid I am too busy. But I will always help my friend Leo, when he needs me. Better get back to your stool, Leo. Your act is over. (LION *hops back on stool.*)

RINGMASTER: A big hand for the Trainer and his wild beasts of the jungle. (*On applause, the animals and* TRAINER *exit.*) And another round of applause for our brave little visitor. (*More applause. Four* CHILDREN *enter from audience.*)

FIRST CHILD: May we please come in? We know that the Wolf was in "Little Red Riding Hood."

SECOND CHILD: Wolves really get around in books and stories. There's a big, bad wolf in "The Three Little

Pigs" and another wolf who puts on sheep's clothing in "The Wolf and the Seven Little Kids."

THIRD CHILD: The Fox is in the Uncle Remus stories and I've also read about him in fairy tales—"The Fox and the Geese," "The Fox and the Crow," and lots of others.

FIRST CHILD: I am sure the Tiger was Mr. Tigger who builds a house in "The House at Pooh Corner."

SECOND CHILD: And the first lion was the Cowardly Lion who went to see the Wizard of Oz with Dorothy.

THIRD CHILD: The Limping Lion was in *two* stories. One was called "The Lion and the Mouse." The other was about a Greek slave who pulled a thorn out of a lion's paw.

BARKER: I can see you have used your library cards well. You may go in and see the rest of the show. (CHILDREN *take places on bleachers.*)

MR. MOUSE (*To audience*): But what about me? We mice are very important characters in Bookland. If you go to your library, you will find all sorts of stories about us. There's "The Town Mouse and the Country Mouse," "*Ben and Me*," and a book your teacher might read to you about a mouse named Stuart Little. And don't miss the "Mousewife"—and oh-me-oh-my—there are so many I can't remember them all. (*Starts to exit, stops and turns*) Oh yes, be sure to wave at Mickey and Minnie when you see them in the movies. They're my cousins.

RINGMASTER: Thank you, Mr. Mouse. Thank you for

coming. Won't you stay and see the rest of the show?
MR. MOUSE: Sorry, Mr. Ringmaster. I must get back to the library. And besides, I see that your next act is elephants, and elephants are afraid of mice. Goodbye and good luck with your circus. (MR. MOUSE *exits*.)
RINGMASTER: Ladies and gentlemen, your attention please. For our final act, we proudly present The Skating Elephants. (*To the strains of "The Skaters' Waltz," three* ELEPHANTS *enter and do a comedy routine on roller skates. One* ELEPHANT *wears a crown. During the applause at end of act, three* CHILDREN *come up from the audience.*)
FIRST CHILD (*Indicating* ELEPHANT): This is Babar, the French elephant. I know him by his crown. He is the only elephant in Bookland who ever drove an automobile and set out on his honeymoon in a bright yellow balloon. (BABAR *bows*.)
SECOND CHILD (*Indicating* ELEPHANT): This is the Elephant's Child in the "Just-So-Stories." He was spanked for his "*satiable* curiosity" by all his aunts and uncles in the jungle. (ELEPHANT *bows*.)
THIRD CHILD (*Indicating* ELEPHANT): This is the Circus Baby. His mother brought him up like the Clown Baby and even taught him to eat at the table. (ELEPHANT *bows*.)
BARKER: I see you know your elephants. Welcome to our circus.
FIRST CHILD: But the circus is over!
SECOND CHILD: The Ringmaster said this is the last act.
THIRD CHILD: Now we won't see any more.

BARKER: Pray do not be offended,
  For the circus is *not* ended.
  You may come again tomorrow
  And again and yet again!
RINGMASTER: We'll show you story rabbits
  With the most enchanting habits,
  And the ducks and barnyard creatures—
  Chicken Little and Red Hen.
CLOWNS: And, of course, we'll have the kittens
  Those who lost their pretty mittens,
  And the donkeys and the monkeys
  You will find upon the shelf.
BARKER *and* RINGMASTER: If you keep on turning pages
  You will open up the cages
  For a jolly *Reading Circus*
  You can run all by yourself!
BARKER: So, what do you say, everybody?
CHILDREN (*On bleachers singing to tune of* "Row, Row Your Boat," *as* CLOWNS *caper about directing them.*):
  Read, read, read your books, read them every one!
  Merrily, merrily, merrily, merrily,
  Reading's lots of fun! (*Curtain*)

THE END

THE MOTHER GOOSE BAKESHOP

Characters

PITACAKE ⎫
PATACAKE ⎬ *three little bakers*
CHIEF BAKER ⎭
MR. FROSTING
MOTHER HUBBARD
FIDO
BO PEEP
SIMPLE SIMON
MISS MUFFET
JACK SPRATT
MRS. SPRATT
WOMAN IN THE SHOE
TOMMY TUCKER
CHILDREN
TEACHER
BIRTHDAY BOY *or* GIRL

SETTING: *A bakeshop.*
AT RISE: *The* THREE LITTLE BAKERS, *armed with big wooden spoons, are at the table. Each* BAKER *wears a white apron and a tall chef's hat. They sing to the tune of "Looby Loo."*

BAKERS:
Here we will mix the dough,
Here we stir round and round,
Then we will beat and beat,
Making you goodies to eat.
(*Suiting actions to the words*)

We put our big spoons in,
We take our big spoons out,

We give our big spoons a shake, shake, shake,
And turn the bowl about.
(*Taking up shakers*)

We shake some sugar in,
We shake some sugar out,
We give our shakers a shake, shake, shake,
And turn the bowl about.

We put our beaters in
(*Taking up egg beaters*)
We take our beaters out,
We give our beaters a shake, shake, shake,
And turn the bowl about.

CHIEF BAKER: That should do the trick. I think the batter is finished.

PITACAKE: Do you think there's enough sugar?

PATACAKE: Do you think there's enough flour?

CHIEF BAKER (*Tasting*): Umm. Just right. This should be a beautiful cake.

PITACAKE: Now we will pour the batter into the pans. (*Pours batter*)

PATACAKE: And I will put them into the oven.

CHIEF BAKER: Don't forget to prick it and nick it and mark it with "B." That's what the order says.

PITACAKE: Who ordered this beautiful cake?

CHIEF BAKER: I don't know. Didn't you get the name?

PITACAKE: No. Didn't you get it?

CHIEF BAKER: Patacake, did you get the customer's name?

PATACAKE: Not me. What does the order say?

CHIEF BAKER (*Takes order sheet from apron pocket and holds it so* PITACAKE *and* PATACAKE *can see it*): This is what it says. (*All sing to the tune of* "*Pat-a-cake*"):
Pat-a-cake, Pat-a-cake, Baker's man,
Bake a cake, master, as fast as you can.
Prick it and nick it and mark it with "B",
And have it all ready and waiting for me.
All ready for me, all ready for me,
And have it all ready and waiting for me!
PITACAKE: But there's no name.
PATACAKE: I can't think of any customer whose name starts with "B".
CHIEF BAKER: Oh well, someone will call for it. Better get it into the oven so it will be ready. Pitacake will help me with the customers. (PATACAKE *exits with cake pans, as* MOTHER HUBBARD *and* FIDO *enter from opposite side.*)
PITACAKE (*From behind counter*): Good morning. What can I do for you?
MOTHER HUBBARD:
I'm old Mother Hubbard,
I went to the cupboard
To get my poor dog a bone.
But when I got there,
The cupboard was bare,
And so my poor dog had none.
PITACAKE: And there was nothing there for you, either! How would you like some nice fresh bread?
MOTHER HUBBARD: That will be fine.
FIDO: Arf! Arf!

MOTHER HUBBARD: And a coffee cake, too, if you have one.
PITACAKE: We do indeed: a nice fresh one, right out of the oven.
FIDO: Arf! Arf!
MOTHER HUBBARD: Hush, Fido! You know it isn't nice to bark when we go shopping!
FIDO (*Sitting up*): Bow, wow, wow,
I'm hungry now!
Ask him for
Some puppy chow!
MOTHER HUBBARD: Isn't he clever? Please put in a box of doggie biscuits, and deliver it all to my house just as soon as you can.
FIDO: Arf! Arf! Thank you! Thank you!
CHIEF BAKER: Excuse me, Mother Hubbard, but did you order a cake for today?
MOTHER HUBBARD: A cake? Dear me, I'm not sure. (*To* FIDO) Did I order a cake for today, Fido?
FIDO (*Shaking his head*): Arf! Arf!
MOTHER HUBBARD: Fido says no, I didn't. Perhaps some other day, Mr. Baker.
CHIEF BAKER: I can't think who ordered it. It is to be marked with the letter "B".
MOTHER HUBBARD: Maybe it was Bo Peep. I saw her coming this way. Come along, Fido. We must be on our way. Say goodbye to the bakers.
FIDO: Arf! Arf! (MOTHER HUBBARD *and* FIDO *exit as* PATACAKE *enters from the other side.*)
PATACAKE: The cake is in the oven and I told Mr. Frost-

ing to put on a big "B" with pink icing. (BO PEEP *enters crying loudly*.) Dear me! Who is it?
BO PEEP: I'm little Bo Peep. I've lost my sheep! And can't tell where to find them!
PATACAKE: Leave them alone, and they'll come home, Wagging their tails behind them.
BO PEEP: That's what everybody tells me, but I can't help worrying about them.
CHIEF BAKER (*At counter*): Here, have a sugar cake, and you'll feel better. (*Takes sugar cake from beneath counter*)
BO PEEP (*Taking sugar cake from* CHIEF BAKER): Oh, thank you, thank you very much. (*Eats it*) Yum! This is good. You always have good things in here.
THREE BAKERS: Thank you, Bo Peep.
BO PEEP: Dear me! I've been so worried about my sheep, I've forgotten what I came for.
CHIEF BAKER: Was it a cake?
BO PEEP: I don't think so.
PITACAKE: A lovely big cake, marked with a "B"?
BO PEEP: My name begins with "B". What kind of cake is it?
PATACAKE: A great big cake with yellow dough!
BO PEEP: Dough! Dough! Now I remember what I came for. Mother said to buy a dozen doughnuts!
PITACAKE: Oh! Doughnuts! (*Puts doughnuts into box*) Here they are, all nice and fresh.
BO PEEP (*Pretending to pay for them*): Thank you.
PATACAKE: And don't worry about your sheep.
BO PEEP: I'll try not to. Thank you for the sugar cake.

THREE BAKERS: You're welcome. (BO PEEP *exits*.)
CHIEF BAKER: We still haven't found out who ordered that cake.
PITACAKE: Maybe it was Simple Simon. It would be just like him to order a cake and forget all about it.
PATACAKE: Yes, he does the silliest things—like the time he met the Pieman.
CHIEF BAKER: Yes, I remember. (SIMPLE SIMON *enters as* CHIEF BAKER *is reciting*):
Simple Simon met a Pieman,
Going to the Fair.
Said Simple Simon to the Pieman,
"Let me taste your ware."
PITACAKE: And what did the Pieman say?
SIMPLE SIMON: I'll tell you what he said:
Said the Pieman to Simple Simon,
"Show me first your penny."
Said Simple Simon to the Pieman,
"Indeed, I have not any!"
PITACAKE: And did the Pieman give you one of his pies without the money?
SIMPLE SIMON: Indeed he didn't. But I have a penny today, and I want a nice fresh cherry pie.
PITACAKE (*Handing him a pie*): Here it is, Simon.
SIMPLE SIMON: Thank you, and here's the penny. That's all the money I have.
PITACAKE: What about the cake?
SIMPLE SIMON: What cake?
PITACAKE: Didn't you order a big cake marked with a "B"?

SIMPLE SIMON: No, indeed. I never eat cake—just pie. (*Exits*)
CHIEF BAKER: Here come Mr. and Mrs. Spratt. They have a little girl with them. She looks frightened. (MR. *and* MRS. SPRATT *enter with* MISS MUFFET.)
MISS MUFFET: He's after me! He's after me! I know he is!
MRS. SPRATT: Now! Now! Now! Don't get so excited. There's nothing to be afraid of!
MR. SPRATT: This is little Miss Muffet. She has just had a terrible experience. (MR. *and* MRS. SPRATT *and* MISS MUFFET *sing or recite*):
"Little Miss Muffet sat on a tuffet,
Eating some curds and whey,
There came a big spider, and sat down beside her
And frightened Miss Muffet away."
MISS MUFFET: Oh, it was a terrible spider, Mrs. Spratt! It was this big! (*Holds her hands several inches apart*) I was so scared, I dropped my bowl of curds and whey and ran! Now I am hungry.
MRS. SPRATT: Then you shall have a cinnamon bun.
PATACAKE: Here's a nice one all full of raisins. (*Gives bun to* MISS MUFFET) And what will you have, Mrs. Spratt?
MRS. SPRATT: Oh dear, I hardly know. Meals are such a problem at our house. (*Recites*):
Jack Spratt will eat no fat,
And I will eat no lean.
And so, between us both, you see
We lick the platter clean.

MR. SPRATT: But the Doctor says we must eat other things besides meat. He says we should start the day with a good breakfast, so we'll take a loaf of toast!

PATACAKE (*As all laugh*): I'll give you a loaf of bread, Mr. Spratt, but you'll have to make the toast yourself. (*Gives bread to* MR. SPRATT) That will be twenty-five cents, please.

CHIEF BAKER: By the way, did you order a cake for today?

MRS. SPRATT: No, sir. But I think I'd like to have one for tomorrow.

CHIEF BAKER (*Taking notebook and pencil from beneath counter*): And what kind would you like?

MRS. SPRATT: I'd like chocolate.

MR. SPRATT: I'd like vanilla!

MRS. SPRATT: Chocolate!

MR. SPRATT: Vanilla!

CHIEF BAKER: We'll make you a two-layer cake: one layer chocolate, the other vanilla.

MR. *and* MRS. SPRATT: That will be fine.

MRS. SPRATT (*To* MISS MUFFET): And you may come for lunch and have a piece, my dear.

MISS MUFFET: Thank you. You are very kind to me. (MR. *and* MRS. SPRATT *and* MISS MUFFET *exit as* MR. FROSTING *enters with birthday cake on a cake stand. It is decorated with a* "B" *and has candles on it.*)

MR. FROSTING: Here's the cake. I've nicked it and pricked it and marked it with "B", just the way you said.

ALL: It's beautiful!

CHIEF BAKER: Put it here on the counter, Mr. Frosting. (MR. FROSTING *puts cake on counter.*) And here is an order for tomorrow from Mr. and Mrs. Spratt. (*Hands* MR. FROSTING *a page from his notebook*) One layer is to be chocolate, and the other, vanilla.

MR. FROSTING (*As he exits*): Very good, sir. (WOMAN IN THE SHOE *enters with as many* CHILDREN *as desired.*)

PITACAKE: Good morning. I believe you are a stranger in town.

WOMAN IN THE SHOE: Yes, we just moved into the shoe-house across the street.

PATACAKE: Are all of these your children?

WOMAN IN THE SHOE: Every one of them! They say I'm the Old Woman in the Shoe who has so many children she doesn't know what to do.

CHIEF BAKER: They certainly are well behaved.

WOMAN IN THE SHOE: They ought to be! Last night I gave them some broth without any bread and whipped them all soundly and put them to bed! Now today they are so good I want to give them a treat. Do you have any cookies?

CHIEF BAKER: Yes, indeed. (*Takes large shopping bag from beneath counter*) How about these?

WOMAN IN THE SHOE: That should be enough to go around.

TOMMY: Don't forget my nice white bread, please, Mother.

WOMAN IN THE SHOE: I won't forget, Tommy. (*To*

PITACAKE) A loaf of white bread, please. This is Tommy Tucker. Tell the bakers about Tommy, children. (CHILDREN *sing the following song*):
"Little Tommy Tucker, sing for your supper,
What shall he sing for, white bread and butter.
How can he cut it without any knife?
How can he marry without any wife?" (PITACAKE *puts loaf of bread into shopping bag.*)

WOMAN IN THE SHOE: Of course, they're just teasing about Tommy's getting married, but the part about the white bread and butter is very true. He eats it all the time.

CHILDREN: Look, Mother, look at the big cake! It must be somebody's birthday.

WOMAN IN THE SHOE: Well, it's none of yours, so don't think you're going to get any. Cookies are enough for you. Now come along.

CHILDREN: Goodbye, Mr. Baker. (*Exit*)

CHIEF BAKER: That's the last of our customers, and no one has called for the fancy cake.

PITACAKE: But now we know that the "B" stands for Birthday.

PATACAKE: It must be a birthday cake—but whose?

CHIEF BAKER: Wait a minute! I remember! I remember! I remember who ordered the birthday cake.

PITACAKE *and* PATACAKE: Who?

CHIEF BAKER: It was a lady—a teacher! Let me see, her name was . . . (*Reaches into pocket for slip of paper*) Her name was Miss (*Fill in with name of teacher giving the play*) and she teaches . . . . grade in .... school. The birthday cake is for (*Names either boy or girl or both*). Is Miss .... in the audience? (*Real teacher enters with boy or girl whose birthday is being celebrated. This may be a surprise if the teacher desires.*) Ah! Here she is, and here is our Birthday Boy (*or Birthday Girl*).

TEACHER (*With child or children for whom party is to be given*): It's a beautiful cake, Mr. Baker. Thank you so much. And now we want to invite all of your Mother Goose customers back on stage to share in our birthday party for (*name child*). We are sure this is a birthday he (*or she*) will never forget. (*To music of "Happy Birthday to You" all characters march on stage and close by singing a birthday greeting to the child who is to be honored. Curtain. Curtain may close and reopen on actual party or it may remain open as teacher helps Birthday Boy or Girl cut the cake.*)

THE END

THANKFUL'S RED BEADS

Characters

THANKFUL	MOTHER
COMFORT	RED FEATHER
DAVID	YELLOW FEATHER
DANIEL	GREEN FEATHER
FATHER	BLUE FEATHER

TIME: *The day before the second Thanksgiving.*
SETTING: *The main room of a colonial cabin.*
AT RISE: THANKFUL *is on her knees by an open chest, examining the contents.*

THANKFUL: Oh, what beautiful silver buckles! I wonder if they will fit me. (*Holds up a pair of bright buckles sewn on elastic bands. She slips them on over her shoes, and stands up to admire them.*) I almost feel like dancing! But that would never do for a Puritan maid! (*Kneels before chest and pulls out a bright-colored shawl*) O-o-oh! A shawl! I've never seen one so pretty! (*Puts it on and pulls out a long, blue scarf which she drapes over her head.*) I never knew Mother had such wonderful things in here. I wonder what else she has. (*Takes out small box, opens it and draws out a long string of bright red beads.*) Oh, they're beautiful! I've never seen anything so pretty! (*Calling*) Comfort, come see what I found!

COMFORT (*Entering right*): Thankful, you naughty girl! You have opened Mother's chest! You know we are not allowed to do that!

THANKFUL: But look at all the pretty things I found. Aren't they beautiful? Why doesn't she ever wear them?

COMFORT: You know Puritan women do not wear bright colors. Put them back right away before she catches you.

THANKFUL: But why does she have such things if she can't wear them?

COMFORT: She keeps them because they belonged to her mother. Now put them back. If Mother sees you, she'll skin you alive!

THANKFUL: All right! All right! I'll put them back. (*Slowly returns scarf to the chest.*)

COMFORT: Be sure to fold them neatly so they won't muss.

THANKFUL (*Putting back the shawl*): There! That's just the way I found it. Oh, Comfort, don't you think she'd let me wear these buckles just for a little while?

COMFORT: I should say not. Put every single thing back where you got it.

THANKFUL: All right. I'll put everything back—all but the beads. They're much too pretty.

COMFORT: Put the beads back, too. Now hurry. Mother and Father will be here any minute.

THANKFUL (*Rising*): I'm not going to put the beads back, Comfort. I'm going to wear them.

COMFORT: You wouldn't dare!

THANKFUL: I would so! They're mine! They're mine!

COMFORT: They are not yours, and if Father sees you wearing them, you'll really catch it!

THANKFUL: Why?

COMFORT: Because it's wicked to wear such things and red is an evil color!

THANKFUL: I don't care! I like it. I'm going to wear my beautiful red beads. (*Puts them on and dances about.*)

COMFORT: You'll be sorry when Father catches you. Ask the boys, if you don't believe me. (DAVID *enters with armload of wood, followed by* DANIEL *carrying a pail of water.*) Look, David, look! See what Thankful is wearing!

THANKFUL (*Dancing up to* DAVID *and showing him the beads*): Aren't they pretty?

DAVID (*Dumping wood at fireplace*): Where did you get them?

THANKFUL: Out of Mother's big chest.

DAVID: Then put them back right away.

DANIEL (*Putting water bucket on bench*): And shut the lid. I still remember the switching David and I got when we took a pair of silver buckles out of that chest!

DAVID: Mother never lets us play with anything in that chest. She brought all those things over from England.

THANKFUL: I'm not *playing* with them. I'm *wearing* them.

DAVID: That's even worse. Puritan maids don't wear beads. They're wicked!

THANKFUL: Who says so?

ALL: Father!

THANKFUL: I don't believe Father would say these are wicked. I think he would say they are pretty.

COMFORT: Very well. Have it your own way. (*Closing lid of chest*) But I'm closing this lid just the same. I don't want Father and Mother to think *I've* been meddling in that chest.

DANIEL: And don't come crying to us when Father takes a switch to you!

THANKFUL: Do you really think he would?

DANIEL: I know he would.

THANKFUL: Then I won't let him see them! I'll hide them under my collar. (*Tucks beads under collar.*) There! Now he will never know!

DANIEL: Suppose we tell him!

THANKFUL: I know you wouldn't do that. And besides, if you did, I know some things I could tell, too. I saw you and David whispering and giggling at meeting last Sabbath! And you were making faces, too, when Father wasn't looking!

DAVID: You see too much, little sister.

DANIEL: Where is Father? We were supposed to help him cut more wood this afternoon.

COMFORT: He and Mother went to the Brewster

cabin to talk about the feast tomorrow. Here they come now. (FATHER *and* MOTHER *enter*) Father looks worried.

FATHER: Well, boys, I see you have done your work. The wood is in and the water bucket is filled.

COMFORT: I made the beds and did the dusting.

MOTHER: I hope Thankful has been working at the spinning wheel as she was told.

THANKFUL: I did work some of the time, Mother. But I will finish this afternoon.

FATHER: Not this afternoon, child. We are all going out in the woods to help Mother look for some wild grapes for tomorrow's feast.

THANKFUL: That will be fun. I can hardly wait for tomorrow to come.

FATHER: You think too much about fun, my child. Tomorrow's feast day is a day of prayer and thanksgiving.

COMFORT: Are the Indians coming, Father?

FATHER: I don't know. They came last year to the Thanksgiving feast at Plymouth. But this year there has been some trouble.

DAVID: Do you think there will be fighting?

MOTHER: Of course not. The Indians will be kind to us as long as we are kind to them.

FATHER: They are having a council now. If only we had more presents to give them! The Indians are like children. Presents always make them happy—the brighter the better!

MOTHER: We can be thankful they have let us live here in peace.

FATHER: We can be thankful for many blessings, my dear. I am thankful that you and I and the children have all been well and happy this year.

MOTHER: The children have much to be thankful for, too.

FATHER: Tomorrow as we sit around the table, we will each give thanks for our own special blessings. David, you are the oldest son. You may speak first. What have you to be thankful for?

DAVID: I am thankful for many things, Father. But I am most thankful that we came to this new land. I like it here.

FATHER: Well spoken, lad. Daniel, what have you to be thankful for?

DANIEL: I am thankful that I have a big strong brother like David to help chop wood and carry water.

FATHER (*Smiling*): That is, at least, an honest answer. Comfort, what have you to be thankful for?

COMFORT: I guess I am most thankful for you and Mother and this good, warm house that you built for us.

MOTHER: We are all thankful for our home, Comfort. Now, Thankful, it's your turn.

THANKFUL (*Hesitating*): I'm thankful for the same things as Comfort said.

FATHER: Come now, child. Surely you have some special blessing. What makes you feel most thankful of all?

THANKFUL: Well—I guess I am *most* thankful for my beautiful red beads! (*The other children utter a horrified "ah!"*)

FATHER: Beads? Beads? What red beads?

THANKFUL: Oh, dear! The others warned me not to tell! But I am so thankful I found them!

MOTHER: Thankful, what do you mean? What beads are you talking about?

THANKFUL (*Pulling beads out from under collar*): These! These beads! I found them in your chest.

MOTHER (*Shaking her*): You naughty child! You know you are forbidden to open that chest! Take those beads off and give them to me!

THANKFUL: Oh, please, Mother. Let me keep them! They are so pretty!

FATHER: Do as your mother says. You are a wicked girl and must be punished. David, go outside and bring me a good, stout switch!

THANKFUL: Please, Father, I'll take them off right away. (*Gives beads to* MOTHER *who puts them into chest.*)

DAVID: She's a very little girl, Father, and she didn't understand.

FATHER: She's old enough to understand that a Puritan maid does not wear red beads! Now get that switch.

COMFORT: Please, Father. Let her go this time.

DANIEL: She was brave enough and honest enough to tell you about them, sir.

FATHER: Don't try to stand up for her. David, if I have to go for that switch myself, I'll use it on both of you!

DAVID: Yes, sir. Yes, sir. (*Exits*)

MOTHER: These beads as well as everything else in that chest belonged to my mother. That is why I have kept them and they are very precious to me. You knew you were not allowed to touch them.

THANKFUL: I'm sorry, Mother. I'll never do it again, I promise! The beads were so pretty.

FATHER: That is no excuse.

DAVID (*Running in wildly excited*): Quick, Father! Quick! The Indians are coming!

ALL: Indians!

FATHER: Where? Where?

DAVID: They are surrounding the house. And they are in war paint!

FATHER: How many are there?

DAVID: Four or five—maybe six. I didn't stop to count.

MOTHER: What shall we do? What shall we do?

FATHER: Try to be natural. Comfort, go to the spinning wheel. Thankful, help your mother get some food ready.

DANIEL: I'll get the guns.

FATHER: There will be no shooting. They would kill us and attack the settlement. We must prove our friendship.

DAVID: Here they come! (*There is a bang at the door.*)

FATHER: I will open the door. You boys stand back. (*Pretends to open door. Four* INDIANS *enter with tomahawks*) Welcome! We bid you welcome!

INDIANS (*Brandishing tomahawks*): We want firewater! We take scalps!

FATHER: We have no firewater, but my wife and daugh-

ter will serve you food. (THANKFUL *and* MOTHER *advance with trays of bread or rolls. The* INDIANS *dash the trays out of their hands.* MOTHER *shrinks back against table.* THANKFUL *runs to chest and opens it.*)
RED FEATHER: No food! Firewater!
YELLOW FEATHER: We want scalps!
FATHER: But we are your friends!
BLUE FEATHER: White man take our land—now we take white man's scalp!
GREEN FEATHER (*Seizing* COMFORT *by the hair*): Yellow hair make good scalp!
COMFORT: Help! Help!
MOTHER (*Running to* COMFORT): Let her go! Let her go!
FATHER: Stop! Stop! (RED FEATHER *tangles with* FATHER *as he rushes toward* COMFORT. BLUE FEATHER *and* YELLOW FEATHER *grapple with* DANIEL *and* DAVID. *During the struggle,* THANKFUL *takes red beads from chest. She runs to* GREEN FEATHER *and dangles them in front of his face.*)
THANKFUL: Look! Look! See the pretty beads! These are for you. See! (*Shaking them*) Aren't they pretty? (GREEN FEATHER *lets* COMFORT *go and reaches for beads.* THANKFUL *moves away from him, beads outstretched.*) These are for you. We are your friends.
GREEN FEATHER (*Following* THANKFUL, *his eyes on the beads*): For me?
THANKFUL: Yes, they are for you. Take them.
GREEN FEATHER: Heap pretty beads! Brothers let pale-

faces go. See pretty beads. (*As he grabs them, the string tears and beads scatter in all directions. The other* INDIANS *release their victims and hunt for beads, exclaiming with delight as they find them.*)

RED FEATHER: Presents! Presents! We want more presents!

MOTHER (*Running to chest*): You shall have lots of presents. See, here is a pretty shawl for you. (*Tosses shawl to nearest* INDIAN) And here is a scarf! (INDIAN *grabs scarf*) And here are some buckles—all for you! (INDIANS *caper about, trying on their gifts.*)

FATHER: See, we are your friends.

RED FEATHER: Now we believe. You give us fine presents.

YELLOW FEATHER: Paleface girl is friend. She gives us red beads.

BLUE FEATHER: Paleface squaw is friend. She, too, gives us presents.

FATHER: We want you to come to our feast tomorrow. Tell your people there will be food for all.

RED FEATHER: Red man bring presents, too. Bring fish, corn. Bring feathers and blankets for girl child and squaw.

GREEN FEATHER: We came to take scalps and burn house. We go now. Paleface and red man—we friends.

YELLOW FEATHER: We go in peace.

GREEN FEATHER: We come tomorrow to white man's feast.

BLUE FEATHER: We smoke peace pipe. (INDIANS *exit*.)
MOTHER: Thank heaven, they are gone.
FATHER: Tomorrow will, indeed, be a day of Thanksgiving.
COMFORT: Oh, Father, have they really gone? Are we safe?
DANIEL: They will not hurt us now.
DAVID: And we owe it all to little Thankful's red beads.
MOTHER: What made you think of opening the chest?
THANKFUL: I know I said I never would again, but then I remembered what Father said about Indians being like children. I thought they would like the red beads.
FATHER: You were right, child. Your quick thinking saved us all.
DAVID (*Laughing*): Do you still want me to go for that switch, Father?
FATHER: No, indeed. (*Stooping and picking up two beads from the floor*) Thankful shall have her beads and my blessing. The Indians didn't find them all. (*Each member of the family picks up several beads, exclaiming:* "Here's one," "Here's another.")
MOTHER: I think there might be enough to string and make a small bracelet.
THANKFUL: Oh, Mother, do you really mean it?
MOTHER: If your father would let you wear it!
FATHER: I think a brave little girl who saved her whole family might wear a red bracelet, even if she is a Puritan maid.
THANKFUL: Oh, thank you, Father.

FATHER: And now let us give thanks to our Heavenly Father by raising our voices in a hymn of praise. (ALL *bow their heads, fold their hands, and sing The Doxology—"Old Hundred." Curtain*)

THE END

A THANKSGIVING RIDDLE

Characters

BILLY	CINDY
JOHNNY	ROSE
MIKE	PENNY
RALPH	MABEL
SAM	MISS HARPER
MOLLY	

TIME: *Just before Thanksgiving.*
SETTING: *A classroom.*
AT RISE: *The* CHILDREN *are grouped around their teacher,* MISS HARPER, *who is reading a story.*

MISS HARPER: So the Puritans bowed their heads and gave thanks to God for bringing them safely across the sea to find freedom in a new land. (*Closing book*) That is the story of the first Thanksgiving.
BILLY: That was a good story, Miss Harper.
JOHNNY: I liked the part about the Indians.
MIKE: I'd like to shoot a turkey for Thanksgiving.
ROSE: I'd rather get mine at the supermarket.
MOLLY: Puritans didn't have supermarkets, silly!
CINDY: Puritans didn't have a lot of things we have today.

RALPH: No ice-cream cones!
SAM: No movies!
PENNY: No TV!
BILLY: But they had other things.
MABEL: They had woods, and trees, and grass, and flowers.
MIKE: They had Indians and bows and arrows.
ROSE: But they had to work hard.
CINDY: And sometimes they were sick and hungry.
MABEL: Did Puritan children have fun?
SAM: Did they play games?
MISS HARPER: Oh, yes. We still play some of the games today that Puritan children enjoyed.
ROSE: Did they play hide-and-go-seek?
MISS HARPER: I'm sure they did. Hide-and-go-seek is a very old game, and I know they enjoyed riddles.
MABEL: Oh, I love riddles.
MISS HARPER: Do you know any riddles about Thanksgiving?
BILLY: I don't know any riddles about Thanksgiving, but I know one about something the Indians had at their Thanksgiving feast.
ALL: What is it?
BILLY: What has an ear but cannot hear?
MABEL: I know! I know! It's an ear of corn!
BILLY (*Disappointed*): Aw, you guessed it!
MABEL: Sure. That was easy. But the Puritans would have starved without their corn crop.
MISS HARPER: Can you think of any other riddles about things the Puritans might have used?

PENNY: I know one.
ALL: Let's hear it.
PENNY: Little Nancy Etticoat
In a white petticoat
And a red nose.
The longer she stands,
The shorter she grows.
ALL: That's a candle.
MISS HARPER: The Puritans made their own candles out of bayberries.
SAM: I know one, Miss Harper. Let me tell mine.
MISS HARPER: Go ahead, Sam.
SAM: As soft as silk, white as milk,
As bitter as gall, a strong wall,
And a green coat covers me all.
MIKE: I've heard that one before. That's a walnut, before it's picked.
ROSE: Miss Harper told us that the Puritans ate lots of nuts and berries.
BILLY: That gives me an idea. Listen to this one.
As white as milk and not milk,
As green as grass and not grass,
As red as blood and not blood,
As black as soot and not soot.
MOLLY: That must be a blackberry. First it's white, then it's green, then it's red, and, finally, it's black.
RALPH: I'll bet the Puritan children had fun picking berries in the woods.
MISS HARPER: Do you think you would like to be Puritans?

SOME: Yes.
OTHERS: No.
ALL: We don't know.
MISS HARPER: Let's find out.
ALL: How?
MISS HARPER: Let's play Puritans and see how we like it.
JOHNNY: How do we play?
MISS HARPER: First we'll make a long table such as the Puritans used for their Thanksgiving feast. The boys may set up the card tables. (*Boys set up three card tables.*) Molly and Rose may cover the tables with some of our clean, white paper. (*Girls do so.*)
MABEL: We should have a centerpiece.
MISS HARPER: We will use the turkey we made in art class. Penny, you may get it from the closet. (PENNY *exits and returns with a large, cardboard turkey. There are eleven feathers in the tail. The feathers can be pulled out of their cardboard slots.*)
MISS HARPER: Now we will each ask the turkey a riddle. Girls, line up on one side, boys on the other. (*They do so.*)
MOLLY: What is the riddle?
MISS HARPER: It's very simple: Turkey, turkey, tell me true
What would a little Puritan do?
BILLY: How will the turkey answer us?
MISS HARPER: The riddle has many answers. You will find them written on the turkey feathers.
ALL: This will be fun.
MISS HARPER: When you find the answer, you must act

it out. The rest of us will guess what you are doing. You may use any object in the room to help you. Mabel, you may begin.

MABEL (*Advancing to table*): Turkey, turkey, tell me true
What would a little Puritan do? (*Pulls out turkey feather and reads it. Then looks around, finds a toy broom and begins to sweep.*)

MISS HARPER: You should be able to guess what this little Puritan is doing. (*Children raise hands eagerly, calling out, "I know! I know!"* MISS HARPER *calls on* RALPH.)

RALPH: I think she is helping her mother clean up for the Thanksgiving feast.

MABEL: That's right. My turkey feather says:
A Puritan child, like any other,
Would sweep and clean to help her mother.

MISS HARPER: Since the children have guessed what you were doing, Mabel, you may go to the cloakroom and put on one of the Puritan caps and aprons you will find there. Then you may take your place at the table. (*Exit* MABEL.) Billy, you're next.

BILLY (*At table*): Turkey, turkey, tell me true
What would a little Puritan do? (*After selecting feather and reading it, he collects a pile of rulers or other pieces of wood and pretends to lay a fire.*)

MISS HARPER (*Calling on* MOLLY): What is this lad doing?

MOLLY: He's bringing in wood for the fire.

BILLY: Right. My feather says:
A Puritan lad would carry wood

And help his father all he could.
MISS HARPER: Now, Billy, you may wear one of the Puritan hats you will find in the closet. (*As* BILLY *exits,* MABEL *returns in cap and apron and takes her place at the table.*)
ROSE: Now, it's my turn. (*Goes to table*) Turkey, turkey, tell me true
What would a little Puritan do? (*After consulting the feather, she finds a sewing basket, pulls up a stool, sits down, and sews.*)
CINDY (*Raising hand*): Rose is sewing. Maybe she is sewing a quilt patch.
ROSE: Yes. My feather says:
One thing a little maid must know,
And that is how to stitch and sew.
Now, Miss Harper, may I get my costume?
MISS HARPER: Yes, indeed. (BILLY *enters as* ROSE *exits.*) Mike, it's your turn.
MIKE (*At table*): Turkey, turkey, tell me true
What would a little Puritan do? (*Finds toy hoe, a paper fish and pair of scissors. He pantomimes digging a hole, cuts the fish into three pieces and drops them on the floor. Reaches into pockets for seeds and pretends to plant them. Then kneels and covers the hole with dirt, patting it into place.*)
BILLY: It looks as if Mike is planting something. But I don't understand what he did with the fish.
PENNY (*Excited*): I know! I know! He is planting corn. The Indians taught the Puritans to put a few pieces of fish into every hill of corn.

MIKE: That's right. My feather says:
A Puritan lad at early morn
Would help his father plant the corn.
MISS HARPER: You did very well, Mike. You may get your hat. (MIKE *exits as* ROSE *enters.*)
MOLLY (*Approaching turkey*): Turkey, turkey, tell me true
What would a little Puritan do? (*Looks around for book. Studies it for a second, puts it behind her back, and pretends to recite. Looks at book again, squeezes her eyes shut and recites again as if memorizing.*)
MISS HARPER: What is this little maid doing?
JOHNNY: I think she is learning her ABC's.
MOLLY: That's right. My feather says:
A Puritan child must say with ease
His numbers and his ABC's. (MOLLY *exits as* MIKE *returns to stage.*)
RALPH (*Moving up to turkey*): Turkey, turkey, tell me true
What would a little Puritan do? (*He seizes a yardstick for a gun. Then he stalks about, kneels, takes aim, fires, and holds up the imaginary animal he has shot.*)
MABEL: That's easy. I think Ralph is shooting the Thanksgiving turkey.
RALPH: It *could* be a turkey. My feather says:
In Puritan times a little lad
Would go out hunting with his dad. (*Exits for costume as* MOLLY *returns.*)

CINDY (*At table*): Turkey, turkey, tell me true
What would a little Puritan do? (*After consulting feather, she picks up a basket and pretends to gather berries. She drops them into the basket, a handful at a time, occasionally popping one into her mouth. She might even make a face and spit out a sour one.*)

SAM: I know what Cindy is doing. She is picking berries.

CINDY: I love to pick berries. They make good pies. Here's what my feather says:
Little Puritan Sue's and Mary's
Often picked wild fruits and berries.

MISS HARPER: And they ate lots of wild fruits and berries at the first Thanksgiving dinner. (*Exit* CINDY; *enter* RALPH) Johnny, you're next.

JOHNNY (*At table*): Turkey, turkey, tell me true
What would a little Puritan do? (*After reading feather, he picks up a pointer, ties a string to it and attaches a paper fish. Then he walks around, whistling proudly.*)

ALL: Johnny went fishing and caught a big fish!

JOHNNY: My turkey feather says:
All Puritan children liked to fish
And brought home many a tasty dish.

MISS HARPER: They got most of their food from the woods and streams. Johnny, you have earned your Thanksgiving hat. (*He exits as* CINDY *returns.*) Now, Penny, it's your turn.

PENNY (*At table*): Turkey, turkey, tell me true

What would a little Puritan do? (*She finds a wooden bowl and block of wood. She sits on floor and pounds bowl with wooden block.*)

ROSE: Penny is pounding something, but I don't know what it is.

PENNY: Do you give up?

BILLY: Maybe she is pounding corn.

PENNY: I am making cornmeal. (*Reading from feather*)
Puritan children by the hour
Would pound the kernels into flour.

MISS HARPER: And their mothers baked corn pudding for the Thanksgiving feast. (PENNY *exits as* JOHNNY *enters.*)

SAM: Now it's my turn to ask the riddle. (*At table*)
Turkey, turkey, tell me true
What would a little Puritan do? (*Reads feather, picks up yardstick which he shoulders as a gun. Walks up and down as if on sentry duty.*)

MIKE: I think Sam is on guard duty. Is he a soldier?

SAM: No, I am not a soldier. I am just a little boy. My feather says:
The Puritans met many dangers
And always watched for enemy strangers.

MISS HARPER: But the Indians were kind to them, and most of the strangers who came were friendly strangers.

SAM: The Puritans were grateful to the Indians for their help.

MISS HARPER: So they invited the Indians to their Thanksgiving feast. Sam, you may put on your cos-

tume and join us at the table. (*Exit* SAM; *enter* PENNY.)
PENNY: We are all Puritans now, Miss Harper.
RALPH: Puritan boys and girls weren't very different after all.
CINDY: They worked and they played, just as we do.
MIKE: Sometimes they were good, and, I guess, sometimes they were bad.
SAM (*Entering with hat*): Miss Harper, there is one feather left. That one must be for you.
MISS HARPER (*At table now occupied by children in costume*): Then I will ask my riddle. (*Pulling out feather*) Turkey, turkey, tell me true
What would a Puritan teacher do? (*Reading from feather*)
She'd teach her boys and girls to say the Bible verses every day. And this is the verse we should all say together in honor of our first American Thanksgiving: "Enter into His gates with thanksgiving, and into His courts with praise."
CHILDREN: "Enter into His gates with thanksgiving and into His courts with praise."
MISS HARPER: "Be thankful unto Him and bless His name."
CHILDREN: "Be thankful unto Him and bless His name."
(CHILDREN *all fold their hands and sing any simple prayer of Thanksgiving as the curtains close.*)

THE END

A VISIT TO GOLDILOCKS

Characters

MAMMA BEAR
PAPA BEAR } *The Three Bears*
BABY BEAR

HOOTIE
TOOTIE } *Three Owls*
CUTIE

GOLDILOCKS
MOTHER, *Goldilocks' mother*
FATHER, *Goldilocks' father*

SCENE 1

TIME: *Early afternoon in spring.*
SETTING: *A clearing in the woods.*
AT RISE: *The* THREE BEARS *enter.* BABY BEAR *is between* MAMMA BEAR *and* PAPA BEAR, *holding their hands.*

THREE BEARS (*Singing to the tune of "Farmer in the Dell"*):
A-walking we will go,
A-walking we will go.
Ha, ha, ha and ho, ho, ho,
A-walking we will go.
(*They repeat song until they reach center stage.*)

BABY BEAR: Where are we going?
MAMMA *and* PAPA BEAR (*Singing*):
   We're walking through the woods,
   We're walking through the woods,
   Ha, ha, ha and ho, ho, ho,
   We're walking through the woods.
BABY BEAR: I don't want to walk through the woods. I've been there before—lots of times.
MAMMA *and* PAPA BEAR (*Singing*):
   Where would you like to go?
   Where would you like to go?
   Ha, ha, ha and ho, ho, ho,
   Where would you like to go?
BABY BEAR: I'd like to go visiting.
MAMMA *and* PAPA BEAR: Visiting! Whoever heard of visiting? Besides, where would we visit?
BABY BEAR: I'd like to visit Goldilocks.
MAMMA *and* PAPA BEAR: Goldilocks!
BABY BEAR: Yes. She came to see us. Now I'd like to visit her.
MAMMA BEAR: What do you think, Papa Bear?
PAPA BEAR: Whatever you say, my dear.
BABY BEAR (*Jumping up and down*): Please! Please!
MAMMA *and* PAPA BEAR (*Nodding their heads and singing*):
   It seems a happy thought,
   It seems a happy thought,
   Ha, ha, ha and ho, ho, ho,
   It seems a happy thought.
BABY BEAR: Then we're really going! We're really going

to visit Goldilocks. Come on, let's hurry. (BABY BEAR *tugs at* MAMMA *and* PAPA BEAR *in an effort to hurry them, but they are halted by the entrance of the three owls,* HOOTIE, TOOTIE *and* CUTIE.)

THREE OWLS: To-whit-to-whoo!
   What's this you do?

THREE BEARS: We're going to visit Goldilocks.

HOOTIE: My word!

TOOTIE: Whoever heard—

CUTIE: Of such a thing!

THREE OWLS: What will you do when you get there?

PAPA BEAR: I'm going to taste the big bowl of porridge to see if it's too hot.

MAMMA BEAR: I'm going to taste the middle-sized bowl of porridge to see if it's too cold.

BABY BEAR: I'm going to taste the little, wee bowl of porridge, and if it's just right I'm going to eat it all up!

HOOTIE: Land sakes.

TOOTIE: What a lot of mistakes—

CUTIE: Each one of you makes!

THREE OWLS: That's not the way to go visiting!

PAPA BEAR: Then I'm going to sit in the great, big chair to see if it's too hard.

MAMMA BEAR: I'm going to sit in the middle-sized chair to see if it's too soft.

BABY BEAR: I'm going to sit in the little, wee chair, and if it's just right, I'm going to rock and rock till the bottom falls out!

HOOTIE: Dear me,

A VISIT TO GOLDILOCKS

TOOTIE: It's dreadful to see—
CUTIE: How rude you will be!
THREE OWLS: That's not the way to go visiting!
PAPA BEAR: Then I'm going upstairs and try the great, big bed to see if it's too hard.
MAMMA BEAR: I'm going to try the middle-sized bed to see if it's too soft.
BABY BEAR: I'm going to try the little, wee bed and if it's just right, I might fall fast asleep.
HOOTIE: Fie! Fie!
TOOTIE: Oh, me and oh, my!
CUTIE: You're making me cry!
THREE OWLS: That's not the way to go visiting! You'll never be invited again!
BABY BEAR: But that's what Goldilocks did when she came to our house!
PAPA BEAR: She tasted our porridge!
MAMMA BEAR: She sat in our chairs!
BABY BEAR: And she went to sleep in my bed!
THREE OWLS: But Goldilocks is older now! She knows better! She's learned how to be polite.
PAPA BEAR: Is it very hard?
MAMMA BEAR: Does it take very long?
BABY BEAR: Could *we* learn to be polite?
THREE OWLS: It's easy. We'll teach you. (*As the* THREE OWLS *sing the following song to the tune of "Old MacDonald," they pantomime the action. The* THREE BEARS *join in on some of the lines. If desired, children in audience or rest of classroom may sing this song.*)

A VISIT TO GOLDILOCKS

First you knock upon the door.
Knock, knock, knock, knock, knock.
If no one comes, you knock again.
Knock, knock, knock, knock, knock.
With a knock knock now, and a knock knock then,
Now a knock, then a knock,
Every time a knock, knock.
First you knock upon the door,
Knock, knock, knock, knock, knock.

Then you wait till someone says:
"Won't you please come in?"
And then you bow and then you say,
"Thank you, ma'am," and grin.
With a handshake here, and a handshake there,
Here a shake, there a shake,
Everywhere a handshake,
That's the way to greet your hosts,
Shake them by the hand.

Once inside, your host will say:
"Won't you please sit down?"
And then you say, but not until,
"Thank you, ma'am, I will."
With a chat about this, and a chat about that,
Now a chat, then a chat,
All the time a chit-chat.
Then you talk of this and that,
Till it's time to go.

When you leave, be sure to say:
"Thank you very much.

I had a very pleasant time,
Thank you very much."
With a thank you here, and a thank you there,
Here a thank, there a thank,
Everywhere a thank you,
You'll be sure your host will then
Ask you back again.

THREE BEARS: Thank you, thank you very much.
PAPA BEAR: Now we know just what to do and say.
MAMMA BEAR: I am sure Goldilocks will be glad to see us.
BABY BEAR: And maybe she will ask us to come again. (*They skip off.*)
THREE OWLS: To-whit-to-whoo!
 Goodbye to you!
 And have a good time!

CURTAIN

* * * * *

SCENE 2

TIME: *Later the same day.*
SETTING: *The home of Goldilocks. A screen at one side of the stage serves as a door. There are three empty chairs in the room.*
AT RISE: FATHER *is reading his paper.* MOTHER *is sewing.* GOLDILOCKS *is playing with her doll on the floor. The* THREE BEARS *enter near screen.*
THREE BEARS (*Singing to the tune of "Old Mac-*

Donald"): First we knock upon the door. (*All three knock on screen.* GOLDILOCKS *stops playing,* MOTHER *stops sewing, and* FATHER *stops reading.*)

MOTHER, FATHER *and* GOLDILOCKS (*Looking toward the door and singing to the tune of* "*Who's That Knocking at My Door*"):
Who's that knocking at the door?
Who's that knocking at the door?
Who's that knocking at the door?
Who is here to see us?

PAPA BEAR (*Singing*): It is I, the Papa Bear.
MAMMA BEAR (*Singing*): It is I, the Mamma Bear.
BABY BEAR (*Singing*): It is little Baby Bear.
THREE BEARS (*Singing*): We have come to see you.
MOTHER, FATHER *and* GOLDILOCKS: The Three Bears!
GOLDILOCKS: What shall we do?
FATHER: Let's call the police!
GOLDILOCKS: Let's run and hide!
MOTHER: Don't be silly. They are our guests. (*Singing*)
We will hurry to the door,
We will hurry to the door,
We will hurry to the door,
And say: "How do you do."

FATHER: Of course, Mother. You are quite right. (*Singing*)
We will shake them by the hand,
We will shake them by the hand,
We will shake them by the hand,
And say: "Please, do come in."

GOLDILOCKS: I am not afraid any more, Mother. (*Singing*)
We will lead them to a chair,
We will lead them to a chair,
We will lead them to a chair,
And say: "Please, do sit down."
(*All three go to door.*)
MOTHER: How do you do.
FATHER (*Shaking hands with* PAPA BEAR): Please come in. (THREE BEARS *enter room.*)
GOLDILOCKS (*Indicating chairs*): Please do sit down.
FATHER: The big chair is for Mr. Bear.
MOTHER: The middle-sized chair is for Mrs. Bear.
GOLDILOCKS: The little wee chair is for Baby Bear.
MOTHER: We are so glad you came.
PAPA BEAR: It was such a fine day for a walk through the woods.
MAMMA BEAR: And Baby Bear wanted to go visiting.
BABY BEAR: So we came to see our friend, Goldilocks.
MOTHER: Goldilocks, you will find some milk and cookies for our guests on the dining room table. (GOLDILOCKS *exits.*)
PAPA BEAR: I'm so glad you were at home today, so we could visit you.
FATHER: We like to have company. (GOLDILOCKS *enters with milk and cookies, which she passes to her guests and her parents. Each thanks her.*)
MAMMA BEAR: These cookies are delicious.
PAPA BEAR: This milk is good and cold.

BABY BEAR: Everything is just right.
MAMMA BEAR: When you come to visit us, I will bake some honey cakes.
PAPA BEAR: I will show you my garden.
BABY BEAR: I will let you play with my toys.
MOTHER, FATHER *and* GOLDILOCKS: Thank you very much.
MAMMA BEAR: We really must be going. (*Rises*)
PAPA BEAR (*Rising*): Thank you for a pleasant afternoon.
BABY BEAR: Thank you for the milk and cookies. (*Rises*)
MAMMA BEAR: Do come to see us soon.
FATHER: Thank you. I would like to see your garden.
MOTHER: I have always wanted to see your house in the woods.
GOLDILOCKS: And I will not break your chairs or eat up your porridge.
MOTHER: Goldilocks knows better now. She would never go into a house when folks are not at home.
FATHER: It's more fun to go visiting when you know the rules.
ALL (*Joining hands, skipping around in a circle, and singing to "Farmer in the Dell"*):
We've had a lot of fun,
We've had a lot of fun,
Ha, ha, ha and ho, ho, ho,
We've had a lot of fun.
MOTHER, FATHER *and* GOLDILOCKS (*Singing as the* THREE BEARS *move off-stage*):

Be sure to come again,
Be sure to come again,
Ha, ha, ha and ho, ho, ho,
Be sure to come again.
THREE BEARS (*Turning and singing*):
Be sure to visit us,
Be sure to visit us,
Ha, ha, ha and ho, ho, ho,
Be sure to visit us. (*Curtain*)

THE END

THE LOST CHRISTMAS CARDS

Characters

POSTMAN
TRUDY
BILL
LYNN
MARY
TOMMY
JANE
CARL

BETH
BOB
ANDY
SARAH
JOE
FOUR CHILDREN
SEASON'S GREETING QUARTET

SCENE 1

TIME: *Just before Christmas.*
SETTING: *A street corner. There is a mailbox in front of the curtain.*
BEFORE RISE: *A group of twelve* CHILDREN *come in to mail Christmas cards. They sing to the tune of "Skip to My Lou."*

TRUDY (*Singing to the tune of "Skip to My Lou"*): I have a card for Emmy Lou. (*Drops in card*)
BILL: I have a card for dear Aunt Sue. (*Mails card*)
LYNN: I have a card for you guess who.
ALL: We all have our Christmas cards.

THE LOST CHRISTMAS CARDS 113

MARY: I have a card for Uncle Pete.
TOMMY: I have a card that is really neat!
JANE: I have a card that is mighty sweet.
ALL: We all have our Christmas cards.
CARL: I have a card to send the preacher.
BETH: I have a card to send my teacher.
BOB (*With a grin and a wink*): I have an extra special feature!
ALL: We all have our Christmas cards.
SARAH: I have a card for Cousin Joe.
ANDY: I have a card with falling snow.
JOE: I have some cards—and here they go!
ALL: We all have our Christmas cards! (POSTMAN *enters as song ends.*)
POSTMAN: Good morning, children. Mailing your cards, I see.
ALL: Yes, Mr. Postman and a Merry Christmas.
POSTMAN: Merry Christmas to you. Mailing Christmas cards is a lot of fun, isn't it?
ANDY: Getting Christmas cards is even better. I have a whole stack of them already.
LYNN (*As* POSTMAN *takes cards from box and puts them into his pouch*): Be careful, Mr. Postman. Don't lose any of the cards.
POSTMAN: Don't worry. I won't.
LYNN: Last year my very best friend didn't get the card I sent her because the Postman lost it.
POSTMAN: Are you sure the Postman lost it?
LYNN: Of course. I mailed it with the others, and she never got it.

THE LOST CHRISTMAS CARDS

POSTMAN: Did you have the right postage?

LYNN: My Daddy stamped all the cards last year.

POSTMAN: Was the card clearly addressed?

LYNN (*Proudly*): In my best writing!

TOMMY (*Laughing*): Miss Parker says you scribble, Lynn. Maybe the Postman couldn't read the name and address.

POSTMAN: Did you have your return address on the envelope?

LYNN: Return address? What's that?

POSTMAN: That is your street, number, town and state. You write it on the top left corner of the envelope. Then if a letter is lost, the Post Office can send it back home.

TOMMY: That's a good idea. I'll have to remember that.

CARL: Why do Christmas cards get lost, Mr. Postman?

POSTMAN: Because people are careless. That's why. Let's look at some of the cards I just pulled out of this box. (*Takes a handful of cards from mailbag*) Now here! Look at this one. It's not sealed and already the card is falling out of the envelope.

MARY (*Catching card as it falls out of envelope*): Oh, dear! I hope this one doesn't get lost. It is for a shut-in. (*Reads*)
Just a cheery greeting
With wishes fond and true
That you will have a happy day
And know we think of you.

POSTMAN: Here's another careless card. Can you read the address? (*Hands card to* TRUDY)

THE LOST CHRISTMAS CARDS

TRUDY: It looks like Miss . . . No. . . . It's Mr. Harry Hays.
MARY (*Taking card*): Let me see it. No, that's not Mr. Harry Hays. That's Mrs. Mary Hawes.
TOMMY (*Taking card*): And the address is 53 Pine Street.
JANE (*Taking card*): It looks like 35 Vine Street to me. What do you think, Bill?
BILL (*Taking card*): I don't know. It could be Pine Street, Vine Street or Lime Street.
CARL (*Taking card*): The city is very plain. It's Springfield.
SARAH: What state? There are a lot of Springfields.
CARL: There isn't any state.
BETH: What will happen to this Christmas card, Mr. Postman?
POSTMAN: Just another lost card, I'm afraid. Someone will be disappointed. (*Shakes envelope and card flutters out.*)
LYNN (*Picking it up*): Oh, dear! It's a card to somebody's mother. (*Reads*)
Of all the mothers in the world,
You are the dearest one.
So here's a Merry Christmas
From your ever loving son. It's signed *Joe*.
JOE: Joe? That's *my* name. I sure would hate to have my mother disappointed on Christmas Day.
ALL: So would I.
TOMMY: If this card had a return address on the envelope, it would go back to Joe, wouldn't it?

POSTMAN: That's right. But now, this poor little lost Christmas card will go to the Dead Letter Office.
BETH: That sounds sad.
POSTMAN: It *is* sad. Every year people spend hundreds of dollars for cards that never get where they're going. It's all because of carelessness.
LYNN: Mr. Postman, I have an idea. Would you visit our school on Monday and tell the rest of the children in our room about the lost Christmas cards?
POSTMAN: I will if you boys and girls will help me. Will you do that?
ALL: You bet we will.
POSTMAN: Then come along down to the Post Office with me right now and we'll talk things over with the Postmaster. (CHILDREN *and* POSTMAN *exit*.)

CURTAIN

* * * * *

SCENE 2

TIME: *The next week.*
SETTING: *A schoolroom. There are two tables on stage. At one table are seated* FOUR CHILDREN, *each with a tray of Christmas cards. At the other is a big box, overturned to show piles of Christmas cards spilling out. There is also a white flannel board with the outline of an envelope in black.* LYNN *and the* POSTMAN

are center stage. Other children are seated in the first row of the audience or, if space permits, may be seated at one side of the stage.

LYNN: This afternoon, our good friend, the Postman, is going to tell us a story. It's a sad story, and the name of it is "The Lost Christmas Cards." Let's give our Postman a Christmas welcome.

CHILDREN (*Singing to "Happy Birthday"*): Merry Christmas to you, Merry Christmas to you. Merry Christmas, Mr. Postman, Merry Christmas to you.

POSTMAN: Thank you, boys and girls. As you know, I am the Postman. I collect the mail from the corner mail boxes and take it to the Post Office. There it is sorted and put into the bags we Postmen carry on our rounds. Every morning, I pick up my bag and deliver the mail to your homes. At Christmas time this is a big job. Down at the Post Office we call it the Christmas rush. We work very hard but every year, in spite of all we can do, hundreds of cards and packages are lost. Today we are going to tell you the story of some of these lost Christmas cards. Our story begins over here. (*Indicates table where* FOUR CHILDREN *are sitting with cards.*)

1ST CHILD: I wonder why I didn't get a card from Cousin Fred.

He always used to send me one. I wonder if he's dead!

2ND CHILD: I'm feeling low! No card from Bill! I must be off his list!

THE LOST CHRISTMAS CARDS

And nothing here from Kathy Lou. I wonder how she missed!

3RD CHILD: I'm very far away from home, as lonely as can be.

I hate to think my neighbors have all forgotten me.

4TH CHILD: I never heard a single word from my dear sister Kate.

Oh, well! I guess she mailed the card a little bit too late.

ALL: It's really very, very sad to get no Christmas mail. We don't see how at Christmas time our dearest friends could fail!

POSTMAN: Maybe all those dear friends didn't forget after all. Maybe they were just careless. (*Indicating box of cards*) Here are just a few of the Christmas cards that were lost last year. We'll ask Beth and Tommy to take a look. (BETH *and* TOMMY *go to box.*)

BETH (*Pulling card from box and reading*):
I hope that Santa brings you
The best of Christmas cheer,
A very happy holiday,
And gay and glad New Year.
It is signed *Cousin Fred*.

POSTMAN: See! Cousin Fred wasn't dead after all. He was just careless! Tommy, what do you have there?

TOMMY: I have two cards. This one is signed *Bill*. It says *Merry Christmas to a good pal!* The other one is from Kathy Lou. I'll read it to you.
Christmas bells are ringing! Happy children singing!

THE LOST CHRISTMAS CARDS

Christmastide is in the air! Merry Christmas everywhere!

POSTMAN: Beth, what have you found?

BETH (*Reading another card*): This one is the lost Christmas card from sister Kate.
Christmas makes me glad anew.
I have a sister just like you.

POSTMAN: Poor sister Kate! Her card got lost in the rush. Now, Tommy, it's your turn.

TOMMY: This card is a good-neighbor greeting. (*Reads*)
I send this little greeting gay
To a friendly neighbor, far away.
With dearest love and wishes, too,
For a very special friend like you.

POSTMAN: It's too bad that all these lovely cards were lost in the Christmas rush. You can make sure that your Christmas card story will have a happy ending, if you mail your cards early this year, and make sure that each one is properly addressed. Trudy and Bill will show you how. (TRUDY *and* BILL *take their places at flannel board and stick the prepared materials in place.*)

TRUDY (*Pointing to board*): This is an envelope. Make sure you write the name and address plainly. (*Sticks on a name. Example: Miss Mary Jones.*) On the second line, write the street and number. (*Sticks on street and number.*)

BILL (*Putting up the name of a city*): Next, the city to which the card is going.

TRUDY: If it is a very large city, be sure to put the zone number. (*Adds zone number to city.*)

BILL: Don't forget the state. In America we have many towns of the same name. The state is important. (*Sticks name of state on board*)

TRUDY: In the upper left-hand corner of the envelope goes the return address. (*Sticks on a return address*) This is your own street and number, town and state.

BILL (*Sticking the stamp in place*): Now for the stamp. If you seal the envelope, you must use a four-cent stamp, and if a card is worth mailing, it is worth sealing the envelope so the card doesn't fall out.

POSTMAN: When you mail your Christmas cards this year, boys and girls, look them over. Make sure they won't get lost. Then your friends and relatives will have a happier Christmas because of your cards.

TRUDY (*Pointing to flannel board*): Write the name and address plainly.

BILL: Check the number, street, city and state.

TRUDY: Put on a return address.

BILL: Be sure you have the right postage.

BOTH: And mail your Christmas cards early this year.

POSTMAN: We'll have no more lost Christmas cards, if you listen to our Season's Greeting Quartet. (*Enter* FOUR CHILDREN *wearing large placards addressed as Christmas cards. They sing to the tune of "I'm a Little Tea Pot."*)

1ST GREETING: I'm a cheery greeting,
Saucy scamp!

Here is my address! Here is my stamp!
Just before you mail me,
Stop and grin.
Look me over
And drop me in!

2ND GREETING: I'm a little greeting,
Short and sweet.
Here is my number! Here is my street!
Just before you mail me,
I repeat,
Look me over
So I'm complete.

3RD GREETING: I'm a little greeting,
I can't wait!
Here is my city! Here is my state!
Just before you send me,
Check the date!
Mail me early
Or I'll be late!

4TH GREETING: I'm another greeting,
Pitched and tossed.
Four cents to mail me! Ten cents I cost!
If my street or number's
Scratched and crossed,
Write me over
Or I'll get lost!

ALL GREETINGS: We are little greetings,
Gay and bright.
Some of us red, and some of us white.

Just before you send us
On our flight,
Look us over
So we'll be right. (*Curtain*)

THE END

WAKE UP, SANTA CLAUS!

Characters

SANTA CLAUS
MRS. SANTA
ROLY ⎫
POLY ⎭ *Santa's elves*
MR. TICK-TOCK
REINDEER MASTER
RHYTHM BAND ELVES
MR. COCKADOODLE DOO
MR. QUACK-QUACK
MRS. WADDLE-WADDLE
ROVER
FIDO
PLUTO
TABBY
TOMMY
OOPAH, *an Eskimo boy*
SEE-GLOO, *an Eskimo girl*

TIME: *Christmas Eve.*
SETTING: *Santa's bedroom.*
AT RISE: SANTA *is asleep on a small cot.* MRS. SANTA *sits in a rocking chair beside his bed. She dozes from time to time over her knitting, and rouses herself with a start.* SANTA *is snoring deeply. After a short pause allowing* SANTA *a few snores and* MRS. SANTA *a few catnaps,* ROLY *and* POLY *enter.*

ROLY: Santa, Santa, wake up! Wake up!
POLY: It's a quarter to Christmas Eve.
ROLY *and* POLY: We'll be late! We'll be late!
MRS. SANTA (*Wide awake*): Dear me! Dear me! What's all the clatter?
ROLY: Santa has overslept.

POLY: We should be on our way.

MRS. SANTA: The alarm has not gone off yet. (*Reaching for clock*) Dear me! It's stopped. It must be broken.

ROLY: Hurry, Mrs. Santa. Wake him up.

POLY: We don't want to keep the children waiting.

MRS. SANTA (*Shaking* SANTA *gently*): Wake up. Wake up, Santa. It's time to go. (SANTA *does a few fancy snores.*)

ROLY: Shake him harder, Mrs. Santa. There's no time to lose.

MRS. SANTA (*Shaking harder and talking louder*): Santa, Santa, wake up. Wake up!

ROLY: Why is he asleep at this hour?

POLY: He's always ready ahead of time.

MRS. SANTA: The poor dear was so tired, I told him he should lie down for a little nap, but you know what a sound sleeper he is. (*More shaking*) Santa, Santa, it's time to get up. (SANTA *turns over and resumes snoring.*)

ROLY (*Also shaking* SANTA): Come on, Santa. It's time to get on the job.

POLY (*Shaking* SANTA *from the other side of the bed*): Santa, Santa, you *must* wake up. If we don't get started, we'll never finish our rounds.

MRS. SANTA: Oh, dear! It's no use. He'll never wake up without that alarm clock. It's the only sound he ever hears once he's fallen into a deep sleep.

ROLY: Then we must get it fixed. Poly, run and see if you can find Mr. Tick-Tock.

POLY: I think he's still in the workshop. I'll get him.

(*Exit* POLY. MRS. SANTA *and* ROLY *keep trying to wake* SANTA.)

ROLY: My mother used to pour water on me when I wouldn't get up in the morning.

MRS. SANTA: We'll not pour water on Mr. Santa, young man. Not if he sleeps straight through till Christmas morning. I don't want him catching a chill.

ROLY: We *must* do something!

MRS. SANTA: Maybe Mr. Tick-Tock will be able to fix the alarm. Here he comes now. (*Enter* POLY *with* MR. TICK-TOCK, *who wears coveralls and carries a tool kit.*)

POLY: Here he is, Mrs. Santa. Here's Mr. Tick-Tock.

MR. TICK-TOCK: I knew when Roly and Poly wanted me, it must be an important job.

MRS. SANTA (*Handing clock to* MR. TICK-TOCK): Here's the clock, sir. Please see what you can do with it.

MR. TICK-TOCK (*Sitting down on floor with his back to the audience. In this position, he can pull out all sorts of springs, wires, and wheels from his bag, as if he is taking them out of the clock*): I'll have to take it apart first. Looks like a ticklish job.

ROLY: Please hurry. Every minute counts.

MR. TICK-TOCK (*Hammers and bangs as if working on the clock*): There! I have it. Now let me see what the trouble is. Oh, oh! Look at this. A bad spring! (*Holds up a big spring and tosses it over his shoulder*) Dear me! These wires are in bad shape. (*Pulls out several feet of wire or cord which he tosses over his shoulder*)

MRS. SANTA: Maybe the mainspring is broken.

MR. TICK-TOCK: I can't even find the mainspring. None of these wheels seems to be right. (*Tosses out a handful of wheels*)

POLY: Can't you please hurry?

MR. TICK-TOCK: Patience. Patience. You can't rush a job like this. (*Pulls out more wire*) This poor clock is really in bad shape. I'm afraid I'll have to take it out to the workshop.

ROLY: Then we'll be late.

POLY: We can't possibly get around the world tonight.

MRS. SANTA: Can't you fix the bell so it will ring just once?

MR. TICK-TOCK (*Rising with clock and tool kit*): I'm afraid not. I'll have to make some new parts. These are all worn out.

MRS. SANTA: How long will that take?

MR. TICK-TOCK: I'm afraid I couldn't possibly get it done before tomorrow morning.

ROLY: But tomorrow will be Christmas.

MR. TICK-TOCK: Sorry, but that's the way it is.

MRS. SANTA: I'm sure you'll do your very best.

MR. TICK-TOCK: Isn't there some other bell that would wake him? Isn't there another clock in the house?

MRS. SANTA: Not a single one.

ROLY: We could try another bell, couldn't we?

POLY: What about sleigh bells?

MR. TICK-TOCK: A splendid idea. I'll speak to the Reindeer Master as I go by the stables, and send him in at once. (*Exit* MR. TICK-TOCK.)

MRS. SANTA (*Shaking* SANTA *again*): Please, Santa, please, wake up. It's almost Christmas Eve.

ROLY: Couldn't we throw just a few drops of water on him, Mrs. Santa?

MRS. SANTA: Not a single drop. I won't have him catching cold. Santa, Santa, wake up! Wake up!

POLY: How about tickling him with a feather? That should wake him up in a hurry.

MRS. SANTA: I'll get my feather duster. Santa's very ticklish. (*Exit* MRS. SANTA.)

ROLY: If only she'd let us try the water.

POLY: Maybe the feather will work. We'll try. (MRS. SANTA *returns with a feather duster.*)

MRS. SANTA: Now be very gentle with him.

ROLY (*Bending over* SANTA *with feather duster*): Just a few tickles under the nose should do the trick. (*As he tickles* SANTA, *the sleeper stirs, sneezes violently, and goes on snoring.*)

POLY: You almost had him that time. Try it again. (*This time* SANTA *sneezes again, turns over and buries his head in the pillow.*)

MRS. SANTA: It's no good. Nothing will wake him up but that old alarm clock. (REINDEER MASTER *enters with several* ELVES *carrying sleigh bells.*)

REINDEER MASTER: What's the trouble? Mr. Tick-Tock told me to come at once and bring the sleigh bells.

ROLY: We can't wake Santa, and it's time to leave with the toys.

REINDEER MASTER: I wondered what was keeping him. Dancer and Prancer won't stand still much longer.

POLY (*To* ELVES *with sleigh bells*): Now come right over here, boys, close to the bed. Ring the sleigh bells good and loud. (ELVES *ring the sleigh bells for all they're worth.* SANTA *doesn't even stir.*)

MRS. SANTA: Look! He's smiling. He must hear the bells in his sleep.

REINDEER MASTER: Louder! Louder! Faster! Faster! Keep on ringing. (ELVES *ring sleigh bells violently for several seconds.*)

ROLY: It's no use. He's still sleeping like the dead.

REINDEER MASTER: This is bad business. Shall I unharness the reindeer?

MRS. SANTA: Oh, no! Not yet. There *must* be some way to wake him.

REINDEER MASTER: Maybe a deeper noise would wake him. Are there any drums handy?

ROLY: There are lots of drums here in the toy bags.

POLY: I'll get more elves to play them. (*Exit* POLY.)

ROLY: I'm sure there must be drums in one of these bags. Help me look. (REINDEER MASTER *and* ROLY *find drums in one of the bags as* MRS. SANTA *tries shaking* SANTA *again.*) Here are the drums.

REINDEER MASTER (*As* ELVES *enter with* POLY): Here are the boys to beat them.

POLY (*Passing drums to* ELVES): Here, beat the drums as loud as you can.

ELF: But we'll wake Santa.

ROLY: That's the idea. Now beat 'em good and loud. (ELVES *march around the bed beating the drums.*)

REINDEER MASTER: Try ringing the bells again. (*Repeat*

drum march with addition of sleigh bells. SANTA still snores.)

POLY: Maybe there are some other musical toys in these bags. (*Opens bags and produces wood blocks, triangles, and sand blocks*)

ROLY (*Shouting offstage*): Elves! Elves! We need more elves. (ELVES *run in and seize instruments.*)

POLY: Here you are, fellows. Make all the noise you can. We must get Santa to wake up. (ELVES *make a terrific din with rhythm instruments.*)

MRS. SANTA (*Holding her ears*): That sounds terrible. I think some Christmas music might have a better effect.

REINDEER MASTER: Let's try "Jingle Bells." I'll lead the band. (*The rhythm band assembled by the* ELVES *plays a rousing chorus of "Jingle Bells" with piano accompaniment.*)

ROLY: Santa is snoring louder than ever.

POLY: I give up!

REINDEER MASTER: We can't give up. Isn't there some other noise that might wake him?

ROLY: What noise seems to disturb Santa when he is resting?

MRS. SANTA: He sometimes wakes up when the roosters crow or when the dogs bark.

REINDEER MASTER: That's it. We'll call on our animal friends. Elves, go round up everything that barks or crows or cackles or meows. We'll try a barnyard chorus to wake Santa. (*Several* ELVES *exit.*)

REINDEER MASTER: In the meantime, let's try another

chorus of "Jingle Bells." (RHYTHM BAND *repeats* "*Jingle Bells.*")

ELF (*Entering*): The animals are ready.

MRS. SANTA: Send them in, but make sure they wipe their feet.

ELF: Mr. Cockadoodle Doo. (ROOSTER *enters.*)

ROOSTER: Merry Christmas, Mrs. Santa.

ROLY: Don't be so polite. Just crow as loud as you can.

ROOSTER: It isn't time to crow.

ROLY: Crow anyhow. We want to wake Santa Claus.

ROOSTER: I hope he won't be angry. (*Crows loud and long*)

POLY (*After a look at* SANTA): No good. What's next?

ELF: Mr. Quack-Quack and Mrs. Waddle-Waddle. (*Enter two* DUCKS.)

MR. QUACK-QUACK *and* MRS. WADDLE-WADDLE: Quackity, quackity, quack!
Yackity, yackity, yack!
Wake up! Wake up! Wake up!
It's time to take your pack.
(*The* DUCKS *stand beside* SANTA's *bed and quack very loudly, and the* ROOSTER *joins in.*)

ELF: Rover, Fido and Pluto!

ROVER, FIDO *and* PLUTO: Bow-wow, bow-wow, bow-wow!
Bow-wow, bow-wow, bow-wow!
Wake up! Wake up! Wake up!
The time to go is *now*. (*The* DOGS *caper about* SANTA's *bed, barking wildly.*)

MRS. SANTA: I'm sure Tabby and Tommy would like to try. Here, kitty, kitty, kitty—
TOMMY *and* TABBY (*Entering*):
  Meow, meow, meow!
  Meow, meow, meow!
  Wake up! Wake up! Wake up!
  We're here to show you how.
  (TABBY *and* TOMMY *frolic around the bed, with loud meows, and the other animals join in the chorus.*)
MRS. SANTA: It's no use. Santa just won't wake up.
ROLY: We can't give up.
REINDEER MASTER (*Opening one of the bags and pulling out an Indian headdress, a cowboy hat and a toy gun*): Let's make one more try. I've always heard that "Cowboys and Indians" is a noisy game.
POLY: Elves, do your duty! (*A few* ELVES *put on Indian headdresses, and cowboy hats. They circle the bed with Indian war whoops, cowboy yells and "bang-bangs."*)
MRS. SANTA: Stop it! Stop it! I can't stand the noise! Stop it, I say.
ROLY: You might as well unharness the reindeer. Santa won't be going out tonight.
POLY: By the time Santa wakes up, Christmas will be over.
REINDEER MASTER: The children will be so disappointed.
MRS. SANTA (*Wiping her eyes*): Poor Santa! This will be a sad Christmas for him. (*Sound of door-knocker*)
ELF: We have visitors. May they come in?

MRS. SANTA: Of course. Everyone is welcome on Christmas Eve. (*Enter* OOPAH *and* SEE-GLOO.)

OOPAH (*Bowing*): Good evening. I am Oopah, and this is my little sister, See-Gloo. We are your neighbors.

SEE-GLOO: Is this really where Santa Claus lives? (*The large group on the stage conceals* SANTA'S *bed*.)

MRS. SANTA: This is where he lives and I am Mrs. Santa.

OOPAH: We have brought Santa Claus a present.

SEE-GLOO: It is such a cold night, we knew his hands would get cold on his long drive.

OOPAH: So we brought him a pair of fur mittens.

MRS. SANTA: Thank you, children. That was very nice of you, but I am afraid Santa will not be going out tonight.

OOPAH: What's the matter?

SEE-GLOO: Is he sick?

MRS. SANTA: No, he is not sick. But he is sound asleep. We can't wake him.

OOPAH: I am sure he would wake up if we talked to him.

SEE-GLOO: Where is he? Won't you let us speak to him?

ROLY: Stand back! Stand back! Let the children speak to Santa Claus. (*As the group divides revealing* SANTA, *snoring away for dear life*, OOPAH *and* SEE-GLOO *stand on either side of the bed*.)

OOPAH *and* SEE-GLOO (*Speaking softly*): Santa, Santa! Can you hear us? (SANTA *stirs*.) Santa, Santa, it's Christmas Eve—(SANTA *stirs even more*.) The children are waiting for you—all over the world!

SANTA (*Half sitting up*): What's that? What's that you say?

OOPAH *and* SEE-GLOO: In every land beneath the sun,
  The children wait till night is done.
  "Their stockings are hung by the chimney with care
  In hopes that Saint Nicholas soon will be there."
SANTA (*Sitting up, wide awake*): Bless my soul! The children are calling me. It's Christmas Eve!
ALL: He's awake! He's awake!
SANTA: Awake? Of course I'm awake! I've no time to be sleeping on Christmas Eve. Mrs. Santa, please help me with my coat. Where are my spectacles? Roly and Poly, help me with my boots. (*There is a scramble to get* SANTA *into his costume.*) Dear me! Dear me! Why did you let me sleep so long?
ROLY: We thought you'd never wake up, Santa.
POLY: We tried everything.
REINDEER MASTER: You kept right on snoring.
ELVES: We beat our drums and rang our bells,
  But you kept right on snoring.
COWBOYS *and* INDIANS: We fired our guns and gave our yells,
  But you kept right on snoring!
ROOSTER *and* DOGS: We crowed and crowed and said "Bow Wow!"
  But you kept right on snoring.
DUCKS *and* CATS: We quackity-quacked and said "Meow"
  But you kept right on snoring!
OOPAH *and* SEE-GLOO: But when we spoke to you, you woke up right away.
MRS. SANTA: I don't see how you could sleep through

all that racket! Yet you heard the children the minute they spoke to you.

SANTA: Of course, I heard the children. Old Santa always keeps one ear open for little children, especially on Christmas Eve. (MR. TICK-TOCK *runs in with the alarm clock which is ringing.*)

MR. TICK-TOCK: It's fixed! It's fixed! Now Santa will wake up in time for Christmas Eve.

REINDEER MASTER: We won't need the alarm clock now, Mr. Tick-Tock. Santa is awake and ready to go.

ALL: Let's give him a royal send-off. (*All sing to the tune of "Up on the Housetop" as* SANTA *puts on his gloves handed to him by* OOPAH *and* SEE-GLOO, *and picks up two of the toy bags ready to go.*)

Out in the courtyard reindeer pause,
Here comes good old Santa Claus.
Laden with bags full of jolly toys,
All for the good little girls and boys.
Ho, ho, ho, now he will go,
Ho, ho, ho, now he will go,
Up on the housetops, click, click, click
All round the world comes our good Saint Nick!
(*Curtains close as* SANTA *walks off stage, waving to audience.*)

THE END

THE REAL PRINCESS

*Adapted from the story by
Hans Christian Andersen*

Characters

KING
QUEEN
PRINCE
SIX WISE MEN
PAGE
PRINCESS MONDAY
PRINCESS TUESDAY
PRINCESS WEDNESDAY
PRINCESS THURSDAY
PRINCESS FRIDAY
PRINCESS SATURDAY
PRINCESS SUNDAY
SERVANT

SETTING: *A room in the palace.*
AT RISE: *The* SIX WISE MEN, *the* KING, QUEEN *and* PRINCE *are seated at a long table. All prop their elbows on the table and lean their chins in their hands and look very worried.*

KING: I am the King!
QUEEN: I am the Queen!
PRINCE: I am the Prince!
WISE MEN: We are the wisest men in the land!
KING, QUEEN *and* PRINCE: We have a problem.
WISE MEN: What is it?
KING: We must find a Princess for the Prince to marry.

PRINCE: She must be beautiful.
KING: She must be good.
QUEEN: She must be a *real* Princess.
KING, QUEEN *and* PRINCE (*Singing to tune of "Rise, Sally, Rise"*):

> Wise men, arise!
> Open your eyes!
> Search in the East,
> And search in the West,
> And bring us the Princess
> We'll like best!

WISE MEN (*Stand and sing*):
> We will arise,
> Open our eyes,
> Search in the East
> And search in the West
> And bring you the Princess
> You'll like best.

(WISE MEN *march out singing.*)

PRINCE: How long will it take the Wise Men to find a Princess?
KING: Not long. They are very wise, you know.
QUEEN: But a *real* Princess is hard to find. It may take a whole week!
PRINCE: Tomorrow is Monday. Perhaps one of the Wise Men will find me a Monday Princess.
QUEEN: We'll have to wait and see.
KING (*Yawning and stretching*): Ho hum! I think I'll take a nap.

QUEEN: I think I shall, too.

PRINCE (*Yawning*): That's a good idea. I'm tired. (*All three stretch, yawn and fall asleep, their heads pillowed on their arms on the table. Enter* PAGE. *He wears a placard which reads,* MONDAY.)

PAGE (*As he crosses the stage*): Monday! Monday! Make way for Monday! (*Repeats this line as often as necessary to make the crossing and exit on opposite side of stage*)

QUEEN: Wake up! Wake up! It's Monday morning.

KING: Ho hum! What a happy sleep!

PRINCE: I do hope one of the Wise Men will bring me a Princess today. (*Enter* WISE MAN *with* PRINCESS MONDAY.)

FIRST WISE MAN: Happy Monday morning, Your Majesties! I have found a Princess for our Prince to marry.

KING (*To* PRINCESS): What is your name, child?

PRINCESS MONDAY: I am the Princess Monday.

QUEEN: Are you sure you are a *real* princess, my dear?

PRINCESS MONDAY: Oh, yes. My father is the King of Tomorrow.

PRINCE: Come, let me show you the gardens. We must get to know one another. (PRINCE *exits with* PRINCESS MONDAY *and* WISE MAN.)

KING: How do you like the Princess Monday, my dear?

QUEEN: We cannot be sure that she is a *real* Princess until she has spent a night in the royal bed I have prepared for her.

KING: I don't understand you!

QUEEN: Have patience, husband. In the morning I will be able to tell if the Princess Monday is a *real* Princess or only a pretender. Just wait and see. (PAGE *enters from opposite side of stage and crosses, but this time his placard announces* TUESDAY.)

PAGE: Tuesday! Tuesday! Take time for Tuesday! Tuesday! Tuesday! Take time for Tuesday! (*Exits.* PRINCE *enters.*)

PRINCE: Good morning, Mother. Good morning, Father. Have you seen the Princess Monday?

QUEEN: She has not yet come downstairs.

KING: I hope she slept well.

PRINCE: Ah, here she is. Good morning, Princess Monday.

PRINCESS MONDAY (*With a curtsy*): Good morning.

QUEEN: Did you sleep well, my dear?

PRINCESS MONDAY: Very well, thank you. My bed was like a downy cloud.

KING: Silence! The Second Wise Man is coming. (*Enter* SECOND WISE MAN *with* PRINCESS TUESDAY.)

SECOND WISE MAN: Allow me to present the Princess Tuesday.

ALL: Welcome, Princess.

QUEEN: Are you sure you are a *real* Princess, my dear?

PRINCESS TUESDAY: Oh, yes, my father is King of Yesterday.

PRINCE: Would you like to walk in the gardens with me and the Princess Monday? Then we will get to know each other. (*Exit* PRINCESSES, PRINCE, *and* WISE MAN.)

KING: Surely this is a *real* Princess, my dear. She is so beautiful.
QUEEN: Wait until tomorrow, Sire. Wait until she has rested in the little gold bed I have prepared for her.
KING: Oh, well! Wednesday will soon be here. (PAGE *enters as before with* WEDNESDAY *placard.*)
PAGE (*Crossing stage*): Wednesday! Wednesday! Welcome to Wednesday! Wednesday! Wednesday! Welcome to Wednesday! (*Enter* PRINCE.)
PRINCE: Good morning, Father. Good morning, Mother.
BOTH: Good morning, son.
KING (*As* PRINCESS MONDAY *and* PRINCESS TUESDAY *enter*): Good morning, ladies.
PRINCESS MONDAY *and* PRINCESS TUESDAY: Good morning. What a lovely day!
PRINCESS TUESDAY: And what a happy sleep I had in that little gold bed. I felt as if I were floating on air.
KING: Sit down, my dears. It is time for our Third Wise Man to arrive.
THIRD WISE MAN (*Entering with* PRINCESS WEDNESDAY): Allow me to present the Princess Wednesday.
ALL: Good morning, Princess Wednesday.
PRINCESS WEDNESDAY (*With curtsy*): Good morning.
KING: Welcome to our kingdom, my child.
QUEEN: Are you sure you are a *real* Princess, my dear?
PRINCESS WEDNESDAY: Oh, yes. My father is the King of Today.
THIRD WISE MAN: We have had a long journey, Sire. Perhaps the Princess would like to rest.

QUEEN: Come, my child, I will show you to your room, where I hope you will rest like a true Princess. (*Exit* QUEEN *and* PRINCESS WEDNESDAY, *followed by* WISE MAN.)

PRINCESS MONDAY: Every day a new Princess arrives.

PRINCESS TUESDAY: It is very exciting.

PRINCE: I can hardly wait until tomorrow.

KING: Tomorrow will be here before we know it. (*Enter* PAGE *with* THURSDAY *sign.*)

PAGE: This is Thursday! This is Thursday! This is Thursday! (*Enter* QUEEN *with* PRINCESS WEDNESDAY.)

QUEEN: You look rested, my dear.

PRINCESS WEDNESDAY: I never slept better in my life. We don't have such fine mattresses in our own kingdom.

QUEEN: Thank you, child. Would you like to join the others? (*All sit down.*)

KING: Our Fourth Wise Man is right on time, and he is bringing a lovely lady. (*Enter* FOURTH WISE MAN *with* PRINCESS THURSDAY.)

FOURTH WISE MAN: Good morning. I have brought you the lovely Princess Thursday.

KING: Welcome to our land. You are truly a beautiful Princess.

PRINCESS THURSDAY (*With curtsy*): Thank you, Sire.

QUEEN: But are you sure you are a *real* Princess, my dear?

PRINCESS THURSDAY: Oh, yes. My father is the King of Seven Days.

THE REAL PRINCESS

KING: Wise Man, you have done well. I am sure by the end of the week we will celebrate our son's wedding.
WISE MAN: Thank you, Sire. (*Exits*)
PRINCESS WEDNESDAY: I should like to show Princess Thursday to her room.
QUEEN: Certainly, my dear. She must be tired.
PRINCESS WEDNESDAY: You will have a fine rest in the little gold bed with the silken coverlets. Let me show you. (PRINCESS WEDNESDAY *and* PRINCESS THURSDAY *exit.* PAGE *enters with* FRIDAY *placard, crossing stage as before.*)
PAGE: Friday! Friday! A fine day for Friday! Friday! Friday! A fine day for Friday! (*Enter* PRINCESS WEDNESDAY *and* PRINCESS THURSDAY.)
PRINCESS THURSDAY: You were right, Princess Wednesday. Never have I had a better night's rest. Those mattresses must be made of powder puffs.
PRINCE: Please hurry and take your places. The Fifth Wise Man is coming. (*As girls are seated,* FIFTH WISE MAN *enters with* PRINCESS FRIDAY.)
FIFTH WISE MAN: Hail to you, gentle people. I bring you the Princess Friday.
ALL: Good morning, Princess Friday.
PRINCE: You are very beautiful.
KING: You look just like a princess, my dear.
QUEEN: But are you quite sure you are a *real* princess, my child?
PRINCESS FRIDAY: Oh, yes. My father is the King of the Week.

PRINCE: Please sit down and tell us about your country. (PRINCESS FRIDAY *takes place at table.*)
KING (*To* WISE MAN): Wise Man, you have done well.
QUEEN: Tomorrow we will hear our last report.
PRINCE: I can hardly wait until tomorrow.
FIFTH WISE MAN: Please excuse me, Sire. I have many things to do before tomorrow comes. (*He exits.* PAGE *enters as before with placard,* SATURDAY.)
PAGE: Saturday! Saturday! See what a Saturday! Saturday! Saturday! See what a Saturday!
PRINCESS FRIDAY: I am sure I will enjoy this day. I had such a good rest last night in the little gold bed with the soft, puffy mattresses.
QUEEN: Did you sleep well, my child?
PRINCESS: Like a baby, Your Majesty.
QUEEN: Then you will be bright and smiling to greet the new Princess. (*Enter* SIXTH WISE MAN *with* PRINCESS SATURDAY.)
SIXTH WISE MAN: Good morning to the court. May I present the most beautiful lady in the world, the Princess Saturday.
ALL: Welcome, Princess Saturday.
QUEEN: Excuse me, my dear, but are you sure you are a *real* princess?
PRINCESS SATURDAY: Oh, yes. My father is the King of Right Now.
QUEEN: How nice! We will spend a happy day together and this evening you shall rest in a little gold bed, made especially for you.
OTHER PRINCESSES: And what a wonderful bed it is!

KING: My son, will you please take your visitors into the garden so they may enjoy themselves?
PRINCE: Come, ladies, I have many things to show you. (*Exit* PRINCE *and* PRINCESSES)
KING (*To* SIXTH WISE MAN): You have done well, Wise Man.
WISE MAN: But with so many beautiful girls, which one will the Prince marry?
QUEEN: I am not sure that any of these is a *real* princess.
KING *and* SIXTH WISE MAN: Not a *real* princess!
QUEEN: We will wait until tomorrow. Then the Prince will decide. Come, Sire. I must make up the little gold bed for Princess Saturday. (*Exit* KING *and* QUEEN *followed by* WISE MAN, *who mutters.*)
SIXTH WISE MAN: Not a *real* princess! What can she mean by that? (PAGE *enters bearing placard,* SUNDAY.)
PAGE (*Crossing stage*): Sunday! Sunday! What a stormy Sunday! Sunday! Sunday! What a stormy Sunday! (WISE MEN *enter and take places, each one standing behind the chair of his princess.*)
WISE MEN (*Singing to tune of "Rise, Sally, Rise"*):
>We are so wise!
>We are so wise!
>Here from the East,
>Here from the West,
>We've brought the Princess
>The Prince loves best.

ALL: But which one will it be? (*Each in turn*) Princess Monday? Princess Tuesday? Princess Wednesday?

Princess Thursday? Princess Friday? Princess Saturday? (*Enter* KING, QUEEN *and* PRINCE, *taking their places at center of table.*)
KING: Today is the day you must choose your bride.
PRINCE: But which one? They are all so beautiful.
QUEEN: You must choose the *real* princess, my son. (*The* SIX PRINCESSES *enter and take their places, three on either side of the royal family.*)
PRINCESSES (*Singing to tune of "Rise, Sally, Rise."*):
>We are not wise,
>We are not wise.
>We're from the East,
>We're from the West!
>Now take the Princess
>That you love best!

KING: If the ladies form a circle around the Prince, perhaps he will be able to choose.
WISE MEN: A fine idea. (PRINCE *takes center stage with the six girls in a circle around him. They dance in a circle around the* PRINCE *as everybody sings.*)
ALL (*To tune of "Rise, Sally, Rise"*):
>Rise, master, rise,
>Don't hide your eyes,
>Turn to the East,
>Turn to the West
>And turn to the one that
>You love best.

(*Before the* PRINCE *points to any one of the* PRINCESSES, *a* SERVANT *enters*)

THE REAL PRINCESS

SERVANT: Stop! Stop! There is a beggar maid at the gate. She begs leave to come into the palace.
KING: We can have no beggar maid here.
SERVANT: But she says she is a Princess, a *real* Princess.
QUEEN: What is her name?
SERVANT: She says she is the Princess Sunday!
ALL: The Princess Sunday!
QUEEN: Let her enter. (*Exit* SERVANT)
KING: I do not believe that she is a Princess at all.
PRINCE: I would like to see her.
ALL: Here she comes. (*Enter* PRINCESS SUNDAY, *dressed in rags.*)
KING: So you say you are a Princess?
PRINCESS SUNDAY: Yes, Sire. I am the Princess Sunday. My father is the King of the Calendar.
PRINCE: But you do not look like a Princess.
PRINCESS SUNDAY: That is because I have been lost for many days. My clothes are torn, and I am cold and wet.
QUEEN: Come with me, my dear. I will see that you have dry clothing. You shall take a nap in a little gold bed.
PRINCESS SUNDAY: Thank you, my Lady. (*Exit* QUEEN *and* PRINCESS SUNDAY.)
WISE MEN: We do not think she is a *real* princess. (PRINCESSES *giggle.*)
PRINCESS MONDAY: Look at her dress!
PRINCESS TUESDAY: Look at her hair!
PRINCESS WEDNESDAY: She wears no crown!
PRINCESS THURSDAY: And her feet are bare!

PRINCESS FRIDAY: She is not a *real* princess! (*Re-enter* QUEEN)
QUEEN: The little Princess Sunday has had some hot milk, and now she is tucked into bed. She will feel better soon.
KING: Shall we go on with the wedding plans?
QUEEN: Let us wait until the new Princess has finished her nap.
KING: Do you think she is *really* a Princess?
QUEEN: I will know after she has had her nap. (*Enter* PRINCESS SUNDAY.)
PRINCE: Have you finished your nap already?
PRINCESS SUNDAY: Nap? How could anyone sleep in such a bed?
QUEEN: What is wrong with the bed, Princess?
PRINCESS SUNDAY: It is so humpy and lumpy, I am black and blue all over.
QUEEN: Did anyone else find the bed humpy and lumpy?
ALL PRINCESSES: No, indeed.
PRINCESS SATURDAY: It was the softest bed in the world.
PRINCESS SUNDAY: It was hard as a rock.
KING: What is the matter with this beggar maid?
QUEEN: She is not a beggar maid, sire. She is a *real* Princess.
ALL: A *real* Princess?
QUEEN: Each time I made up the little gold bed, I put a hard, dry pea under the twenty quilts and mattresses. The other girls did not mind it.
PRINCESS SATURDAY: We never felt a thing.

QUEEN: Only a true princess would be able to feel that hard lump under the soft padding.

KING: My dear, you are wiser than all the Wise Men in our land.

PRINCE: Let the Princess Sunday join our circle, Mother. (QUEEN *leads* PRINCESS SUNDAY *into the circle.*) Now I am ready to make my choice. (PRINCESSES *dance around* PRINCE, *singing to the tune of* "Rise, Sally, Rise")

> Rise, master, rise,
> Don't hide your eyes.
> Turn to the East (*He turns in one direction.*)
> Turn to the West (*He turns the other way.*)
> Turn to the one that
> You love best.

PRINCE (*Takes hand of* PRINCESS SUNDAY *and leads her to his parents*): Princess Sunday shall be my bride.

ALL: Long live the Princess Sunday! Hurrah! Hurrah! Hurrah! (*Curtain*)

THE END

THE SAFETY CLINIC

Characters

DR. WISE
THE NURSE
MRS. JONES
BILLY JONES
MRS. HORNER
JACK HORNER
DR. SPECK
MRS. SMITH

SUSIE SMITH
DR. SWALLOW
GILDA, GLENDA *and* GLADYS
MRS. SIMON
CYCLE SIMON
DR. STEPP
MRS. BROWN
JACK *and* JILL

SETTING: *The waiting room of a clinic.*
AT RISE: *The patients, wearing plasters and bandages, are sitting with their mothers on benches and chairs.* DR. WISE *is seated at his desk, with the* NURSE *standing beside him. The mothers stand and sing to the tune of "Oh, Dear! What Can the Matter Be?"*

MOTHERS: Oh, dear, what can the matter be?
Dear, dear, what can the matter be?
Oh, dear, what can the matter be?
Doctor, please tell if you can.
Our children are covered with bruises and scratches,

> And some of the naughty ones will play with matches.
> We've used up our Bandaids and plasters and patches
> Since all of this trouble began. (MOTHERS *sit*.)

NURSE: Mrs. Jones, the Doctor will see you now. (MRS. JONES *brings* BILLY *to* DR. WISE, *then sits in chair beside desk*.)

MRS. JONES: Doctor, Doctor, can you tell
> What will make my Billy well?

DR. WISE: What seems to be the matter with him?

MRS. JONES: Look at him! (*Recites*):
> He's covered with scratches and bruises and patches,
> No wonder the poor fellow cries!
> He's all the time falling, and so we came calling
> Because you're so good and so wise.

DR. WISE: Well, Billy, you *do* look the worse for wear. Tell me, where did you get this bump on your head?

BILLY: I fell out of a tree.

DR. WISE: And how did you get these scratches on your arm?

BILLY: I fell off a fence.

DR. WISE: And how did you get this bruise on your knee?

BILLY: I fell off a wall.

DR. WISE: Dear me, I must take your temperature. (NURSE *puts thermometer in* BILLY'S *mouth*.) I'm afraid you have monkey fever.

MRS. JONES: Monkey fever? What's that?

DR. WISE: Monkey fever makes a child think he's a monkey instead of a boy. Humpty Dumpty had the same trouble. The children can tell you about him.

PATIENTS (*Sing*):
> Humpty Dumpty sat on a wall,
> Humpty Dumpty had a great fall.
> All the king's horses and all the king's men
> Couldn't put Humpty together again.

NURSE: But Doctor Wise put Humpty together again, and now he's as good as new.
> He never climbs fences, he never climbs trees.
> He stays on the ground with the greatest of ease.
> He never tries leaping or jumping through space.
> He leaves that for monkeys who do it with grace.

DR. WISE (*Taking thermometer out of* BILLY'S *mouth and holding it up for a reading*): Just as I thought! (*Nods head seriously*) A bad case of monkey fever!

MRS. JONES: Can you cure him, Doctor?

DR. WISE: I hope so. (*Takes enormous bottle of pills from desk*) Billy, every time you feel like jumping down a pair of steps, or leaping over a wall, or swinging from a railing, I want you to take one of these pills.

BILLY: I feel like jumping now.

NURSE: Then take a pill quickly. (*Opens bottle and gives him "pill"*) Chew it up. It will taste good. (BILLY *chews, and immediately begins to chant.*)

BILLY: I'm a boy, not a monkey; I'm a boy, not a monkey; I'm a boy, not a monkey (*etc.*).

MRS. JONES: Oh, thank you, thank you, Doctor. Come

along, Billy. (*They exit,* BILLY *still saying "I'm a boy, not a monkey" until they get off-stage.*)

DR. WISE: Next case, please.

MRS. HORNER: Come along, Jack. It's our turn. (JACK *is considerably bandaged and walks with cane or crutch.*)

MRS. HORNER: Doctor, Doctor, can you tell
What will make my Jackie well?

DR. WISE: What happened to him?

PATIENTS (*Sing to tune of "Little Jack Horner"*):
Little Jack Horner, crossing the corner
Watching the traffic light.
He darted ahead, although it was red,
And now he's a pitiful sight!

MRS. HORNER: I'm afraid it's his eyes. I think he needs glasses.

DR. WISE: In that case, we must call Dr. Speck, the eye doctor. (*Presses buzzer and* DR. SPECK *enters.*)

DR. WISE: Dr. Speck, this is Mrs. Horner. She thinks her little boy needs safety glasses.

DR. SPECK: I will examine him. (DR. WISE *exits*) Nurse, the color chart, please. (NURSE *crosses to easel and puts up a placard with a big, red circle.*)

DR. SPECK: Jackie, do you know what color this is?

JACK: Red.

PATIENTS (*Sing to tune of "'Round the Mulberry Bush"*):
Red is the color says you must stop, you must stop, you must stop,
Red is the color says you must stop,

When you are crossing the corner.
(NURSE *puts up card with green circle*.)
DR. SPECK: What color is this, Jackie?
JACK: Green.
PATIENTS (*To same tune*):
Green is the color says go ahead, go ahead, go ahead,
Green is the color says go ahead
When you are crossing the corner.
(NURSE *puts up placard with yellow circle*.)
DR. SPECK: And what color is this?
JACK: Yellow.
PATIENTS (*To same tune*):
Yellow's the color says stop and look, stop and look, stop and look,
Yellow's the color says stop and look
When you are crossing the corner.
DR. SPECK: This boy doesn't need glasses, Mrs. Horner.
MRS. HORNER: Then what is the trouble?
DR. SPECK: I think Jackie needs a big shot of anti-killin.
JACK: What's that?
DR. SPECK: Dr. Wise will explain. You are his patient.
(*Buzzes and* DR. WISE *enters*.)
JACK: Dr. Speck says I need a shot of anti-killin. What's that?
DR. WISE: It's like penicillin, only it kills all the carelessness germs in your body. Thank you, Dr. Speck, for examining this boy.
DR. SPECK: I hope the anti-killin works, Dr. Wise. Good day, Mrs. Horner. (DR. SPECK *exits*.)

DR. WISE: Nurse, bring the needle.

JACK: I'm not afraid of needles. I've had all kinds of shots. (NURSE *brings huge syringe of the type used to baste turkeys and roasts.*)

JACK: Wow! That's the biggest needle I've ever seen! Wait till I tell the kids about this!

DR. WISE (*Scrubbing* JACK's *arm with cotton*): It's big medicine, Jackie, but it won't hurt. (DR. WISE *pretends to inject medicine.*)

JACK: That feels good. I feel more careful already.

DR. WISE: We'll see how it works. Watch him carefully, Mrs. Horner, and see how he acts at traffic lights. If you have any more trouble, come back next week.

MRS. HORNER: Thank you, Doctor. Come along, Jackie. (*They exit.* MRS. SMITH *comes forward with* SUSIE.)

MRS. SMITH: Please, Doctor, will you see my little girl right away? I'm afraid she swallowed a pin.

DR. WISE: I'll buzz for Dr. Swallow, the throat doctor, at once. (*Buzzes and* DR. SWALLOW *enters.*) Dr. Swallow, here is a patient for you. Her mother thinks she swallowed a pin.

DR. SWALLOW: Sit right here, child. (SUSIE *sits down.*) I'll have a look. (*Pretends to examine her throat with throat stick*) You're a lucky little girl. There is no pin in your throat. (*To* MRS. SMITH) How did this happen?

MRS. SMITH: Susie was making doll clothes and I gave her a paper of pins.

PATIENTS (*Sing to tune of "I'll Give You a Paper of*

Pins"): She gave to her a paper of pins, and that is where the pain begins, for she did not take care, take care, for she did not take care.

DR. SWALLOW: You must never put pins in your mouth, Susie. And it is not safe to drop them on the floor or stick them into the furniture. I will give you something so this will never happen again. (*Pulls from his jacket pocket a small red pincushion on a ribbon, and hangs it around her neck.*) Wear this whenever you are using pins and needles. If you remember to use it, you will always be safe.

SUSIE: Thank you, Doctor. I will try to remember.

MRS. SMITH: I have also brought my neighbor's children, Doctor. They have terrible colds and sore throats. (GILDA, GLENDA *and* GLADYS *come forward. They each carry a box of tissues and all are sneezing.* MRS. SMITH *and* SUSIE *resume their seats.*)

DR. SWALLOW: My goodness! What happened to you?

GILDA, GLENDA *and* GLADYS:
We went ice skating! Kerchoo!
And we fell in! Kerchoo!
And we all have wheezes and sneezes! Kerchoo!

DR. SWALLOW: Let me see your throats. (*All stand in a row with mouths open, as* DR. SWALLOW *looks in.*) Aha! I see! You all need my Glorious Gargle. Nurse, will you please pass the gargle glasses? (NURSE *gives each child an empty glass.*)

DR. SWALLOW: Now, all together, please—1-2-3-Go! (GIRLS *make gargling noises.*)

DR. SWALLOW: Excellent! Excellent! I would now like

to hear you sing the Safe Skating Song. Nurse, will you please post the words? (NURSE *places placard with words on easel. Patients sing to tune of "Sailing, Sailing"*)

PATIENTS:
>Skating, skating, never where ice is thin,
>So better beware and have a care
>Or you may tumble in.
>Skating, skating, never where ice is thin,
>For maybe you'll stop, and go ker-plop!
>And you may fall right in!

GILDA, GLENDA, *and* GLADYS: Thank you, Dr. Swallow. (*Going to seats.*) Mrs. Simon, it's your turn now. (MRS. SIMON *goes to* DR. SWALLOW *with* CYCLE SIMON)

DR. SWALLOW: Does your little boy have a sore throat?

MRS. SIMON: My little boy is sore all over. He's covered with bruises.

DR. SWALLOW: Then you had better see Dr. Wise. (*Buzzes for* DR. WISE. *He exits as* DR. WISE *appears.*)

DR. WISE: Good afternoon, ma'am. And what is your little boy's trouble?

MRS. SIMON: He fell off his bicycle. He's always riding it, you know. That's why the children call him Cycle Simon.

PATIENTS (*Sing to tune of "Simple Simon"*):
>Cycle Simon, Cycle Simon
>Tried to do a trick.
>He let go of his handlebars
>And now he's feeling sick.

DR. WISE: That's too bad. Why did you let go of your handlebars, Cycle?

CYCLE SIMON: I was pretending I was a circus rider.

DR. WISE: But you're not a circus rider. You're just a little boy riding a bicycle. Nurse, please hand me my Sticky Salve. (NURSE *hands him a jar from desk.*) I will put some of this on your hands. (*Pretends to rub salve on* CYCLE's *hands.*) Now you will never let go of the handlebars. It doesn't pay to do tricks when you ride a bike. Next patient, please. (CYCLE SIMON *and* MRS. SIMON *sit down.*)

MRS. BROWN (*Coming forward with* JACK *and* JILL):
        Doctor, Doctor, can you tell
        What will make my children well?

DR. WISE: What are your names, children?

JACK: I am Jack.

JILL: I am Jill.

MRS. BROWN: They are always having accidents because they never walk. They always run. Just listen to what happened yesterday. (*All sing "Jack and Jill."*)

DR. WISE: These children need a foot doctor. I will call Dr. Stepp. (*Buzzes and* DR. STEPP *enters.*) Dr. Stepp, I have two patients for you. I would like you to look at their feet. (NURSE *moves two chairs forward for* JACK *and* JILL. DR. STEPP *examines their feet.*)

DR. STEPP (*To* JACK): Do you always run and race?

JACK: Always.

DR. STEPP (*To* JILL): And do you always run with a hop, skip and jump?

JILL: Always.

DR. STEPP: No wonder you fall down. You are wearing the wrong kind of shoes.

MRS. BROWN: What is wrong with their shoes, Doctor?

DR. STEPP: These are running shoes. They should wear walking shoes. (*Takes a notebook from pocket and writes a note which he tears out and gives to* MRS. BROWN.) Take them downtown and buy them the shoes I have named here. They are the very best walking shoes. If they wear these—no more accidents.

MRS. BROWN: We will buy the walking shoes this very afternoon.

DR. STEPP: I am sure you will find them helpful. Good day, Mrs. Brown. (*Exits*)

NURSE (*To* DR. WISE): You have seen all of your cases for today, Doctor. But I think your patients have something to say to you. (PATIENTS *and* MOTHERS *stand, and are joined by* MRS. JONES *and* BILLY *and* MRS. HORNER *and* JACK. *They sing, to the tune of* "Sing a Song of Sixpence"):

ALL:
Sing a song of safety, we need a watchful eye,
Crossing street and highway, we must be spry.
Thank you kindly, Doctor, for curing all our ills.
Safety rules are better than the very finest pills. (*Curtain*)

THE END

TEN PENNIES FOR LINCOLN

Characters

SERGEANT AT ARMS	FREDDY GATES
PRESIDENT	SHIRLEY SMITH
SECRETARY	TOBY TAYLOR
TWELVE MEMBERS	MARTHA SCOTT
TOMMY HALL	JERRY JONES

SETTING: *A club meeting. Stage decorations include an American flag and a picture of Lincoln. On the table is a bowl or bank for pennies.*

AT RISE: PRESIDENT, SERGEANT AT ARMS, *and* SECRETARY *of the Rail Splitters' Club sit at table.* TWELVE MEMBERS *sit in front of table.*

SERGEANT AT ARMS:

We have a little Lincoln Club,
We bring you friendly greeting,
And hope you have a happy time
At this, our birthday meeting.

Our president will now take charge.
The meeting will begin
And you will see just what we do
To take new members in.

PRESIDENT: The meeting of the Rail Splitters will please come to order. Our secretary will explain the name of our club.

SECRETARY: We call our club the Rail Splitters. We chose this name because we try to do some of the things that Lincoln did, and Lincoln was a Rail Splitter, too.

MEMBERS (*Singing to the tune of "Reuben and Rachel"*):
Lincoln, Lincoln, we've been thinking of the things that we might do
So we'd grow up strong and fearless, brave and honest, just like you.

SECRETARY: As I call the roll, every Rail Splitter will respond with an important fact about Abraham Lincoln. (*Calls roll*)

1ST MEMBER: Abraham Lincoln was born on February 12, 1809.

2ND MEMBER: He was born in Hardin County, Kentucky.

3RD MEMBER: When he was a small boy, Lincoln moved to Indiana.

4TH MEMBER: Lincoln's nickname was Honest Abe.

5TH MEMBER: Lincoln's mother was Nancy Hanks Lincoln.

6TH MEMBER: His father was Thomas Lincoln.

7TH MEMBER: Lincoln's mother died when he was eight years old.

8TH MEMBER: He had a stepmother who was very good to him. Her name was Sarah Bush Lincoln.

9TH MEMBER: Abraham Lincoln was the sixteenth President of the United States.

10TH MEMBER: He was President during the Civil War or the War Between the States.

11TH MEMBER: President Lincoln signed the paper that ended slavery.

12TH MEMBER: President Lincoln was shot and killed by John Wilkes Booth. (*Extra facts may be added according to number of pupils.*)

PRESIDENT: Every year in honor of Lincoln's birthday, we take new members into the Rail Splitters' Club. Our Secretary will tell you what the new members must do.

SECRETARY: Each new member of the Rail Splitters' Club must earn ten pennies for Lincoln. This means the money must be earned by doing something that Lincoln might have done or doing something that is connected with Lincoln's life. Each new member will now come forward and tell how he earned his ten pennies. If the old members agree that his pennies were earned in the Lincoln manner, he will become a real Rail Splitter. We will hear first from Tommy Hall.

TOMMY (*Enters and stands at the table*): Mr. Frazer, the man next door, got a load of wood for his fireplace. I remembered that Lincoln chopped down trees and carried wood, so I offered to carry the wood to the kitchen door and stack it into piles. Mr. Frazer paid me ten cents.

PRESIDENT: You have heard how Tommy Hall earned his ten pennies. All in favor of admitting Tommy to the Rail Splitters, raise your hands. (*All* MEMBERS *raise hands.*) You may now drop your pennies into our Lincoln bank. This money will be used to buy a new Lincoln book for our school. (TOMMY *drops pennies into the bank.* PRESIDENT *shakes hands with* TOMMY.) Tommy, you are now a member and may join the rest of the Rail Splitters.

MEMBERS (*As* TOMMY *takes his seat with the others*): Welcome to the Rail Splitters!

SECRETARY: Our next Rail Splitter is Freddy Gates.

FREDDY (*Enters and stands by table*): I earned my ten pennies for Lincoln by helping my dad in the grocery store. When Lincoln was a young man, he kept store in Salem, Illinois.

PRESIDENT: All in favor of admitting Freddy Gates to the Rail Splitters, raise your hands. (*They do so.*) Freddy, you are now a member. (FREDDY *drops pennies into the bank.* PRESIDENT *shakes hands with him.*)

MEMBERS: Welcome to the Rail Splitters.

SECRETARY: Shirley Smith will now tell us about her ten pennies.

SHIRLEY (*Entering and standing by table*): I had a hard time thinking of a way to earn ten pennies for Lincoln. Then Mother said she would give me ten cents if I learned a poem about him. Would you like to hear it?

MEMBERS: Let's hear the poem.

SHIRLEY:

>Mr. Lincoln was a farmer.
>He walked behind a plow,
>And he would plant and harvest
>If he were living now.
>
>Mr. Lincoln was a lawyer.
>He lived by rule and book,
>And he would seek for justice now
>Were he alive to look.
>
>Mr. Lincoln was a President.
>He ruled with sword and pen,
>And he would serve his country well
>Were he alive again.
>
>Mr. Lincoln was a man of God.
>He often knelt in prayer;
>Now he would pray for freedom
>That all the world might share.

PRESIDENT: If you think Shirley has truly earned ten pennies for Lincoln, please raise your hands. (*All raise hands.*) Shirley, your poem has taught us something about Lincoln, so you may drop your pennies into our Lincoln bank. (*She drops pennies into the bank and* PRESIDENT *shakes hands with her.*)

MEMBERS: Welcome to the Rail Splitters.

SECRETARY: Toby Taylor is our next new Rail Splitter.

TOBY (*Enters and stands beside the table*): I did not earn my ten pennies on purpose. I was just lucky. One day I found a book in our bookcase. It was a book my dad had borrowed from Mr. Kelley. Mr. Kelley lives way over on the other side of town and Dad had forgotten to return it. I remembered how Lincoln had walked many miles to return a book he had borrowed so I decided to return it. Mr. Kelley was so glad to get his book back that he gave me ten cents for my trouble.

PRESIDENT: We will now vote on Toby Taylor. (MEMBERS *raise their hands.*) Toby, that was a fine way to earn your Lincoln pennies. (TOBY *drops them into the bank.* PRESIDENT *shakes hands.*) Congratulations.

MEMBERS: Welcome to the Rail Splitters.

SECRETARY: Martha Scott is now ready to tell us about her Lincoln pennies.

MARTHA (*Entering and standing by table*): My Lincoln pennies are really Lincoln pennies. For a long time Mother and Father have been helping me save Lincoln pennies. One day Daddy told me to take my Lincoln pennies to Mr. Free who buys and sells coins. Mr. Free liked my collection and bought some of my Lincoln coins. That is how I earned my ten pennies for Lincoln.

PRESIDENT: If you are in favor of admitting Martha Scott to the Rail Splitters, raise your hands. (CHILDREN *raise hands.*) Martha, you are now a member. (*Shakes hands after* MARTHA *deposits her pennies.*) Perhaps more of us might start to collect Lincoln pennies for the Rail Splitters.

MEMBERS: Welcome to the Rail Splitters.

SECRETARY: Our last new member is Jerry Jones.

JERRY (*Enters and takes place at table*): I do not think you will let me join the Rail Splitters.
SECRETARY: Why not, Jerry?
JERRY: Because I don't have my ten pennies. I have only five.
SECRETARY: Then you will have to come back next year. Our rules say you must have ten pennies.
PRESIDENT: Maybe we should hear Jerry's story anyhow. Jerry, what happened? Why couldn't you earn your ten pennies for Lincoln?
JERRY: Well, I had the same idea as Freddy. My uncle has a grocery store and he said he would let me help in the store to earn my Lincoln money.
PRESIDENT: Did you take the job?
JERRY: Yes, I did, and my uncle paid me a quarter.
PRESIDENT: That's twenty-five pennies. What did you do with them?
JERRY: I made a mistake. A lady bought some candy bars and I gave her the wrong change. My uncle told me where she lived so I took the money back to her. I had to spend twenty cents for bus fare, so now I don't have enough Lincoln pennies.
1ST MEMBER: Mr. President, I think we should let Jerry become a Rail Splitter because he did just what Lincoln would have done.
2ND MEMBER: After all, he did *earn* his ten pennies in the Lincoln way.
3RD MEMBER: And he *spent* them in the Lincoln way, so that makes him a true Rail Splitter.
4TH MEMBER: When Lincoln worked in a country

store, he also made a mistake in change. But he corrected it, just as Jerry did.
SECRETARY: This calls for a special vote.
PRESIDENT: All those in favor of making Jerry a Rail Splitter, raise your hands. (*All raise hands.*) Jerry, you are now a member of the club—a real Honest Jerry.
JERRY: Thank you. Thank you very much. I will try very hard to earn another five pennies for the Lincoln book fund.
MEMBERS: Welcome to the Rail Splitters.
PRESIDENT: We will ask our new members to stand and sing the Rail Splitters' Code.
NEW MEMBERS (*Singing to the tune of "Sweet Betsy from Pike"*):
A Rail Splitter's honest,
A Rail Splitter's kind.
He works with his muscles,
He works with his mind.
To God and to country
He's loyal and true,
And does things that Lincoln
Would want him to do.
ALL MEMBERS (*Singing to the tune of "Old Gray Mare"*):
Our Abe Lincoln came out of the wilderness, out of the wilderness, out of the wilderness,
Our Abe Lincoln came out of the wilderness,
    Down in Illinois.
PRESIDENT: We will close our birthday meeting of the

Rail Splitters by pledging allegiance to our flag and singing "America." (*They pledge allegiance and sing "America." Curtain*)

THE END

THE COUNTRY STORE CAT

Characters

CLERK
BILLY THE STOREKEEPER
NINE STOREKEEPERS
PETER
MARY
SUSIE
RUTH   } *customers*
SARAH
JACK
ANN
JIM *and* JANE
OTHER CUSTOMERS
THE COUNTRY STORE CAT
SIX MICE

SETTING: *A country store.*
AT RISE: *The* CUSTOMERS, *equipped with shopping bags and market baskets, are lined up, half on one side of the stage, and half on the other. The* NINE STOREKEEPERS *are hidden behind the counter. The* CLERK *stands behind the counter and sings to the tune of "This Old Man":*

CLERK:
    Come on friends, let's play store!
    Buy and sell and buy some more.

Clerks and customers, each will take a turn.
How much money will we earn?

PETER (*Stepping forward from line of* CUSTOMERS): I want to be the storekeeper. Please let me be the storekeeper.

CLERK: It's all right with me. But what kind of store are you going to keep?

PETER: I don't know.

CLERK: You'd better make up your mind. Watch the Parade of the Storekeepers, and take your choice. (*The* CUSTOMERS *sing the following verses to the same tune. Each* STOREKEEPER *pops up from behind the counter as he is described and pantomimes the action of the song. On the final verse, they all march around the counter and off-stage.*)

This old man, he looks sweet,
He sells candy on our street,
Nick-nack, paddy whack, sing the song some more,
This old man keeps a candy store.

This old man, he keeps shop,
He sells grape and lemon pop.
Nick-nack, paddy whack, sing and never stop,
This old man keeps a soda shop.

This old man, he works hard,
He sells dress goods by the yard,
Nick-nack, paddy whack, sing the song some more,
This old man keeps a dry goods store.

This old man, he sells nails,
Also hammers, locks and pails,

Nick-nack, paddy whack, sing the song some more.
This old man keeps a hardware store.

This old man, he sells pills,
Big and small to cure your ills,
Nick-nack, paddy whack, sing the song some more,
This old man keeps a big drug store.

This old man, he sells hats,
Coats and dresses, shoes and spats.
Nick-nack, paddy whack, sing the song some more,
This old man keeps a clothing store.

This old man, he sells bread,
Cabbage, lettuce by the head,
Nick-nack, paddy whack, sing the song some more,
This old man keeps a grocery store.

This old man, he sells trains,
Also drums and dolls and planes.
Nick-nack, paddy whack, sing the song some more,
This old man keeps a big toy store.

These old men, they keep store,
Buy and sell and buy some more.
Nick-nack, paddy whack, cheer them every one,
These old men have lots of fun!
   (STOREKEEPERS *exit*.)
CLERK: Now that you have seen all these different storekeepers, what kind would you like to be?
PETER: I still don't know.
BILLY (*Coming forward*): I know what kind of store I want to have. I want a *general* store.

CUSTOMERS: What's a *general* store?
MARY: Is it a place where they sell generals?
BILLY: Don't be silly. A general store is where they sell everything in general.
SUSIE: I know. It's like a country store.
BILLY: General store or country store, it's all the same.
RUTH: What can you buy there?
BILLY: Listen. I'll tell you. (*Goes behind counter*) But first I must dress up like a storekeeper. (*Stoops behind counter and puts on a white apron, cardboard cuffs, a pair of glasses and a big, black, handle-bar mustache.*) Now I am the storekeeper, and this is my clerk. (*Indicates* CLERK)
CUSTOMERS: Good morning, Mr. Storekeeper.
BILLY: Good morning to you. Just look around and help yourselves. We have everything you need. (*Recites*)
You can buy laces
And Halloween faces,
And apples so juicy to eat.
You can buy candles,
And baskets with handles,
And candy all sticky and sweet.

You can buy dishes,
And oysters and fishes,
And, oh yes, a thousand things more.
You can even buy onions
And plasters for bunions,
When you deal at a real country store.
SARAH (*Coming forward*):
Can I get potatoes

And big red tomatoes,
And maybe a trinket or two?

BILLY:

Oh, yes, indeed, madam,
We always have had 'em,
And keep them in stock just for you.

JACK (*Coming forward*):

Can I buy a collar
And tie for a dollar,
And maybe a new pair of shoes?

CLERK:

Right here, at your service,
And please don't get nervous,
We've plenty of styles you can choose.

ANN (*Coming forward*):

Can I buy a dolly
For Susan or Molly,
And maybe just one for myself?

BILLY:

Oh, yes, indeed, honey
If you have the money,
You'll find them right here on the shelf.

ALL (*Singing*):

Come on, friends, let's play store,
Buy and sell and buy some more,
Anything, everything, anything at all,
Our new store is the place to call.

BILLY:

Welcome, folks, to the Country Store,
And all our crowded shelves.

I'll make you out a proper bill
When you have helped yourselves.
(CUSTOMERS *move about the stage pretending to fill their baskets and bags.*)

GIRL CUSTOMERS:
I'll take this and I'll take that!
I'll take a dress and a brand-new hat!

BOY CUSTOMERS:
I'll take a rake and I'll take a hoe.
I'll take seeds that will grow and grow.

JIM *and* JANE (*At cracker barrel.* JIM *and* JANE *each wear glasses.*):
I'll take crackers and I'll take cheese.
Let's help ourselves to some of these! (*Leaning over and reaching into barrel, then coming up empty-handed*) Look! Look! The cracker barrel is empty!

CAT (*Pops out of cracker barrel*): Meow! Meow! Meow! Go away! Go away! You woke me up! You've ruined my nap!

CUSTOMERS: A cat! A cat!

CAT: Well, what are you staring at? Haven't you ever seen a cat before?

JIM *and* JANE:
Of course we've seen a cat before,
But you don't belong in a country store!

CAT: I most certainly *do* belong here. This is my home and besides I *work* here. The storekeeper couldn't get along without me!

BILLY: So there you are, you good-for-nothing cat! Sleeping in the cracker barrel again! (*Seizes broom*

and comes out from behind the counter) I have a good notion to sweep you out of here! You haven't caught a mouse for over a year! All you do is eat and sleep and let the mice eat all my crackers and cheese!
JIM: Why don't you get a new cat?
CAT: Don't say that! What will become of me if he turns me out?
BILLY: And what will become of me if I keep you here? The mice will eat me out of house and home!
CAT: Meow! Meow! Meow! I am the unhappiest cat in the world! If only I could catch a mouse!
JIM: Then why can't you? You *are* a cat, aren't you?
CAT: Of course, I'm a cat. (*Suddenly scratching* JIM) Just feel my sharp claws!
JIM: Ouch! Ouch!
JANE: Why don't you use your claws to catch the mice? All cats can catch mice if they really try.
CAT: Not me! Not any more! I don't know what's the matter with me. I sneak up on them, the way I used to. (*Crouches*) I crouch! (*Leaps*) I spring! But they always get away.
BILLY: Your sad tale touches my heart, but unless you get rid of all our mice by tomorrow, out you go!
CAT: It's a bargain. I'll do my very best. And if I fail, I'll go away and I'll never come back! I promise.
JIM: I think he really means it.
BILLY: I hope so. But now, it's closing time. (*Removes apron, cuffs, and glasses and lays them on counter*) Come on, everybody, it's time to shut up shop!
JANE: Let's all come back tomorrow. Good luck with

the mice, Mr. Country Store Cat!

CUSTOMERS *and* CLERK (*Singing to opening tune*):
Come on, folks, let's go home,
Time to leave this store alone.
Shut it up, lock it up, everybody pay,
We'll come back another day!
(*All march off-stage singing.* JIM *and* JANE *are at end of line.*)

CAT (*Pacing up and down, paws behind his back*):
Meow! Meow! Meow!
A most unhappy cat!
I cannot catch a single mouse,
Or sneak up on a rat!

Meow! Meow! Meow!
The mice are laughing, too!
They always get away from me,
No matter what I do!

JIM *and* JANE (*Re-entering*): We came back to help you.

CAT: What can you do?

JIM: Maybe we can watch and see what you are doing wrong.

CAT: The mice won't come out of their holes if you are here. They are more afraid of children than they are of me!

JANE: We'll hide so they won't see us.

JIM: We'll hide behind the cracker barrel.

CAT: Then be quick, because I hear them coming now.
(*As* JIM *and* JANE *duck behind the cracker barrel,* SIX MICE *enter. They are marching in a line, each*

MOUSE *grasping the tail of the* MOUSE *ahead. They sing to the tune of "The Farmer in the Dell."*)
MICE: The cat is in the house,
The cat is in the house,
Shame, shame on kitty-cats
Who cannot catch a mouse!

We'll eat up all the cheese,
We'll eat up all the cheese!
Shame, shame on kitty-cats
When we do as we please!

We'll eat up all the rice,
We'll eat up all the rice,
Shame, shame on kitty-cats
Who cannot catch the mice!
(*The* MICE *circle round the* CAT, *acting out each of the following verses. The* CAT *meows ferociously and leaps at them in vain. The* MICE *squeal in delight at the end of each verse.*)
We'll twist his bushy tail,
We'll twist his bushy tail,
Shame, shame on kitty-cats
Who can't put us in jail!

We'll tweak his tender ears,
We'll tweak his tender ears,
Shame, shame on kitty-cats
Whom not a mousie fears!

We'll pull his whiskers out!
We'll pull his whiskers out!

Shame, shame on kitty-cats
Who cannot drive us out!

CAT: It's no use! I give up! I can't catch a mouse to save my life!

MICE: Ho, ho, ho! Tee-hee-hee!
Poor old kitty-cat can't catch me!

CAT (*Makes another lunge.* MICE *scatter.*): I almost had one that time. If only I had jumped a little farther!

JIM *and* JANE (*Coming out from behind barrel*): We have it! We have it! (MICE *exit, scattering in all directions.*)

CAT: Now see what you've done! You've scared them all away.

JIM: Don't worry. They'll come back again.

JANE: The important thing is that we've found out why you can't catch any mice.

CAT: Tell me! Tell me!

JIM: You're nearsighted.

JANE: You need glasses. I was nearsighted, too, before I got mine.

CAT: Don't be silly!

JANE: We can prove it.

JIM: Pretend I'm a mouse. Try to catch me. (CAT *jumps, but not far enough.*)

JIM: I didn't even move, but you didn't jump far enough.

CAT: But how does that help me? I'm a cat, remember. Cats don't wear glasses.

JANE: You can try a pair. Here. Try these. (*Hands* CAT *the glasses left on counter by* STOREKEEPER.)

JIM: I'll tie them on you with a piece of string. (*Ties glasses onto* CAT)
CAT: Things look better already.
JANE: Now try to catch me. (CAT *leaps and catches* JANE.)
CAT: I did it! I did it!
JIM: Now try to catch me. (CAT *leaps and catches* JIM.)
CAT: Meow! Meow! I really did it! I do believe I could catch a mouse!
JIM: With these glasses on, you can catch all the mice you want.
CAT: But they're all gone.
JANE (*Dipping into cheese container on counter and sprinkling cheese on the floor*): This cheese will bring them back and Jim and I will hide again.
JIM: Now the trap is set.
JANE (*As she and* JIM *go behind barrel*): Those mice are going to have a big surprise!
CAT: Meow! Meow! Meow! I can hardly wait!
MICE (*Re-enter singing*):
 We'll eat up all the cheese,
 We'll eat up all the cheese!
 Shame, shame on kitty-cats
 When we do as we please! (*As they approach the* CAT, *he leaps and catches a* MOUSE *in each paw.*)
Captured MICE (*Squealing in terror*): Help! Help!
Other MICE: He's caught Squeak and Nibble! Help! Help! (*They cringe in the corner.*)
SQUEAK *and* NIBBLE: Let us go! Let us go!
CAT: Not on your life! I'm having you for supper! Yum! Yum! What a feast!

JIM (*Coming out from behind barrel*): I'll hold these two while you catch the rest.

MICE: No! No! Help! Help! (*They run around in circles.*)

CAT (*Crouches, springs and catches two more*): I'll have these for breakfast!

JANE (*Holding the two struggling* MICE): Now catch the others before they get away.

CAT (*Chases the last two* MICE *and finally catches them*): I'll have these for lunch!

SQUEAK: Please, please, good, kind Mr. Cat, please let us go!

NIBBLE: We'll never come near this store again.

WHISKERS: Please don't eat us, Mr. Cat. We'll go far away and never come back.

LONG-TAIL: And we'll tell all our friends and relations to stay away, too.

SHORT-TAIL: You'll be the Terror of Mouseland for always.

ALL MICE: Please let us go!

CAT: Meow! Meow! Meow! Never! Never! Never!

JIM: Maybe we'd better have a conference. You mice, stand facing the cracker barrel. (SIX MICE *join hands in a circle around the barrel.*) One false move, and Mr. Cat will tear you to pieces.

JANE: He'll swallow you whole!

CAT (*Ferociously*): Meow! (JIM, JANE *and* CAT *withdraw to opposite side of stage.*)

JIM: Maybe you'd better let them go.

CAT: Never! It's been too long since I've tasted a good, tender, little mouse.
JANE: But don't you understand? When the storekeeper comes back he'll take his glasses.
JIM: Then you'll never be able to catch another mouse.
CAT: And all the mice will come back again just as before.
JANE: But if you let these mice go, they'll keep the others away.
CAT: Maybe you're right. Okay, you mice. You may go. (MICE *start to run away.*) But wait, before you go, I must have your mouse-promise.
MICE (*Lining up and each raising right paw*):
By my whiskers and by my tail,
I make a promise without fail.
No mouse for ever, ever more
Will dare set foot inside this store!
CAT: Good enough! And now, get out and stay out! (*He lunges after them with a terrible "Meow" as they exit, almost running into* BILLY THE STOREKEEPER *as he enters.*)
BILLY: Land sakes! What was that? (*Catching sight of* JIM *and* JANE) What are you doing here?
JIM: We came back to help your cat. What are *you* doing here?
BILLY: I came back to get my glasses. (*Suddenly sees them on* CAT) Bless my soul! What are you doing with my glasses? Give them back to me this minute! (JANE *unties string and hands glasses to* STOREKEEPER)

JANE: Here they are, sir. But I'm afraid your cat needs them more than you do.

JIM: He's nearsighted. That's why he couldn't catch any mice.

BILLY: Who ever heard of a nearsighted cat?

CAT: It's true, Boss. With your glasses on, I caught every one of those pesky mice.

BILLY: Then why did you let them go?

CAT: Because they promised to keep all the rest of the mice away from this store for ever and ever.

JIM: It's true, sir. Jane and I were right here.

JANE: You'll never be bothered with mice again.

BILLY: In that case, you're really a champion. I think you should have a medal.

CAT: I'd much rather have a saucer of cream, if you please.

BILLY (*Going behind counter*): One saucer of cream for the champ!

CAT: Meow! Meow! (*Hops up on counter as* BILLY *hands him a large bowl of cream.*)

JIM, JANE *and* BILLY: (*Singing to the tune of "This Old Man"*):
Pussy cat, pussy cat,
You're the champ of mouse and rat.
With a nick-nack, paddy whack, sing the song some more,
You're the Champ of the Country Store! (*Curtain*)

THE END

WAIT AND SEE

Characters

MR. BUTTON	MARY
MRS. BUTTON	JIMMY
BETSY BUTTON	SUSIE
FOUR FAIRIES	KATHY
TOMMY	JOHNNY

TIME: *Morning.*
SETTING: *The dining room.*
AT RISE: MR. *and* MRS. BUTTON *are seated at table eating breakfast.* BETSY *enters skipping and chanting to herself.*

BETSY: I'm having a birthday!
  I'm having a birthday!
  I'm having a birthday today!
MR. BUTTON: Good morning, Birthday Girl.
BETSY: Good morning, Daddy.
MRS. BUTTON: Happy Birthday, Betsy.
BETSY: Thank you, Mother. (*Looking around under table and behind a chair*) Where is it, Mother? Where is my birthday surprise?
MR. BUTTON: What makes you think you're having a birthday surprise?
BETSY: Because I always do. Are you hiding it?

MRS. BUTTON: You'll just have to wait and see.
BETSY: But I can't wait any longer. Today is my birthday.
MR. BUTTON: You heard what your mother said. Wait and see! (*Rises, and takes his cup and saucer*) Goodbye, Betsy. I must go to work.
MRS. BUTTON (*Rising, taking her cup and saucer*): I must go to the store.
BOTH: Be a good girl, Betsy.
BETSY: Won't you please tell me where my birthday surprise is?
MR. *and* MRS. BUTTON: Wait and see, Betsy. You just wait and see. (*They exit, leaving the table clear.*)
BETSY (*Stamping her foot*): No! No! No! I will not wait and see! I will go look for it myself. (*As* BETSY *exits right, six* CHILDREN *enter left. Each* CHILD *carries a gaily wrapped package. They sing to the tune of* "*Lucy Locket.*")
CHILDREN: Betsy Button has a birthday!
We know all about it!
But we will never, never tell,
No, we will never shout it!
Here are her presents. We are going to hide them!
(*As piano continues to play* "*Lucy Locket,*" CHILDREN *hide presents about the stage. When all are hidden,* MARY *speaks.*)
MARY: I wonder where Betsy is.
TOMMY: I'll bet she's gone to look for her birthday surprise.
SUSIE: She'll look in the cellar

    And back of each door.
    She'll look in the pantry,
    And then look some more.
JIMMY: She'll look in the garden,
    She'll look in the shed.
    She'll look in the cupboard,
    And under the bed.
KATHY: She'll look in the attic,
    She'll look on the shelf,
    But she never will find it—
    Not all by herself.
CHILDREN: For secrets are secret,
    As secrets can be.
    You never can find them!
    You *must* wait and see!
    (*They join hands and sing to tune of "London Bridge"*):
    She will have to wait and see,
    Wait and see, wait and see.
    She will have to wait and see!
    Poor, dear Betsy! (CHILDREN *exit as they repeat the song. When stage is clear,* BETSY *enters, tired out.*)
BETSY: I've looked in all the bureau drawers,
    And all the closets too,
    But I can't find my big surprise,
    So I will now boo-hoo!
    (*Wailing*) Boo-hoo-hoo!
    Boo-hoo-hoo!
    Boo-hoo-hoo! (*As* BETSY *boo-hoos, four* FAIRIES *enter, each with a wand.*)

FAIRIES: Betsy Button! Aren't you ashamed?
We never thought you were a boo-hoo baby!
BETSY: Boo-hoo! Boo-hoo!
Now who are you?
FAIRIES: We are the Wait-and-See Fairies!
BETSY: Go away! Go away! I hate you. I hate to wait and see.
First FAIRY: But you don't understand!
Second FAIRY: It's fun to wait and see! (FAIRIES *wave their wands and sing to tune of "London Bridge"*)
FAIRIES: It is fun to wait and see, wait and see, wait and see.
It is fun to wait and see, my dear Betsy.
BETSY: What's fun about it? I can't wait! I won't wait! I hate to wait!
First FAIRY: The longer you wait, the more you'll be surprised.
Second FAIRY: Waiting makes the fun last longer.
Third FAIRY: It's more exciting to wait.
Fourth FAIRY: Just think, if you didn't have to wait, your surprise would be over by now.
BETSY: But the time seems so long.
First FAIRY: That's because you're thinking about yourself.
BETSY: What else can I think about on my birthday?
FAIRIES: Let's tell her.
Let's tell her the wait-and-see secret. (FAIRIES *crowd around* BETSY *and whisper in her ear.*)
BETSY: Really and truly?
FAIRIES: Really and truly.

WAIT AND SEE

First FAIRY: Will you try it, Betsy?
BETSY (*Standing with hands behind her back and singing*):
    You will have to wait and see, wait and see, wait and see,
    You will have to wait and see, my dear fairies.
Second FAIRY: Betsy is catching on to our secret.
FAIRIES: It's time to go! (*As* FAIRIES *exit,* BETSY *busies herself at table with crayons and paper. After a pause,* MRS. BUTTON *enters.*)
MRS. BUTTON: Hello, Betsy. What are you doing?
BETSY: Wait and see, Mother.
MRS. BUTTON: Is it a secret?
BETSY: Mother, you'll just have to wait and see. (*Rises and puts her paper work in her pocket.*)
MRS. BUTTON: Where are you going?
BETSY: I would like to go to the store. May I, Mother?
MRS. BUTTON: What are you going to buy?
BETSY: I can't tell. You will have to wait and see.
MRS. BUTTON: Then run along, and hurry back. Daddy will soon be home. (BETSY *exits right;* MR. BUTTON *enters left.*)
MR. BUTTON: Where is Betsy?
MRS. BUTTON: She has gone to the store.
MR. BUTTON: What for?
MRS. BUTTON: I don't know. She just said: *Wait and see!*
MR. BUTTON: Isn't it time for the birthday surprise?
MRS. BUTTON: Yes, the children should be here now. (*Doorbell rings.*)

MR. BUTTON: Come in, boys and girls. (CHILDREN *enter*.)

CHILDREN: Where is Betsy?

MR. BUTTON: She has gone to the store.

MRS. BUTTON: Find a place to hide. I will bring the birthday cake. (CHILDREN *scurry about and hide behind furniture while* MRS. BUTTON *leaves stage and returns with cake. She places it on table, and lights the candles.*)

MR. BUTTON: Quick! Here she comes! (*As* BETSY *enters with small cardboard box,* CHILDREN *jump out at her, crying* "Surprise! Surprise!")

CHILDREN (*Singing*): Happy birthday to you, happy birthday to you,
Happy birthday, dear Betsy,
Happy birthday to you!

BETSY: It's my birthday surprise!

MARY: Now you must find your birthday presents.

TOMMY: They are all hidden in this room.

SUSIE: We will tell you if you are "hot" or "cold." (BETSY *hunts and finds each of the six presents, the* CHILDREN *aiding her in the hunt by calling* "hot" *or* "cold." *As she finds each gift, she reads the card.* "To Betsy from Mary," "Happy Birthday from Tommy," *etc. As she puts each gift on the table, she thanks the donor, who replies with a polite* "You're welcome." *When all presents are found,* MRS. BUTTON *speaks.*)

MRS. BUTTON: The birthday party is from Daddy and me. And here is your cake!

MR. BUTTON: Was it worth waiting for, Betsy?

BETSY: Oh, yes! I didn't mind waiting after the Fairies told me their secret.
ALL: What fairies?
BETSY: The Wait-and-See Fairies.
ALL: What did they tell you?
BETSY: They told me the easiest way to wait for a surprise was to plan another surprise for someone else.
MRS. BUTTON: But no one else is having a birthday.
BETSY: I would not have this birthday if it weren't for you and Daddy. So I made you a birthday surprise.
MR. *and* MRS. BUTTON: A birthday surprise for us?
BETSY: Yes. I made each of you a birthday card. (*Produces cards for* MR. *and* MRS. BUTTON *from her pocket.*)
MR. *and* MRS. BUTTON (*Reading together*):
Thank you, Parents, both so dear,
Without your love, I'd not be here!
BETSY (*Opening box and taking out two cup cakes, each with a small candle*): And here is a little birthday cake for each of you for your very own.
MR. *and* MRS. BUTTON: Thank you, Betsy. Thank you.
CHILDREN: When are you going to blow out the candles?
BETSY: Wait and see! (*Claps her hand over her mouth*) I'm so used to saying that, I forgot. Come on, let's blow them out right now. (*Curtains close as* CHILDREN *crowd around cake.*)

THE END

THE SHOWER OF HEARTS

Characters

THE KING OF HEARTS
THE QUEEN OF HEARTS
SIX PAGES
KITCHEN MAID
HERALD
WEATHERMAN

CHILDREN
THREE VALENTINE VENDORS
SIX LADIES-IN-WAITING
TWO GUARDS
JACK OF HEARTS

SETTING: *The court of the King and Queen of Hearts. Two throne chairs decorated with hearts occupy the center of the stage.*
AT RISE: *The* KING, *attended by* SIX PAGES *and a* HERALD, *is seated on his throne.*

KING: What time is it?
PAGES: Three o'clock, Your Majesty.
KING: Then where are my tarts? They should have been here at noon.
FIRST PAGE: I have just been to the kitchen, sire. There is no sign of the tarts.
KING: Did you look in the oven?
FIRST PAGE: Yes, indeed, sire.
KING: Did you look on the kitchen table?
FIRST PAGE: Oh, yes, sire.

KING: Then where are they? Here it is three o'clock on the day of my valentine party and no trace of my tarts. What does the Queen say?

SECOND PAGE: She says she finished baking them at eleven, sire. Usually, she puts them on the palace porch to cool.

THIRD PAGE: But we have not seen them, sire.

KING: Then send for the Kitchen Maid. She must have seen them. (THIRD PAGE *exits with bow*.) Unless those tarts are found, there will be no valentine party.

PAGES: No valentine party!

KING: No valentine party! And not a single valentine will be bought or sold this day! (THIRD PAGE *enters with* KITCHEN MAID, *who kneels before the throne*.)

KITCHEN MAID: At your service, sire.

KING: Kitchen Maid, speak up. Have you seen anything of the tarts the Queen baked for me today?

KITCHEN MAID: I saw her take them out of the oven, Your Majesty. But then the third cook called me to scrub the pots and pans, and I didn't see where she put them.

KING: And have you seen them since?

KITCHEN MAID: No, sire. They have disappeared!

KING: Disappeared! We know that already. But what became of them?

KITCHEN MAID: Well, sire, I did see Jack of Hearts sneaking around the cellar door. He had something in his hands.

KING: The Knave has stolen them! (*To one of the* PAGES.) Call the Captain of the Guards! Tell him to arrest Jack of Hearts and bring him to me at once. There will be no valentine party until he is caught and the tarts returned. (*Exit* PAGE.)

KITCHEN MAID: Suppose he has eaten them, Your Majesty!

KING: In that case there will *never* be any valentine parties, or any valentines either. Herald, you will make the announcement at once. No valentines are to be bought or sold this day! Anyone who disobeys this order will be thrown into the dungeon!

HERALD: This will make the people very sad—especially the children!

KING: So much the better! They will work that much harder to catch the thief. (*Rises*) Now I will return to the palace and write a poem about this for the royal records. (KING *exits with all of his* PAGES *and the* KITCHEN MAID. *The* HERALD *sits down on the throne platform and wearily takes off his shoes.*)

HERALD: It's hard work being the King's Herald. My feet hurt! Sometimes I think I will quit and get another job. (*The* WEATHERMAN *enters. He is an old man with a beard. He carries an open black umbrella, trimmed with hearts, and a closed umbrella under one arm.*) Oh dear! More trouble! The Weatherman is carrying his umbrella. Good day to you, Weatherman.

WEATHERMAN: Alas, alas! This is not going to be a good day at all! I have just looked at the weather charts, and there's a strong east wind with black clouds in the north. Mark my word, we'll have storms within the hour.

HERALD: But the valentine party! It's always held here in the courtyard!

WEATHERMAN: Then you'll be rained out. I've just been warning the children to bring their umbrellas and overshoes. Now I must warn the Queen and the rest of the court. (*Gives folded umbrella to* HERALD.) And here is the King's umbrella. Be sure to hold it over him when it rains. (*Exit* WEATHERMAN)

HERALD: Just one thing after the other! (*Three* VALENTINE VENDORS *enter, pushing decorated tea wagons loaded with valentines. Each one is ringing a hand-bell and chanting in a sing-song voice:* "*Valentines! Valentines! Come and get your Valentines!*" CHILDREN *with closed umbrellas run in from either side of the stage, shouting:* "*The valentine men are here! The valentine men are here!*" *They crowd around the valentine carts, singing to the tune of* "*Hot Cross Buns.*")

CHILDREN:
Valentines, valentines!
One a penny, two a penny, valentines!

HERALD (*Running forward*): Stop! Stop! Stop in the name of the King! (*Sings to the tune of* "*The King of France*"):
The King of Hearts has ordered me to say
No valentines will be on sale today!

CHILDREN (*Singing to same tune*):

The King of Hearts has ordered him to say
No valentines will be on sale today!
VALENTINE VENDORS: This is terrible! He can't do this to us!
HERALD: Oh, yes, he can. The King can do anything!
CHILDREN: Down with the King! We will buy valentines in spite of him!
HERALD (*Singing*): The King of Hearts will quickly seize today
Each man or child who dares to disobey!
CHILDREN: Oh dear! Do you think he means it?
HERALD: I am sure he means it. The King is in a terrible temper!
CHILDREN: Why?
HERALD: Because his special valentine tarts have disappeared. He thinks the Jack of Hearts has stolen them.
FIRST CHILD: Jack would never do such a thing!
HERALD: The Kitchen Maid says she saw him running off with them. The King has given orders there will be no valentine party until the tarts are returned and Jack is arrested.
CHILDREN: We will appeal to the Queen! She will help us! The Queen! The Queen! Long live the Queen! (*Enter the* QUEEN *with six* LADIES-IN-WAITING. *Each one carries a closed umbrella.*)
QUEEN: What a lovely greeting! I am happy that the children are so glad to see me. (*All* CHILDREN *curtsy.*)
CHILDREN: Good day to you, Your Majesty.
QUEEN: I see you are making ready for the valentine party.

HERALD: Haven't you heard, Your Majesty? The King has forbidden it until the stolen tarts are returned.
QUEEN: Fiddle-de-dee and fiddle de-dow
We'll have our party anyhow.
VALENTINE VENDORS: But we are not allowed to sell any valentines.
CHILDREN: And we are not allowed to buy them!
QUEEN: Fiddle-de-dee and fiddle-de-dow!
We'll buy and sell them anyhow.
HERALD: But, Your Majesty, listen to this.
ALL, *except* QUEEN *and* LADIES-IN-WAITING (*Sing to tune of "The King of France"*):
The King of Hearts will quickly seize today
Each man and child who dares to disobey!
QUEEN: I am not afraid of the King. He will soon forget what he said. With such lovely valentines as these, who could help but buy? (*Picks up a valentine from the nearest cart and reads*)
Though angry as a bear, my love,
You are, at heart, a singing dove!
I'll buy this one for the King. It just suits him. (CHILDREN *and* LADIES *crowd around carts, all selecting valentines. The* LADIES *read as they pick out their cards.*)
FIRST LADY: This one is perfect for my husband:
Although you sometimes rave and roar,
It's you, my love, that I adore.
SECOND LADY: I'll take this one for my mother:
Oh, Mother, dear, I'm glad you're mine.
I want you for my valentine.

THIRD LADY: This one is just right for my brother:
I hope this valentine will please
A little brother who's a tease!

FOURTH LADY: My sister will like this:
Better than any tall, young mister
I love my darling little sister!

FIFTH LADY: I'll send this one to my father:
This valentine is here to say
That I will love you every day.

SIXTH LADY: I'm buying this for my Secret Pal:
If I should sail the ocean blue,
I'd still love no one else but you!
(*All the* LADIES *and* CHILDREN *now have many valentines.*)

HERALD (*Joining the crowd*): Bless my soul! I think I'll buy one or two myself. (*Just as he, too, has both hands full of valentines, there is an off-stage fanfare and a voice cries:* "Make way for the King! Make way for the King of Hearts!")

ALL: The King! The King!

VALENTINE VENDORS: He'll have us arrested! (*Rush off-stage with carts*)

ALL: He'll have us thrown into the dungeon.

QUEEN: Don't be silly! (*Slipping valentines inside closed umbrella.*) Just follow my example and you'll be quite safe! (*Everybody hides valentines inside umbrellas.*)

KING (*Entering with* PAGES. *He is chuckling over a scroll he is reading.*): If I do say so myself, I never wrote a better poem!

ALL: Greetings, Your Majesty! (*Curtsy*)

KING: Greetings to you, good people. You are here just in time to hear the clever poem I have written about this disgraceful affair of the tarts. (*To* QUEEN) Come, my dear, you must sit beside me while I read it. (KING *and* QUEEN *ascend throne.* HERALD *takes his place at the* KING's *side. The* QUEEN *is seated. The* KING *stands to read his poem. He clears his throat and begins.*)
The Queen of Hearts, she made some tarts,
All on a winter's day.
The Knave of Hearts, he stole the tarts
And took them clean away. (*Hearty applause. The* KING *holds up his hand for silence.*)
Quiet! The next verse is even better.
The King of Hearts called for the tarts,
And beat the Knave full sore.
The Knave of Hearts brought back the tarts
And vowed he'd steal no more. (*No applause. Everyone looks at everyone else.*)
Well, what's the matter? Don't you like it? Isn't it a great poem?

QUEEN: It's a lovely poem, my dear. But . . . well . . . it isn't exactly true, is it?

KING: True? Of course, it's true. Every word of it.

HERALD: But you haven't caught the Jack of Hearts, sire, and the tarts are not yet returned.

KING: No, but I soon will catch him, and when I do, I'll beat him black and blue!

QUEEN: How can you be sure Jack really stole the tarts?

KING: I know he stole them! I know he did! And until

I catch him, there will never be another valentine bought or sold in my whole kingdom. (*Off-stage rumble of thunder*)

FIRST PAGE: Oh, dear! A storm is coming up!

SECOND PAGE: I think it's going to rain!

QUEEN: Maybe we'd better go inside.

KING: Nonsense, my dear! A little rain won't hurt us! Besides, I see the Weatherman has been on the job. You all have your umbrellas. (*Off-stage thunder, louder*)

THIRD PAGE: The storm's coming fast.

FOURTH PAGE (*Holding out his hand*): I felt a raindrop on my hand.

FIFTH PAGE: There's another! And another!

SIXTH PAGE: And another! And another!

KING: Well, don't just stand there! Put up your umbrellas. (*No one makes a move.*) Hurry up! It's going to pour! The Queen's dress will be ruined! (*To* HERALD) You know I catch cold when it rains! Put up that umbrella—at once! (*At the third clap of thunder, all put up umbrellas at the same time, with the result that the* KING *is deluged with valentines.*) What's this! What's this! (*Holding one up*) Valentines! You've been buying valentines! Guards! Guards! Arrest these people at once! Guards! Guards! Where are the Guards?

SIXTH PAGE: The Guards are all out hunting Jack of Hearts, Your Majesty!

FIFTH PAGE: And here they come! They've caught him!

They've caught him! (*Two* GUARDS *drag in* JACK OF HEARTS, *who carries a basket.*)

JACK OF HEARTS: Let me go! Let me go!

GUARDS: Here he is, Your Majesty!

KING: Good work! (*To* JACK) And where are the tarts you stole, you wicked fellow?

JACK OF HEARTS: I didn't steal them! Honestly, I didn't!

GUARD (*Snatching basket out of his hand*): What do you call these?

KING (*Looking into basket*): The stolen tarts!

JACK OF HEARTS: They're not stolen. I didn't steal them!

QUEEN: He's telling the truth! He didn't steal the tarts!

KING: Then how did he get them?

QUEEN: Oh, dear. I'm so ashamed. I told him to take them!

KING: You gave my tarts to him instead of to me!

QUEEN: No, no, no! I told him to take them and put them in the garbage!

ALL: Put them in the garbage!

QUEEN: Yes. I never was a very good cook, and today I made more mistakes than usual. I used salt instead of sugar, pepper instead of cinnamon, cornstarch instead of flour! They were dreadful!

KING (*Indicating basket*): But where did these come from? They look delicious. (*Tastes one*) They *are* delicious.

JACK OF HEARTS: My mother baked them for you, sire. I was just bringing them to you when your guards arrested me.

KING: Thank you, Jack. I apologize for having you arrested as a thief.

FIRST PAGE: What about these people who broke the law and bought valentines? Are they to be arrested?

KING: No, indeed! We will have our valentine party as planned. I don't want any unhappy hearts on Valentine's Day. Look, the rain has stopped and the sun is coming out. (*All put down umbrellas*) I hereby command you all to be joyful and start our party with a song. (*Curtains close as all sing to tune of "Come, Let Us Be Joyful."*)

ALL:
Come, let us be joyful while life is bright and gay,
Come, let us be joyful on St. Valentine's Day.
Oh, we won't worry and we won't fret,
There's lots of fun in the old world yet,
And that's one thing we won't forget,
And go on our way rejoicing.
       (*Curtain*)

THE END

THE WEATHERMAN ON TRIAL

Characters

THE WEATHERMAN
THE DISTRICT ATTORNEY
THE JUDGE
CLERK OF THE COURT
PRETTY POLLY PERKINS
CAPTAIN BABE BOOTH
LITTLE SALLY WATERS
PITTER
PATTER
DRIP } *six little raindrops*
DROP
DRIZZLE
TRICKLE
LADIES AND GENTLEMEN OF THE JURY

SETTING: *A courtroom. The* JURY *is seated in two rows of chairs, right stage. The* JUDGE *occupies a chair mounted on a small platform, center stage. Beside it is the witness stand. The* DISTRICT ATTORNEY *and the* WEATHERMAN *are seated at a table down left.*

JUDGE (*Pounding on desk with gavel*): Hear ye! Hear ye! Hear ye! The court is now in session. Our first case is the Children of (*Name of school, city and state*) against the Weatherman. Who speaks for the children?

DISTRICT ATTORNEY (*Rising*): I, sir. I speak for the children of (*Name of school, city and state*). I will prove their charges against the Weatherman.

JUDGE: Who speaks for the Weatherman?

WEATHERMAN (*Rising*): I will speak for myself, if it please the court.

JUDGE (*Nods to* WEATHERMAN *to be seated*): Mr. District Attorney, you may proceed.

DISTRICT ATTORNEY (*Rising and crossing to* JURY): Ladies and gentlemen of the Jury, I have a question to ask you. (*Sings, to the tune of "The Muffin Man."*)
Oh, do you know the Weatherman, the Weatherman, the Weatherman?
Oh, do you know the Weatherman,
Who brings the sun and rain?

JURY (*Singing to same tune*):
Oh, yes, we know the Weatherman, the Weatherman, the Weatherman.
Oh, yes, we know the Weatherman,
He brings the sun and rain.

DISTRICT ATTORNEY: The boys and girls of this town have some serious complaints about the weather. It will be up to you, the members of the Jury, to decide if the Weatherman is innocent or guilty of these charges. Our first witness is Pretty Polly Perkins.

CLERK (*Calling*): Pretty Polly Perkins! (PRETTY POLLY PERKINS *enters and goes to the witness stand. The*

THE WEATHERMAN ON TRIAL

CLERK, *standing beside the stand administers the oath, to the tune of "Baa! Baa! Black Sheep," singing the following first line of song*): Lady, will you swear to answer true?

POLLY (*Singing next line*): Yes, sir, yes, sir, that I do.

JURY (*Singing the following*):
Now for the questions to praise or to blame
Old Mr. Weatherman for sunshine or rain.

DISTRICT ATTORNEY: Miss Perkins, will you please tell the court what happened to you last Easter Sunday?

POLLY PERKINS (*Reciting*):
In my Easter bonnet,
With all the ribbons on it,
I went to join the others in the Easter Parade.
Alas! My Easter Bonnet!
The rain came down upon it,
And now my hat is ruined and the ribbons sadly frayed!

DISTRICT ATTORNEY (*Goes to table, picks up hatbox, opens it, and takes out a terrible looking hat*): Behold, ladies and gentlemen of the Jury. This is the work of the Weatherman. He sent the rain that ruined Pretty Polly's Easter bonnet.

JURY: Too bad! Too bad! How sad! How sad!

DISTRICT ATTORNEY: Thank you, Miss Perkins. You are excused. Our next witness is Babe Booth, Captain of the Wildcat Nine. (*Exit* PRETTY POLLY)

CLERK (*Calling*): Babe Booth! (BABE BOOTH *enters in baseball uniform. He takes the stand, and the* CLERK *again administers the oath, in song, singing first line as follows*) Mister, will you swear to answer true?

BABE BOOTH (*Singing next line*): Yes, sir, yes, sir, that I do!

JURY (*Singing the following*):
Now for the questions to praise or to blame,
Old Mr. Weatherman for sunshine or rain.

DISTRICT ATTORNEY: Babe Booth, will you please tell the court what happened to you last Fourth of July?

BABE BOOTH (*Reciting*):
On Fourth of July, the Wildcat Nine
Had the biggest game of the year.
But just as I came up to bat,
The storm clouds did appear.
The field became a sea of mud,
It surely was a shame.
Because of that old Weatherman,
We lost our biggest game.

DISTRICT ATTORNEY: And, so, ladies and gentlemen of the Jury, we have another case against the Weatherman—a lost ball game and a disappointed team.

JURY: Too bad! Too bad! How sad, how sad!

DISTRICT ATTORNEY: Thank you, Captain Babe Booth. You are excused. Our next witness is Little Sally Waters. (*Exit* BABE BOOTH.)

CLERK (*Calling*): Little Sally Waters! (LITTLE SALLY WATERS *enters, takes her place at the witness stand and the* CLERK *administers the oath, in song, as before singing first line.*) Lady, will you swear to answer true?

SALLY (*Singing next line*): Yes, sir, yes, sir, that I do.
JURY (*Singing the following*):
  Now for the questions to praise or to blame
  Old Mr. Weatherman for sunshine or rain.
DISTRICT ATTORNEY: Little Sally Waters, will you please tell the court what happened to you last August?
LITTLE SALLY WATERS (*Reciting*):
  Last August Mommy, Dad and I went off on our vacation.
  We had just seven days to spend, the shore was our location.
  We had our brand-new bathing suits, and just one single notion,
  To spend each day down at the beach, a-bathing in the ocean.
  But that old Mr. Weatherman, he spoiled our fun and pleasure.
  He sent the storm clouds every day, and raindrops in full measure.
DISTRICT ATTORNEY: And would you know the Weatherman if you were to see him?
LITTLE SALLY WATERS: I'm not quite sure.
JURY (*Singing, to tune of "Little Sally Waters"*):
  Little Sally Waters, sitting by the bay,
  Crying and weeping for a sunny day.
  Rise, Sally, rise. (*She does so.*)
  Don't hide your eyes.
  Look to the East, look to the West,
  Point to the very one that you know best.

LITTLE SALLY WATERS (*Pointing to* WEATHERMAN):
There he is! There he is! That's the Weatherman!
He's the one who spoiled our vacation!

JURY: Too bad! Too bad! How sad, how sad!

DISTRICT ATTORNEY: Thank you, Little Sally Waters.
You are excused. (*Exit* SALLY) Ladies and gentlemen
of the Jury, you have heard the facts against Mr.
Weatherman. It is now up to you to decide if this man
is to be trusted any further. (*To the* JUDGE) Your
Honor, we rest our case. (DISTRICT ATTORNEY *sits
down.*)

JUDGE: Mr. Weatherman, you have heard the evidence
against you—the ruined Easter hat, the lost ball game,
the spoiled vacation. What have you to say for yourself?

WEATHERMAN (*Rising and approaching the* JUDGE):
Your Honor, I ask leave to present six of my most
trusted workers to speak for me.

JUDGE: Who are they?

WEATHERMAN: They are my busiest raindrops. May
they come in?

JUDGE: You have my permission.

WEATHERMAN (*Picking up a sheet of tin from table and
shaking it so that it makes a sound like thunder*): The
sound of thunder should bring them here right away.
(SIX RAINDROPS *enter. They stand in front of the witness chair.*)

RAINDROPS: You sent for us, sir?

WEATHERMAN: Yes. I have some questions to ask you,

but first, I would like you to tell this gentleman (*Pointing to* JUDGE) who you are.

PITTER *and* PATTER (*Step forward and recite together*):
We're Pitter and Patter,
The Rain twins, you know.
We're always together
Wherever we go.

DRIP, DROP *and* DRIZZLE (*Step forward and recite in unison*):
We're Drip, Drop and Drizzle,
We're triplets, you see,
And where you see one,
You always see three.

TRICKLE (*Stepping forward*):
My folks call me Trickle,
And sadly I moan,
Since I have no partner,
I'm always alone.

JUDGE: I understand you work for the Weatherman. Just what do you do?

PITTER *and* PATTER:
The Weatherman keeps us busy.
We have our work to do.
We keep the wells from running dry,
And fill the rivers, too.

DRIP, DROP *and* DRIZZLE:
We keep the mill wheels turning,
And furnish power and steam.
We wash the leaves in summer,
And keep them fresh and green.

TRICKLE: I spatter here, I spatter there,
And splash about and play,
And yet I help to sail the ships
On ocean, lake, and bay.

WEATHERMAN: And now I would like to ask you some important questions.

JUDGE: Not so fast! The Clerk must swear them in.

CLERK (*Singing as before*): Raindrops, will you swear to answer true?

RAINDROPS: Yes, sir, yes, sir, that we do.

JURY (*Singing*):
Now for the questions to praise or to blame
Old Mr. Weatherman for sunshine or rain.

WEATHERMAN: Pitter and Patter will please take the stand. (PITTER *and* PATTER *go to witness stand; the others sit at table.*) Now think very carefully. Can you remember what you did for me last Easter Sunday?

PITTER *and* PATTER: Oh, yes. That was the day you sent us to look after the poor farmers.

WEATHERMAN: Will you please tell the court what happened?

PITTER *and* PATTER:
On Easter Day the fields were dry.
It had not rained in weeks.
The sun had baked the dusty ground,
And dried up all the creeks.
The farmers knew their crops would fail,
Unless they got some rain.

How glad they were to see us come!
We saved their fruit and grain!
WEATHERMAN: Thank you, Pitter and Patter. You have very good memories. (PITTER *and* PATTER *return to table.*)
JUDGE: So that's what happened on Easter Sunday, the same day that you did such damage to Pretty Polly's Easter hat.
WEATHERMAN: It couldn't be helped, your Honor. The farmers were desperate. May I call my next helpers?
JUDGE: You may.
WEATHERMAN: Drip, Drop and Drizzle will please take the stand. (DRIP, DROP *and* DRIZZLE *go to witness stand.*) I want you to try to remember the job you did for me on July the Fourth.
DRIP: July the Fourth. That was the day we broke up a ball game.
DROP: And ruined a parade.
DRIZZLE: But it was also the day we found Little Lester.
JUDGE: And who is Little Lester?
DRIZZLE: Little Lester was a Cub Scout who got lost from his pack while they were on a camping trip.
WEATHERMAN: Please tell the court what happened.
DRIP, DROP *and* DRIZZLE:

He wandered from the mountain trail,
And soon had lost his way.
He tried to find the road to camp
For many a weary day.
He had no food. The sun was hot . . .

No water—that's the worst.
Without that rain July the Fourth,
He might have died of thirst.

WEATHERMAN: Thank you. You have been a big help and you did a fine job saving Little Lester.

JUDGE: So you broke up a ball game, but saved a little boy's life. I'd say you had a busy day. But you still have some explaining to do. What about that rainy week in August?

WEATHERMAN: I'll ask Trickle to tell you about that. (TRICKLE *takes the stand.*)

TRICKLE: August is a hard month to remember, but I'll try. The first week in August, I had my vacation; but after that, I was very busy.

WEATHERMAN: And why were you so busy during August?

TRICKLE: Because of the careless campers. We have to watch out for fires. I remember there was a bad one during the second week in August last year.

WEATHERMAN: Tell us about it.

TRICKLE: A forest fire was raging.
It was a sorry shame.
The baby deer and rabbits
Were trapped by smoke and flame.
But Mr. Weatherman stood by
And raised an awful shout.
He sent a million raindrops
To put the fire out.

JUDGE: And did it take you a whole week to put out the forest fire?

TRICKLE: We worked for three days and three nights. And then we had to go about soaking the rest of the woods clear down to the ocean so there would be no more fires.

JUDGE: I see. So that is why so many vacations were spoiled.

TRICKLE: It wasn't the raindrops, sir. It was the campers who started the forest fires in the first place.

JUDGE: I understand.

WEATHERMAN: Thank you, Trickle.

TRICKLE: Don't you want me to tell about the summer showers that cooled off the hot city streets, and the thunderstorm that put an end to the heat wave?

WEATHERMAN: Not today, Trickle. You may go. (*Exit* TRICKLE *and other raindrops. To* JUDGE) Well, Your Honor, that is all I can tell you about my raindrops on Easter Sunday, the Fourth of July and the month of August. I am sorry for the damage they caused, but the work they did seemed very important.

JUDGE: We await the decision of the Jury. Ladies and gentlemen, have you reached a verdict?

FOREMAN OF THE JURY: We have, Your Honor. Our verdict is—Not Guilty. In all cases, the Jury has found that the Weatherman has acted for the greatest good of all. (JURY *sings, to the tune of* "*Oats, Peas, Beans and Barley Grow.*")

> Let it rain or let it snow,
> Let the winds begin to blow.
> Can you or I or anyone know
> How much the rain or sun must show.

Tra, la, la, la, la, la,
Tra, la, la, la, la, la,
We're very sure the Weatherman
Will do the very best he can.

JUDGE: You have heard the verdict of the Jury. The Weatherman has been found not guilty of the charges brought against him by the children of (*Name of school, city, state*). Before dismissing this case, I should like to remind you all of the following:
Whether you're wet or whether you're dry,
Sunbeams and raindrops will come from the sky.
Whether you're cold or whether you're hot,
We shall have weather, whether or not!
(JUDGE *raps gavel three times.*) I declare the case against the Weatherman dismissed. (*Raps gavel three more times.*) Court is adjourned! (*Curtain*)

THE END

OLD GLORY GROWS UP

Characters

FIVE SPEAKERS	UNCLE SAM
GEORGE WASHINGTON	NEW MEXICO
BETSY ROSS	ARIZONA
NARRATOR	CONFEDERATE BOY
FRANCIS SCOTT KEY	CONFEDERATE GIRL
VERMONT	ALASKA
KENTUCKY	HAWAII
COLUMBIA	

BEFORE RISE: *On the apron of the stage is an easel bearing a large placard labeled* OLD GLORY. *Underneath this placard are six date cards arranged in order, so that each time a card is removed, another is revealed.* FIVE SPEAKERS *enter, wearing red, white and blue paper caps. As they reach center stage, they bow to the audience and recite:*

FIRST SPEAKER:

> Good gentlemen and ladies,
> We've been sent out to say
> We hope you will be patient.
> There's been a slight delay.

SECOND SPEAKER:
>The costume for George Washington
>We find is much too small,
>Because the boy who plays the part
>Has grown up much too tall.

THIRD SPEAKER:
>Last year the suit we had was right,
>But George has put on inches.
>And now the coat is far too tight.
>In fact, he says it pinches.

FOURTH SPEAKER:
>The trousers are a way too short.
>The sleeves come up to here.
>(*Gestures to indicate*)
>The cotton wig and velvet hat
>Perch right up on his ear.

FIFTH SPEAKER:
We'll do our best to hurry.
We hope it won't be long.
We'll sing while you are waiting
Our Yankee Doodle song. (SPEAKERS *sing verse and chorus of "Yankee Doodle."* NARRATOR *enters.*)

NARRATOR:
We're really very sorry
For causing this delay.
But now the costume's ready,
And we can start our play. (*Five* SPEAKERS *move left stage and remain there as a chorus. The* NARRATOR *moves to easel.*)
We'll tell the story of our flag.

We hope it gets across. (*Removes first placard revealing date—1777.*)
And now you'll meet George Washington
And Mistress Betsy Ross. (*Curtain rises.* GEORGE WASHINGTON *and* BETSY ROSS *are posed at either side of a very large cardboard Colonial flag with thirteen stars arranged in a circle on the blue field. The field is a flannel board arrangement which can be removed and replaced with a new field as the play progresses. Beside* BETSY ROSS *is a small sewing stand or table on which the other fields are placed so they will be available as needed.*)

BETSY ROSS: The flag is finished, General Washington. I trust it meets with your approval.

WASHINGTON: It is a beautiful flag, Mistress Ross. I am sure that the gentlemen of Congress will be pleased.

BETSY ROSS: I have tried to follow their orders, Your Excellency.

WASHINGTON: Everything is exactly right. On June 14th of this year, 1777, Congress ordered that the flag of the United States should have thirteen red and white stripes with a union of thirteen stars on a blue field.

BETSY ROSS: It was hard to arrange the stars. I first put them in three rows, but I liked the circle better.

WASHINGTON: You did well, Mistress Ross. We do not wish to place one state above another. Each one of our thirteen colonies is of equal importance. (*Traces with his finger the outline of the circle*) Then, too, the circle has no end, and there must never be an end to the glory of our country and our flag.

BETSY ROSS: That is a beautiful thought, sir.

WASHINGTON (*With a bow*): And a beautiful flag, Mistress Ross. I propose three big cheers for the red, white and blue.

CHORUS (*Sings chorus of "Columbia the Gem of the Ocean"*) "Three cheers for the red, white and blue, Three cheers for the red, white and blue, The army and navy forever, Three cheers for the red, white and blue." (*Curtain closes. The* NARRATOR *removes the date card, 1777, revealing the date, 1795.*)

* * * * *

NARRATOR: The flag with only thirteen stars
Remained the very same
Until, in seventeen ninety-five,
A change we must explain. (*Curtain opens on same scene with the additional presence of* VERMONT *and* KENTUCKY. *Each child wears a baldric with the name of the state.* VERMONT *carries a white stripe to be affixed to the flag;* KENTUCKY *carries a red stripe.*)

WASHINGTON: Our country is growing, Mistress Ross. Two new states have been admitted to the Union. I present Vermont and Kentucky.

BETSY ROSS (*With a curtsy*): Welcome to the United States of America. And now we must find a place for you in our flag.

VERMONT: The people of Vermont will be proud and happy to have a star of their own.

KENTUCKY: The citizens of Kentucky will always defend their star.

WASHINGTON: A circle of fifteen stars will be far too big for the blue field.

BETSY ROSS (*Removing field with the thirteen stars and replacing it with a field of fifteen stars*): How do you like this design, sir? We will arrange the stars in five rows of three each.

WASHINGTON: Excellent, Mistress Ross, excellent.

VERMONT: If there are fifteen stars, there should be fifteen stripes. (*Attaches white stripe to the flag*) In the name of the state of Vermont, I add this white stripe to the flag of the United States.

KENTUCKY (*Adding red stripe*): This fifteenth stripe represents the people of the state of Kentucky.

WASHINGTON: May every stripe and star stand for America, sweet land of Liberty. (*Curtain closes as* CHORUS *sings the first stanza of* "*America.*")

* * * * *

NARRATOR:
>So fifteen stripes and fifteen stars
>Displayed in just this manner
>Inspired the man who wrote the words
>Of our "Star-Spangled Banner."

(*Curtain opens on same flag with* FRANCIS SCOTT KEY *beside it.*)

FRANCIS SCOTT KEY: My name is Francis Scott Key. It was this flag flying over Fort McHenry in 1814

which inspired me to write the poem in which I called it "the star-spangled banner." You all know the words, but let me read you my favorite lines. (*Reads from notebook*):
"Then conquer we must, when our cause it is just,
And this be our motto: 'In God is our trust!'
And the Star-Spangled Banner in triumph shall wave
O'er the land of the free and the home of the brave!"
Today wherever the star-spangled banner is flown, there are men, women and children to sing my song. But through the years our flag has grown as our country has grown. There have been many flag-makers who have changed the design of our flag, but now to continue the story. The year is 1818. (FRANCIS SCOTT KEY *exits as* COLUMBIA *and* UNCLE SAM *enter. The* NARRATOR *removes the 1795 placard, revealing the 1818 sign.*)

NARRATOR:
    Indiana, Tennessee,
    Oklahoma, Maine,
    Also Mississippi
    Into the Union came.
    Columbia and Uncle Sam
    Now have a new decree
    Of how the stars and stripes should look,
    And how the flag should be.

COLUMBIA: Twenty states in the Union! That would mean twenty stars and twenty stripes! And our country is still growing. It will be hard to design a flag that will represent every new state.

OLD GLORY GROWS UP

UNCLE SAM (*With document*): I have here an official Act of Congress which solves our problem. It is dated April 4, 1818. On this date the flag of the United States shall return to the original design of thirteen stripes. (COLUMBIA *removes the last two stripes.*) A new star shall be added for every new state admitted to the Union. (COLUMBIA *puts up a field with twenty stars.*)

COLUMBIA: Thirteen stripes and twenty stars—and America still growing!

NARRATOR: To twenty add another ten,
And there is room for more, (COLUMBIA *puts up field with thirty-four stars.*)
Until, in 1861
Our flag had thirty-four. (NARRATOR *removes 1818 and reveals placard 1861-1865.*)

UNCLE SAM: The years from 1861 to 1865 were known as the War Years and the flag was called the Flag of the Union. At this time there were thirty-four stars in our flag, but only twenty states remained in the Union. Eleven states had set up a government of their own with a new flag known as the "Stars and Bars." (CONFEDERATE BOY *and* GIRL *enter, each carrying a Confederate flag.*)

BOY: During the Civil War, the Stars and Bars flew over eleven of our southern states, known as the Confederate States of America.

GIRL: The Confederate Flag was carried into all the battles of the Civil War by the men in gray who fought under General Robert E. Lee.

UNCLE SAM: But when the War between the States was over, the stars and stripes once more flew over both the North and the South, "one nation under God, indivisible, with liberty and justice for all."
CHORUS (*As curtain closes*):
>Glory, glory, hallelujah,
>Glory, glory, hallelujah,
>Glory, glory, hallelujah,
>Our flag goes marching on.

* * * * *

NARRATOR (*Removing 1861-1865 and revealing 1912*):
In 1912 the field of stars
Had grown to forty-eight.
As side by side two bright new stars
Were added on that date. (*Curtain re-opens with* NEW MEXICO *and* ARIZONA *standing with* COLUMBIA *and* UNCLE SAM.)
UNCLE SAM: From the Indian Territory, New Mexico and Arizona are admitted to the Union.
COLUMBIA: Welcome to our newcomers from the great Southwest. (*Puts up field with forty-six stars*)
NEW MEXICO (*Affixing the forty-seventh star*):
>I place the forty-seventh star,
>With honor may it glow.
>And with this star I pledge the faith
>Of all New Mexico.
ARIZONA (*Placing forty-eighth star*):
>The cowboys and the Indians
>Who in this state do dwell

OLD GLORY GROWS UP

       All pledge that Arizona
       Will serve her country well.
COLUMBIA: The American flag now has thirteen stripes and forty-eight stars.
UNCLE SAM: It was this flag which was carried in World War One and World War Two. The American Flag with its forty-eight stars has become the symbol of liberty to many other countries of the world. (*Curtain closes.* CHORUS *sings "You're a Grand Old Flag."*)

      *   *   *   *   *

NARRATOR (*Exchanges 1912 for 1960*):
       The story of the stars and stripes
       Is not yet fully told.
       We have another chapter
       All ready to unfold.
       For 1960 is the date
       When two more stars appear
       To take their place upon the flag
       Which we all hold so dear. (*Curtain re-opens on flag of fifty stars.* ALASKA *and* HAWAII *stand with entire company.*)
ALASKA (*Pointing to forty-ninth star*):
       My star shines from Alaska,
       The land of ice and snow,
       The country of the totem pole
       And sturdy Eskimo.
HAWAII (*Pointing to fiftieth star*):
My star shines from Hawaii,

The island of the flowers.
We're proud to join the U.S.A.
And make your country ours. (*The five members of
the* CHORUS *move into tableau with the rest.*)

FIRST SPEAKER:

Good gentlemen and ladies,
We hope you understand
Just how the story of our flag
Has been prepared and planned.

SECOND SPEAKER:

Remember how George Washington
Once had a suit too small,
We said he had outgrown it
Because he was too tall.

THIRD SPEAKER:

America is growing, too,
It's bigger every day,
But we must not outgrow the flag
Of our own U.S.A.

FOURTH SPEAKER:

So every time we add a state
We add another star
To stand for people of our land
From regions near and far.

FIFTH SPEAKER:

And so in 1960
These fifty stars behold,
And thirteen stripes of red and white
Within the flag unfold.

NARRATOR:
> For as our country's growing
> Old Glory's growing, too,
> So let us pledge allegiance
> And loyalty anew. (*All rise and pledge allegiance to the flag.*)

UNCLE SAM:
> May God preserve America
> And guard our liberty
> And grant us peace and union
> From sea to shining sea. (*All sing "America the Beautiful" as curtain closes.*)

THE END

GARDEN HOLD-UP

Characters

GARDENERS, *six or more*
ROBIN
RABBIT
SQUIRREL
JACK FROST
FARMER BROWN
FARMER GRAY

FARMER GREEN
FARMER BLACK
MOTHER ROBIN
PETER RABBIT
BUSHY SQUIRREL
WEATHERMAN

SCENE 1

TIME: *A spring day.*
SETTING: *A garden.*
AT RISE: *On-stage is a row of little* GARDENERS. *Beside each one is a box containing a toy shovel, toy rake, pack of seeds, and small watering can.*

GARDENERS (*Singing to the tune of "Looby Loo"*):
Now it is planting time.
See how the sunbeams shine.
Here we are all in line.
Oh, what a wonderful time.
We pick our shovels up.
  (*Pick up shovels*)

GARDEN HOLD-UP

We point our shovels down.
   (*Poise shovels for digging*)
We give our shovels a dig, dig, dig,
   (*Pretend to dig*)
And turn up all the ground.

We pick our yard rakes up.
   (*Pick up rakes*)
We point our yard rakes down.
   (*Poise rakes for raking*)
We give our yard rakes a scrape, scrape, scrape,
   (*Rake back and forth*)
And smooth out all the ground.

We pick our seed packs up.
   (*Pick up packages of seeds*)
We point our seed packs down.
   (*Poise envelopes for scattering*)
We give our seed packs a shake, shake, shake,
   (*Shake seed packages*)
And scatter them around.

We pick our sprinklers up.
   (*Pick up sprinkling cans*)
We point our sprinklers down.
   (*Poise sprinklers for watering*)
We give our sprinklers a shake, shake, shake,
   (*Sprinkle with cans*)
And water all around.

Now all our work is through,
Off and away we go.
Now all we have to do,

Is wait for our garden to grow. (GARDENERS *return their tools to the boxes and exit. Enter* SQUIRREL, ROBIN, RABBIT, *and* JACK FROST. *They join hands, and dance around, singing to tune of "Little Brown Jug."*)

ROBIN, SQUIRREL, RABBIT, *and* JACK FROST: Ha, ha, ha, and ho, ho, ho,
What those gardeners do not know!
Ha, ha, ha, and hee, hee, hee,
What a garden this will be!

ROBIN: I'm Robber, the Robin.
I'll steal all the seeds
And eat them myself
For my own selfish needs.

RABBIT: I'm Bandit, the Rabbit.
I have a bad habit.
I nibble each stem and each leaf.
My heart I will harden.
I'll ruin this garden
And bring it to sorrow and grief.

SQUIRREL: My name is Spoiler,
A real little toiler.
I dig, and I dig, and I dig.
Then off in a hurry
I scamper and scurry,
To hide in a treetop so big.

JACK FROST:
Jack the Nipper is my name,
Or Jackie Frost, it's all the same.
I nip buds here, I nip buds there,
Just when the springtime seems most fair.

ROBIN: Just wait till I eat up those seeds!
SQUIRREL: Just wait till I dig up that garden!
RABBIT: Just wait till I nibble the lettuce and cabbage leaves!
JACK FROST: Just wait till I nip those tender, green buds!
ROBIN, SQUIRREL, RABBIT, *and* JACK FROST (*Dancing around in glee*):
>Ha, ha, ha, and ho, ho, ho,
>What those gardeners do not know!
>Ha, ha, ha, and hee, hee, hee,
>What a garden this will be!

CURTAIN

* * * * *

SCENE 2

SETTING: *Same as Scene 1.*
AT RISE: GARDENERS *are on the stage. Some are hoeing; some are weeding; some are using the sprinkling cans. After a short time, they pull out red bandannas and wipe their faces.*

GARDENERS (*To the tune of* "Oats, Peas, Beans"):
>First we hoe, and then we weed.
>Then we water all the seed.
>But oh, oh, oh, we do not know
>Why our garden does not grow!

1ST GARDENER: I'm tired.
2ND GARDENER: So am I! Let's give the whole thing up.

OTHERS: No, no, no! We want to have a garden.
3RD GARDENER: If only we knew what to do.
4TH GARDENER: Maybe we're doing something wrong.
5TH GARDENER: I know! Let's ask the farmers for advice.
6TH GARDENER: I think it's time to call for help.
GARDENERS: Farmer Brown, Farmer Gray, Farmer Green, Farmer Black, please come tell us what we lack! (*Enter four* FARMERS)
FARMERS: We heard you call and here we are,
We bring you help from near and far.
(*To the tune of* "*Mistress Mary, Quite Contrary*")
Sally, Mary, John and Harry,
How does your garden grow?
GARDENERS (*Singing to the same tune*):
We hate to tell. It's not so well,
For nothing is starting to show!
FARMER BROWN (*Looking around*): 'Pears to me the birds have been after your garden seed.
FARMER GRAY (*Looking around*): 'Pears to me some squirrel has been digging holes in your garden.
FARMER GREEN (*Looking around*): 'Pears to me some rabbit has nibbled the little green leaves.
FARMER BLACK (*Looking around*): 'Pears to me Jack Frost has been around, nipping the little new buds.
1ST GARDENER: We thought gardening would be easy.
2ND GARDENER: We thought all we had to do was plant the seeds and take care of them.
FARMER BROWN: So much depends on the weatherman.
FARMER GREEN: You have to watch out for insect pests and animals.

3RD GARDENER: What can we do?
FARMER GRAY: A scarecrow might help.
FARMER BLACK: You might put up a fence to keep out the animals.
4TH GARDENER: We thought the birds and animals were our friends.
FARMER BROWN: Most of them are, but there are always some rascals, you know.
FARMER GREEN: When you plant a garden, you have to keep a close watch.
4TH GARDENER: That's what we'll do, Farmer Green.
5TH GARDENER: We'll put up a fence.
6TH GARDENER: We'll keep a close watch.
1ST GARDENER: Maybe we can catch some of those little robbers.
GARDENERS: Thank you! Thank you! Thank you very much.
FARMERS: You're welcome, and good luck with your gardening. (FARMERS *exit*.)
2ND GARDENER: Let's get to work on that fence. (GARDENERS *form a circle, taking hold of each other's hoes or rakes to make circle very large*.)
GARDENERS (*When they are in place*): Shhhh! Shhhh! Shhhh!
And hush, hush, hush!
We'll catch those creatures
With a rush. (ROBIN, SQUIRREL, RABBIT *and* JACK FROST *skip in, shouting*.)
ROBIN, SQUIRREL, RABBIT, *and* JACK FROST: We'll dig and we'll nibble,

We'll peck and we'll nip.
The plants in this garden
We're ready to strip. (*They see the fence and stop.*)
Look! Look! A fence! A fence!

ROBIN: Never mind a silly old fence. I can fly right over the top. (ROBIN *flaps his wings, and goes inside the circle.*)

SQUIRREL: That old fence won't stop me. I can get over that in a single leap. (*Leaps inside circle*)

RABBIT: Who's afraid of a little old fence? I can get over that with one good hop. (RABBIT *hops inside.*)

JACK FROST: There's no fence big enough to keep out Jack Frost. (*He steps over fence. The* GARDENERS *close in the circle, shouting.*)

GARDENERS: We've caught you! We've caught you! (ROBIN, SQUIRREL, RABBIT, *and* JACK FROST *try to plunge out of circle, but* GARDENERS *box them in.*) You're in, but you can't get out! You are our prisoners!

ROBIN, SQUIRREL, RABBIT, *and* JACK FROST: What are you going to do with us?

1ST GARDENER: We don't know yet.

2ND GARDENER: You just wait and see.

3RD GARDENER: You have been stealing our seeds.

4TH GARDENER: And nibbling our plants.

5TH GARDENER: And digging holes in our garden.

6TH GARDENER: And nipping our little green buds.

1ST GARDENER (*To* RABBIT): My mother could use you for rabbit stew.

2ND GARDENER (*To* SQUIRREL): My mother knows how to make a squirrel pie.

3RD GARDENER (*To* ROBIN): My mother needs some feathers for her new hat.

4TH GARDENER: It would be easy to melt Jack Frost into a puddle of water. (ROBIN, SQUIRREL, RABBIT, *and* JACK FROST *become frightened*.)

ROBIN, SQUIRREL, RABBIT, *and* JACK FROST: No, no, no! Help, help, help! Let us go! Let us go! Let us go! Mamma! Mamma! Daddy! Daddy! Help, help! (*Enter* MOTHER ROBIN, PETER RABBIT, BUSHY SQUIRREL *and the* WEATHERMAN)

MOTHER ROBIN, PETER RABBIT, BUSHY SQUIRREL *and* WEATHERMAN: What's the matter? What's the matter?

ROBIN, SQUIRREL, RABBIT, *and* JACK FROST: We're caught! We're caught! We can't get loose! Help, help!

MOTHER ROBIN: What is the meaning of this?

PETER RABBIT: Oh, dear! You are in real trouble.

BUSHY SQUIRREL: What have you done now?

WEATHERMAN: What has happened?

GARDENERS: They're spoiling our garden.

1ST GARDENER: That Robber Robin has been stealing our seeds.

2ND GARDENER: Spoiler Squirrel has ruined our garden with great big holes.

3RD GARDENER: That Bandit Rabbit has eaten the little green leaves.

4TH GARDENER: Jack Frost has nipped all the buds.

MOTHER ROBIN, PETER RABBIT, BUSHY SQUIRREL, *and* WEATHERMAN: Is this true? (ROBIN, RABBIT, SQUIRREL, *and* JACK FROST *nod their heads in shame.*)

MOTHER ROBIN: Then it serves you right. All the good robins help gardeners by eating the bad insects. You know better than to go around eating seeds.

PETER RABBIT: I'm ashamed of having a Bandit Rabbit for a son, and after all I told you about my terrible experience with Mr. McGregor.

BUSHY SQUIRREL: Every good little squirrel buries his nuts in the grass, not in the garden beds.

WEATHERMAN: As for you, Jack Frost, you aren't even supposed to be out at this time of year. You belong home in bed.

ROBIN, RABBIT, SQUIRREL, *and* JACK FROST: Aren't you going to help us?

MOTHER ROBIN, PETER RABBIT, BUSHY SQUIRREL, *and* WEATHERMAN: It's up to the gardeners.

MOTHER ROBIN (*To* ROBIN): Remember when you were a baby this little boy (*Pointing to one of the* GARDENERS) picked you up and put you back in the nest after you had fallen out?

ROBIN: I'm sorry. I forgot.

PETER RABBIT (*Pointing to one of the* GARDENERS): Have you forgotten that this little girl saved you from the big dog who lives next door?

RABBIT: I'm sorry. I forgot.

BUSHY SQUIRREL (*Pointing to another* GARDENER): Have

you forgotten that this little boy put nuts on the window sill for you, every morning last winter?
SQUIRREL: I'm sorry. I forgot.
WEATHERMAN: Have you forgotten that all of us weather people must work to help the farmers and the gardeners raise their crops? That is our job.
JACK FROST: I'm sorry. I forgot.
WEATHERMAN: Have you also forgotten how much these children love you? They even sang a song about you in school.
GARDENERS: We'll sing it for you now, to help you remember. (*Singing to tune of "Jack Spratt."*)

    Jack Frost, we love to see
    Your pictures every year.
    You draw upon our window panes.
    We love to have you near.

GARDENERS (*Shouting*): But we don't want you in our garden!
ROBIN, SQUIRREL, RABBIT, *and* JACK FROST: We're very sorry. We'll never do those naughty things again.
GARDENERS: Is that a promise?
ROBIN: I'll just eat bugs and beetles and worms, the way a good robin should.
RABBIT: I'll never touch those little green leaves.
SQUIRREL: I'll never dig in your garden again.
JACK FROST: I'll stay home where I belong, until it's time for me to go out.
1ST GARDENER: What shall we do?
2ND GARDENER: I think they really mean it.

GARDENERS: Then we'll let them go. (*Break circle.* ROBIN, SQUIRREL, RABBIT, *and* JACK FROST *run to* MOTHER ROBIN, BUSHY SQUIRREL, PETER RABBIT, *and* WEATHERMAN. GARDENERS *sing to the tune of* "*Oats, Peas, Beans.*")

> Now our garden soon will grow,
> Tiny plants begin to show.
> And you and I and all of us know
> Just how you helped to make it so.
>   (*Curtain*)

THE END

THE RABBITS WHO CHANGED THEIR MINDS

Characters

JUMPY
THUMPY } *three little rabbits*
GRUMPY
MAMMA RABBIT
PAPA RABBIT
GRANDPA RABBIT
GUM DROP
LEMON DROP } *three Easter elves*
JELLY BEAN
THE CANDY KING
SIX PEPPERMINT STICK GUARDS
THREE CHEFS

TIME: *Easter morning.*

SETTING: *A forest glade. At right is a worktable, covered with Easter baskets and supplies. At left is a large toadstool, under which sit three* EASTER ELVES.

AT RISE: PAPA, MAMMA, *and* GRANDPA RABBIT *are filling some baskets with colored eggs.* JUMPY, THUMPY, *and* GRUMPY *stand in a row at left. As the curtains open, they bow to the audience.*

JUMPY, THUMPY, *and* GRUMPY:
>We're three little rabbits
>With very bad habits,
>As we have often been told.

JUMPY: Now my name is Jumpy!

THUMPY: I'm Thumpy!

GRUMPY: I'm Grumpy!

THREE LITTLE RABBITS (*Sadly*): Our parents do nothing but scold!

PAPA RABBIT: Just look at Jumpy! He's afraid of his own shadow! (*Loudly*) Boo! (JUMPY *leaps in fright.*) See him jump!

MAMMA RABBIT (*As* THUMPY *clump-clumps toward the table and knocks off one of the baskets*): Look at our Thumpy! Always running into things and knocking them over!

GRANDPA RABBIT: Grumpy is the worst! He never smiles!

OLDER RABBITS: Smile, Grumpy, smile!

GRUMPY: What is there to smile about?

PAPA RABBIT: It's a fine spring day!

MAMMA RABBIT: Easter will soon be here.

GRANDPA: The children will be so happy with their Easter eggs.

JUMPY: Do I have to help with the eggs this year, Papa?

PAPA RABBIT: No, indeed. You are too jumpy.

MAMMA RABBIT: You would be afraid to walk through the forest.

GRANDPA RABBIT: If old Mr. Owl should hoot at you,

THE RABBITS WHO CHANGED THEIR MINDS

you would jump and spill the eggs out of the basket!

THUMPY: Must I help with the eggs this year, Papa?

PAPA RABBIT: You are too thumpy. You would be sure to break them.

MAMMA RABBIT: You make too much noise for a rabbit.

GRANDPA RABBIT: The children would hear you coming and they would not be surprised.

GRUMPY: Please don't ask me to help with the eggs. I am too grumpy.

PAPA RABBIT: Mamma, Grandpa and I can take care of everything.

MAMMA RABBIT: We'll get our wheelbarrows and load the baskets. (PAPA, MAMMA, *and* GRANDPA RABBIT *load toy wheelbarrows with Easter baskets.*)

GRANDPA RABBIT: Dear me! Those bunnies will never grow up to be Easter rabbits. I don't know what the world is coming to. (*When the baskets are loaded on the wheelbarrows,* PAPA, MAMMA, *and* GRANDPA RABBIT *push them around in a circle.*)

OLDER RABBITS (*Singing to the tune of "To Market, To Market"*):

For Easter, for Easter we trundle our eggs,
Hopping along on our short little legs.
For Easter, for Easter, we're now on our way,
Making this Easter the happiest day!
(*They exit.*)

GRUMPY: They took all the eggs and didn't leave any for us.

JUMPY: The eggs are for the children.

THUMPY: Do you think we will be Easter rabbits when we grow up?
JUMPY: Not me! I'm afraid of children. They make me jumpy!
GRUMPY: Not me! I don't like children. They make me grumpy!
THUMPY: Not me! I hate to be quiet. I like to thump, thump, thump, and bump, bump, bump, and make a lot of noise.
THREE LITTLE RABBITS: We'll never be Easter rabbits. Never! Never! Never! (*Sound of thunder off-stage*)
JUMPY (*Clutching at* THUMPY): I hear thunder! I'm afraid!
GRUMPY: Rain! I hate rain. It makes me grumpy.
THUMPY (*Putting out hand*): I feel a raindrop. (*More thunder*)
JUMPY: Let's run and hide.
GRUMPY: I hate to get wet.
THUMPY: We can hide under the toadstool. That will keep us dry. (*The* THREE LITTLE RABBITS *run to the toadstool and attempt to get under it, but the shelter is already occupied by the* THREE EASTER ELVES.)
JUMPY: Oooh! There's someone else under the toadstool! I'm afraid.
THUMPY: Who is it?
GRUMPY: Make room for us. We're coming in. (*As the* THREE LITTLE RABBITS *try to push their way under the toadstool, the* EASTER ELVES *are crowded out.*)
EASTER ELVES: Stop pushing! Stop pushing! We were here first.

THREE LITTLE RABBITS: Who are you?
EASTER ELVES: We are the Easter Elves!
GUM DROP: This toadstool is our umbrella.
LEMON DROP: We always come here when it rains.
JELLY BEAN: If we get wet, we simply melt away.
THREE LITTLE RABBITS: Why?
EASTER ELVES: Because we're made of sugar.
GUM DROP: My name is Gum Drop!
LEMON DROP: I'm Lemon Drop!
JELLY BEAN: I'm Jelly Bean!
EASTER ELVES: We have charge of the Easter candy.
JUMPY: Our name is Rabbit.
THUMPY: We have charge of the Easter eggs.
GRUMPY: Papa, Mamma and Grandpa are out delivering eggs right now.
EASTER ELVES: Why aren't you helping them?
JUMPY: I'm too jumpy. I jump at every noise I hear.
THUMPY: I'm too thumpy. I make too much noise when I walk, and sometimes I bump into things.
GRUMPY: I'm too grumpy. I don't like anything—not even being a rabbit.
GUM DROP: Then why don't you stop being a rabbit?
THREE LITTLE RABBITS: Stop being a rabbit? How?
LEMON DROP: It's easy. The Candy King will be here any minute. He can explain.
JELLY BEAN: Here he comes with his Peppermint Stick Guards.
EASTER ELVES: Make way! Make way! Make way for the Candy King! (*To recorded march music, the* CANDY KING *enters, preceded by* SIX PEPPERMINT

STICK GUARDS. *He is followed by* TWO CHEFS, *carrying a washtub. At the end of the line is a* 3RD CHEF, *who carries a large pitcher and a big brush. If desired, the* PEPPERMINT STICK GUARDS *may do a short marching drill.*)

CANDY KING: Attention! (*All stand at attention*) We have come far enough into the forest. I wonder what has become of our scouts?

EASTER ELVES: Here we are, Your Majesty!

CANDY KING: We are ready for your report.

GUM DROP: We have found three very fine models, Your Majesty.

LEMON DROP: They are nice-looking rabbits, Your Majesty, with short, fluffy tails, and long, pink ears.

JELLY BEAN: They don't like being rabbits, Your Majesty.

CANDY KING: Indeed? Why not?

GUM DROP (*Pushing* JUMPY *forward*): This one says he is too jumpy.

LEMON DROP (*Pushing* THUMPY *forward*): This one says he is too thumpy. Goes around bumping into things and making a lot of noise.

JELLY BEAN (*Pushing* GRUMPY *forward*): This one is too grumpy.

CANDY KING: Excellent! Excellent! Peppermint Sticks, do your duty. (PEPPERMINT STICK GUARDS *surround the* THREE LITTLE RABBITS)

JUMPY: What's going on here? My nose smells danger.

THUMPY: What are you doing?

GRUMPY: I feel grumpier than ever. I don't like this one bit.
CANDY KING: You should be pleased. In a few minutes your life will become very sweet.
GUM DROP, LEMON DROP *and* JELLY BEAN (*Laughing*): That's a good joke, Your Majesty.
GRUMPY: What is so funny?
GUM DROP: We are laughing because your life is going to be *sweet*.
LEMON DROP: The Candy King is making a joke.
JELLY BEAN: He means you are going to become *candy* rabbits, so think how sweet you'll be. (GUM DROP, LEMON DROP *and* JELLY BEAN *laugh*.)
THREE LITTLE RABBITS: We don't want to be candy rabbits!
CANDY KING: Oh, yes, you do! (*To* JUMPY) When *you* are a candy rabbit, you will never jump again! (*To* THUMPY) When *you* are a candy rabbit, you will never bump into anything or go thump! thump! thump! (*To* GRUMPY) When *you* are a candy rabbit, you will never be grumpy again, because you will be as sweet as sugar all day long.
THREE LITTLE RABBITS: Help! Help! We don't want to be *candy* rabbits! We want to be *real* rabbits!
CANDY KING: Who cares what you want? (*To* 1ST CHEF) Master Candy Maker, is the chocolate ready?
1ST CHEF (*Pretending to stir mixture in tub*): It's a little thick, Your Majesty.
CANDY KING: Then add a little more cream. (2ND CHEF *pretends to pour cream into the tub*.)

2ND CHEF: It seems to be just right now—not too thin and not too thick.

CANDY KING: Into the tub with them! (*Pointing to* JUMPY) Take that one first! (TWO PEPPERMINT STICK GUARDS *seize* JUMPY *and put him into the tub.*)

CANDY KING (*As* 2ND CHEF *picks up brush*): Now give him a good, thick, chocolate coat!

JUMPY: No you don't! I'm not called *Jumpy* for nothing! I can jump right out of this tub, and here I go! (*Jumps out and hops about the stage as* PEPPERMINT STICK GUARDS *scramble after him*)

CANDY KING: Quick! Quick! Catch the other one!

THUMPY (*As* PEPPERMINT STICK GUARDS *try to seize him*): Not me! My name is *Thumpy*, and I'm good at bumping into things. Just watch me bump into this tub and knock it over. (*Does so*)

CANDY KING (*Jumping up and down*): What a mess! What a mess! There's only one left. Catch him! Catch him!

GRUMPY (*As* PEPPERMINT STICK GUARDS *advance*): You can't catch me, Mister Candy King! My name is *Grumpy* and I'm the crossest rabbit in the forest! (*Growls*) Ha! Ha! You didn't know a rabbit could growl, did you? (*Growls again*) Hear that? Now call off your guards before I destroy you! (*Loud crash and roll of thunder*)

GUM DROP, LEMON DROP *and* JELLY BEAN: It's raining! It's raining!

CANDY KING: We'll have to get out of here before we

melt! Hurry! Hurry! I order a retreat! (*They scurry off-stage, taking tub with them.*)

THREE LITTLE RABBITS (*Shouting*): Rain, rain, come and stay!

Drive the Candy King away!

JUMPY (*Mopping his brow*): That was a narrow escape!

THUMPY: What's the matter with you, Jumpy? The thunder is very loud and you're not even jumping.

JUMPY: Thunder doesn't bother me! I don't feel jumpy any more. From now on, I'll jump only when there's *real* danger.

THUMPY: I think I'll watch where I'm going. I'm not going to bump into things except when they need knocking over.

GRUMPY: It's funny, but I don't feel a bit grumpy any more. I'm so glad not to be a candy rabbit, that I enjoy being a real one.

ALL: Maybe we'll be Easter rabbits after all. (*Enter* PAPA, MAMMA, *and* GRANDPA RABBIT *with empty wheelbarrows.*)

PAPA RABBIT: This is the busiest Easter ever!

MAMMA RABBIT: If only we had some extra help.

THREE LITTLE RABBITS: Please! Please! Let us help! Please! Please!

GRANDPA RABBIT: You never wanted to help before. You always tried to get out of it.

THREE LITTLE RABBITS: We've changed our minds! We want to learn how to be good Easter rabbits.

PAPA (*To* JUMPY): You are too jumpy!

JUMPY: Not any more. I promise you I won't be jumpy unless there is real danger.

MAMMA (*To* THUMPY): You are too thumpy. You make too much noise.

THUMPY: Not any more. I'll watch where I'm going and I'll be as quiet as a good rabbit should.

GRANDPA (*Pointing to* GRUMPY): Bless my little pink ears! This fellow is smiling! Our Grumpy is grinning a real Easter grin!

PAPA *and* MAMMA: I do believe our little rabbits are ready to help us. Let's give them a chance.

GRANDPA: Then lend a hand with these wheelbarrows, fellows, and we'll practice our Easter song. (ALL *parade around the table singing to tune of "The Campbells Are Coming"*)

    For Easter, for Easter, we trundle our eggs,
    Hopping along on our short little legs.
    For Easter, for Easter, we're now on our way,
    Making this Easter the happiest day.

    (*Curtain*)

THE END

TROUBLE IN TICK-TOCK TOWN

Characters

GRANDFATHER'S CLOCK
GRANDMOTHER'S CLOCK
KITCHEN CLOCK
FRENCH CLOCK
ALARM CLOCK
CUCKOO CLOCK
TRAVELING CLOCK
TOWN CLOCK
COUNCIL OF THE HOURS
DAY *and* NIGHT, *time fairies*
TICK *and* TOCK, *guides*
TOMMY TUCKER

SETTING: *Town Hall of Tick-Tock Town. Directly center is a big cardboard clock face with movable hands.*

AT RISE: *Lined up to the right of the cardboard clock are the* ALARM CLOCK, FRENCH CLOCK, KITCHEN CLOCK *and* GRANDFATHER'S CLOCK. *To the left of the cardboard clock are the* TOWN CLOCK, TRAVELING CLOCK, CUCKOO CLOCK *and* GRANDMOTHER'S CLOCK. *The* COUNCIL OF THE HOURS *is seated at a long table on one side of the stage. Each member of the* COUNCIL *has a pair of rhythm sticks or a wood block.* TICK *and* TOCK *are center stage. Before they speak, there is a long pause, during which the* COUNCIL OF THE HOURS *tap out a tick-tock rhythm. As* TICK *and* TOCK *begin to speak, the tick-tock grows softer.*

TICK *and* TOCK: Ladies and gentlemen, welcome to Tick-Tock Town.
TICK: My name is Tick.
TOCK: My name is Tock.
TICK *and* TOCK: We are the guides who will take you on a tour of this wonderful city and show you the sights.
TICK: First, we will introduce you to the clocks.
TOCK: We will wind them up so they can speak for themselves. (TICK *goes right stage;* TOCK *goes left stage.* TICK *goes to the* GRANDFATHER'S CLOCK *and pretends to wind him.*)
GRANDFATHER'S CLOCK:
Tick-tock, tick-tock!
How do you do!
I'm the Grandfather's Clock.
I have a deep voice and I stand in the hall
To boom out the hours for one and for all. (COUNCIL MEMBER *strikes deep gong or bell three times.*)
TOCK (*Pretending to wind the* GRANDMOTHER'S CLOCK):
And here is another clock we would like you to meet.
GRANDMOTHER'S CLOCK:
Tick-tock, tick-tock.
How do you do!
I'm the Grandmother's Clock.
I'm not quite so tall as my husband out there,
But I tick off the time with the greatest of care. (COUNCIL MEMBER *strikes the time with gong or bell slightly lighter in tone than the one used for the* GRANDFATHER'S CLOCK.)

TICK: The next clock is very important to us all. (*Winds* KITCHEN CLOCK)

KITCHEN CLOCK:
   Tick-tock, tick-tock.
   How do you do!
   I'm the big Kitchen Clock.
   I count off the seconds for three meals a day
   And help with the cooking in my useful way.
   The cook keeps an eye on my hands as they turn,
   So none of her goodies will happen to burn. (COUNCIL MEMBER *strikes the hour with a tiny gong.*)

TOCK (*Winding* CUCKOO CLOCK): This next fellow is the joker in the crowd!

CUCKOO CLOCK:
   Tick-tock, tick-tock,
   How do you do!
   I'm the old Cuckoo Clock.
   I have a wee birdie that's mounted on springs,
   And once every hour, that wee birdie sings. (*Child with bird head-dress sticks his head around the* CLOCK *and shouts:* "*Cuckoo! Cuckoo! Cuckoo!*")

TICK (*Winding the* FRENCH CLOCK): Now we would like you to meet a very beautiful member of Tick-Tock Town.

FRENCH CLOCK:
   Teek-tock, teek-tock!
   How do you do;
   I'm zee leetle French Clock.
   I'm pretty and dainty and sit on zee shelf,

And teek oh so softly I can't hear myself.
But I keep very busy at watching zee time,
And my voice is a clear, little silvery chime. (COUNCIL MEMBER *strikes chime for the* FRENCH CLOCK.)

TOCK (*Winding* TRAVELING CLOCK): This one is not as big as the others, but he is very useful.

TRAVELING CLOCK:
Tick-tock, tick-tock.
How do you do!
I'm a Traveling Clock.
I'm ever so little and fit in a case.
And I have tiny hands and a very small face.
"Have time, will travel"—yes, that's what I say,
And I'll go for a weekend, a year or a day.

TICK (*Winding* ALARM CLOCK): Here is one you all know very well.

ALARM CLOCK:
Tick-tock, tick-tock.
How do you do!
I'm the big Alarm Clock.
My voice is so loud it would waken the dead
And it wakens the family—each sleepy head.
I go off at six, or seven, or eight.
If you listen to me, you will never be late. (COUNCIL MEMBER *sets off alarm clock*.)

TOCK: Our last clock is the most important of all. (*Winds* TOWN CLOCK)

TOWN CLOCK:
Tick-tock, tick-tock.
How do you do!

TROUBLE IN TICK-TOCK TOWN

I'm the mighty Town Clock.
I'm up in the air in a tower or a steeple
And I tell the time to all of the people! (COUNCIL MEMBER *strikes the heaviest sounding gong of all.* TICK *and* TOCK *take up their positions on either side of the table.*)

TICK: These gentlemen are the rulers of Tick-Tock Town.

TOCK: They are the Council of the Hours.

TICK: They wind all the clocks and see that they keep perfect time.

TOCK: They take care of all of the troubles in Tick-Tock Town.

TICK: And today they have a very special problem.

TOCK: We are going to report it right now.

TICK *and* TOCK: Gentlemen, your attention, please. We have a problem for you to solve.

COUNCIL OF THE HOURS: Speak up. What is it?

TICK: There is a boy in Tick-Tock Town
And he is not so wise.

TOCK: For every time he sees a clock,
He cannot believe his eyes.

TICK: When folks step up to ask the time,
He never answers true.

TOCK: No matter where the hands may point,

TICK *and* TOCK: He calls it *half-past two!*

COUNCIL OF THE HOURS: This is terrible! A boy in Tick-Tock Town who can't tell time! What is his name?

TICK *and* TOCK: Tommy. His name is Tommy Tucker.

TICK: Yesterday morning he was late for school.

COUNCIL OF THE HOURS: What happened to the Alarm Clock?

ALARM CLOCK: I rang and rang, but he said it was only half-past two and shut me off. Then he turned over and went to sleep again.

TICK: His mother had to call and call. The clocks can tell you about it. This is what she said.

CLOCKS (*Singing to the tune of "Lazy Mary, Will You Get Up"*):
Lazy Tommy, will you get up, will you get up, will you get up?
Lazy Tommy, will you get up, will you get up today?

COUNCIL OF THE HOURS: And what did he say?

CLOCKS (*Singing second verse*): Oh, no, Mother, I won't get up, I won't get up, I won't get up!
Oh, no, Mother, I won't get up at half-past two today!

TICK: He is also late for meals! His father and mother are very angry with him.

TOCK: Last night they sent him to bed without any supper!

TICK: And they had ice cream! I almost felt sorry for him!

COUNCIL OF THE HOURS *and* CLOCKS (*Singing to the tune of "Little Tommy Tucker"*): Little Tommy Tucker, he's late for his supper,
Now he will not get white bread and butter!
Now he's in trouble with Mother and Dad!
Poor Tommy Tucker; it's all very sad!

TICK (*Handing long paper to* COUNCIL OF THE HOURS): Here is a list of all the trouble he has caused.
COUNCIL OF THE HOURS (*Looking at paper*): This is terrible. We must see this boy at once!
TOCK: The Time Fairies, Day and Night, are bringing him in right now. (TIME FAIRIES *enter. They carry wands with which they poke and prod* TOMMY *on stage.*)
DAY *and* NIGHT: Here he is—Tommy Tucker—the boy who can't tell time.
CHAIRMAN *of the* COUNCIL: Is your name Tommy Tucker?
TOMMY: Yes, sir.
CHAIRMAN: Is it true that you can't tell time?
TOMMY: Not very well, sir.
CHAIRMAN (*Pointing to cardboard clock*): What time is it now?
TOMMY: Half-past two!
ALL: Oh dear, oh dear! (DAY *and* NIGHT *change the hands of the clock to a new position.*)
CHAIRMAN: Let's try again. What time is it now?
TOMMY: Half-past two!
ALL: This is terrible! (DAY *and* NIGHT *change the hands again.*)
CHAIRMAN: We'll give you one more chance. What time is it now?
TOMMY: Half-past two!
CHAIRMAN: Something must be done! I see you are wearing a wrist watch.

TOMMY: Yes, sir.
CHAIRMAN: Take it off and give it to me at once.
TOMMY: But it's a birthday present from my father.
CHAIRMAN: You can't wear a wrist watch if you can't tell time. It's too dangerous.
TOMMY: What's dangerous about it?
CHAIRMAN: When people see you wearing a wrist watch, they ask you the time. We have a record of all the trouble you caused yesterday.
COUNCIL MEMBER (*Standing and reading from record*):
He caused an old lady to miss the last train.
He kept a friend waiting an hour in the rain.
He told the wrong time to a man on the street
So he missed the salesman he wanted to meet.
Another man has this rascal to thank
Because he lost out on a deal at the bank.
His very own brother was half an hour late
With a lovely young lady he wanted to date.
And all of this proves it's a shame and a crime
To have a boy with us who cannot tell time.
CHAIRMAN: Hand over that wrist watch at once. (TOMMY *gives his watch to* CHAIRMAN.) You should not be allowed to live in Tick-Tock Town. I think we will send you away.
TOMMY: Where will you send me?
CHAIRMAN: We'll send you to the Land-Where-Time-Stands-Still.
TOMMY: That suits me fine. I think I'd like that.
CHAIRMAN: Don't be too sure. It will always be half-past two, you know.

TOMMY: Half-past two! Then I'd never have to worry about clocks again!

CHAIRMAN: What were you doing yesterday at half-past two?

TOMMY: I was on the playground and one of the older boys was showing me how to do some exercises—like this. (*Gets down on floor and does several exercises, then stops.*)

CHAIRMAN: Don't stop. Don't stop. Remember it will always be half-past two. (*During the next speeches,* TOMMY *continues to do exercises more and more slowly. The Time Fairies,* DAY *and* NIGHT, *stand beside the cardboard clock face and take turns moving the hands to the times mentioned.*)

GRANDFATHER'S CLOCK: When I strike five and your daddy comes home from work, you'll still be doing exercises.

KITCHEN CLOCK: When I strike six and your mother puts dinner on the table, you'll still be doing exercises.

GRANDMOTHER'S CLOCK: When I strike seven and the other children are doing their homework, you'll still be doing exercises.

FRENCH CLOCK: When I strike eight and zee company comes, you'll still be doing exercises.

CUCKOO CLOCK: When I strike nine and the family is watching TV, you'll still be doing exercises.

TRAVELING CLOCK: When your father puts me in his suit case at ten o'clock, you'll still be doing exercises.

ALARM CLOCK: When your mother winds me at eleven

o'clock and sets me for the next morning, you'll still be doing exercises.

TOWN CLOCK: And when I strike twelve midnight, and the whole town is asleep, you'll still be doing exercises.

TOMMY (*Huffing and puffing*): No! No! Stop! Stop! I must rest!

CHAIRMAN: But it's not time! It's only half-past two!

TOMMY: Please, please, let me stop! I've had enough! I'll learn to tell time! Honest, I will!

CHAIRMAN: I will have to talk it over with the Council. (*The* COUNCIL *confers in pantomime.*) Very well, Tommy, you may stop.

TOMMY (*Standing up*): Oh, thank you, thank you!

CHAIRMAN: Tick and Tock will now take over. (*Sits down*)

TICK: Hasn't anyone ever taught you to tell time, Tommy?

TOMMY: Yes. My mother tried, my father tried and my teacher tried, but I never paid any attention.

TICK: Will you pay attention now?

TOMMY: Oh, yes, yes, I will.

TOCK: Very well, then. We will teach you our secret language.

TOMMY: I didn't know clocks had a secret language.

TICK: Oh, yes! Listen!

CLOCKS (*Recite*):
> We talk with a tick,
> We talk with a tock,
> We talk with a boom and a bong.

And if you give ear,
You'll hear loud and clear
Our tickety-tockety song.

We talk with a tick,
We talk with a tock,
And we also talk with our hands.
All day and all night,
In darkness or light,
We speak out our hourly commands.

DAY (*At cardboard clock*):
 The little hand points to the hour,
 A steady hand, and slow.

NIGHT:
 The big hand moves much faster
 And shows how minutes go.

DAY (*Placing hands at proper position for twelve o'clock*): It's twelve o'clock. Now say with me—

ALL (*As* NIGHT *moves the minute hand to the proper numbers*):
 Five after, ten after, fifteen, and twenty,
 Twenty-five, thirty—half past!
 It's twenty-five of, then twenty, fifteen,
 Ten of (*pause*), five of (*pause*),
 And straight one o'clock at long last!

TOMMY: I have it! I have it! I can tell time! I can tell time!

CHAIRMAN: We'll put him to the test. (DAY *and* NIGHT *move the hands to different times, and* TOMMY *answers correctly. Three different settings should be enough. The* COUNCIL OF THE HOURS *applaud vigorously.*)

COUNCIL: Well done! Well done!

CHAIRMAN: Spoken like a true citizen of Tick-Tock Town. You now have a right to wear your wrist watch and tell the time to anyone who asks you.

TOMMY: Thanks a lot. (*Takes watch*) It wasn't so hard after all.

TICK *and* TOCK:
>Our troubles now are over.
>We have nothing more to say.
>We hope you have enjoyed
>Your visit here today.
>Come back again to Tick-Tock Town,
>And bring a guest with you.
>You'll find the gates are open at
>Exactly half-past two! (*Curtain*)

THE END

MAY DAY FOR MOTHER

Characters

MISS JENNIE JONES	PAGE
MAYPOLE DANCERS	FLOWER GIRL
EMCEE	TRAIN-BEARER
PHOTOGRAPHER	TWO HERALDS
TV CAMERAMAN	FOUR LADIES-IN-WAITING
RADIO INTERVIEWER	HAIRDRESSER
REPORTER	TWO MAIDS
CROWN-BEARER	MRS. JONES

SETTING: *A traditional May Day scene. At center is the throne on a small platform. At left is the Maypole.*

AT RISE: *The* DANCERS *stand around the Maypole, holding the streamers in their hands. The May Queen's attendants—the* LADIES-IN-WAITING, *the* CROWN-BEARER, *the* PAGE, *the* FLOWER GIRL, *the* TRAIN-BEARER *and the two* HERALDS—*stand near the throne. At right are the* EMCEE, *the* PHOTOGRAPHER, *the* TV CAMERAMAN. *At left are the* REPORTER *and the* RADIO INTERVIEWER.

DANCERS (*Singing to tune of "Miss Jennie Jones"*):
We're here to wind the May Day pole, the May Day pole, the May Day pole,

We're here to wind the May Day pole,
And sing a roundelay.
ATTENDANTS (*Singing*):
We are glad to hear it, to hear it, to hear it.
We are glad to hear it,
But who is Queen today?
DANCERS (*Speaking in chorus*): Haven't you heard? It's Miss Jennie Jones. (*Singing*):
We're here to see Miss Jennie Jones, Miss Jennie Jones, Miss Jennie Jones,
We're here to see Miss Jennie Jones,
For she's the Queen of the May!
ATTENDANTS (*Singing*):
We are glad to hear it, to hear it, to hear it,
We are glad to hear it, but where is she today?
DANCERS (*Singing*):
Miss Jennie Jones is dressing, is dressing, is dressing,
Miss Jennie Jones is dressing,
In all her fine array.
ATTENDANTS (*Singing*):
We are glad to hear it, to hear it, to hear it,
We are glad to hear it, and honor her today.
DANCERS: Now you know who *we* are, but what are *you* doing here?
EMCEE:
I am the man who runs the show,
They call me the Emcee.
I see that everything is right
And proper to a "T".

PHOTOGRAPHER (*Carrying camera*):
  I came to take some pictures.
  My camera goes click, click!
  I hope the Queen gives me a smile
  That's bright and flashing quick.
TV CAMERAMAN (*With camera*):
  I am another Cameraman
  To snap our lovely Queen,
  So you will see her face upon
  The television screen.
RADIO INTERVIEWER (*Holding mike*):
  I came to interview the Queen,
  And talk to her alone.
  I hope she speaks up loud and clear
  Into my microphone.
REPORTER (*With notebook*):
  I came to write the story
  For all the daily papers.
  Tomorrow you will read about
  These dances, songs, and capers.
CROWN-BEARER (*Carrying pillow with golden crown on it*):
  This pillow's for the golden crown.
  I carry it just so.
  If I should chance to let it fall—
  There would be grief and woe!
PAGE:
  I am the Page who crowns the Queen,
  The Ruler of our State.

I hope I do the job just right,
And put the crown on straight.

TRAIN-BEARER:
I bear the Queen's long satin train,
And keep it free from dust.
I really did not want the job,
But Mamma said I *must*.

FLOWER GIRL (*Showing bouquet*):
I hand the Queen her big bouquet,
As pretty as you please.
I know just how to curtsy, (*Does so*)
I hope I will not sneeze! (*Kerchoo!*)

TWO HERALDS (*Holding out trumpets*):
We are the Heralds who blow the blast
To set the play in motion.
I bet if we would blow right now
We'd start a big commotion!

FOUR LADIES-IN-WAITING:
We are the Ladies-in-Waiting.
We're here to serve the Queen.
We're waiting here with patience
Till she comes on the scene.

TV CAMERAMAN:
My time is very costly,
I'm charging by the minute.
I cannot wait much longer,
You'd better soon begin it!

LADIES-IN-WAITING: What can be keeping Miss Jennie Jones? (*Enter* HAIRDRESSER *with brush and comb.*

Two MAIDS *follow, one with a dress over her arm, the other carrying a pair of shoes.*)

HAIRDRESSER *and* MAIDS: Oh, dear! Oh, dear! Something terrible has happened!

HAIRDRESSER: Miss Jennie Jones won't let me comb her hair!

FIRST MAID: Miss Jennie Jones won't let me put on her slippers!

SECOND MAID: Miss Jennie Jones won't let me put on her dress!

ALL: What's the matter? What's wrong?

HAIRDRESSER *and* MAIDS (*Singing*):
Miss Jennie Jones is crying, is crying, is crying,
Miss Jennie Jones is crying,
She won't be Queen of the May!

ALL (*Singing*):
We are sorry to hear it, to hear it, to hear it,
We are sorry to hear it,
She won't be queen of the May!

ALL: She won't be Queen of the May! Why not? (*Enter* MISS JENNIE JONES *in a housecoat and bedroom slippers; her hair is in pin curls.*)

MISS JENNIE JONES (*Stamping her foot angrily*): I won't! I won't! I won't! I won't be Queen of the May!

ALL: But you were elected!

MISS JENNIE JONES: I don't care! I don't want to be Queen of the May!

REPORTER (*Moving forward with notebook*): What a story! This will make headlines!

PHOTOGRAPHER *and* CAMERAMAN (*Focusing cameras*): Hold it, please! What a picture! What a picture!

MISS JENNIE JONES: Go away! (*Hiding her face*) I won't have my picture taken.

INTERVIEWER (*Stepping forward with mike*): Miss Jennie Jones, will you please tell our listening audience why you don't want to be our May Queen?

MISS JENNIE JONES: No, I won't. (*Changing her mind*) Yes, yes, I will. (*Speaking into microphone*) Ladies and gentlemen, this is Jennie Jones speaking. I don't want to be Queen of the May because there is someone else who has a better right to be queen.

INTERVIEWER: Someone else? Who? Who could it be?

MISS JENNIE JONES:
Listen. I'll tell you.
Who gets my breakfast every day?
Who puts my toys and games away?

ALL: *Your mother.*

MISS JENNIE JONES:
Who combs my hair and wipes my face?
Who sees my things are all in place?

ALL: *Your mother.*

MISS JENNIE JONES:
Who made my dress for this big show?
Who sees my clothing is just so?

ALL: *Your mother.*

MISS JENNIE JONES:
Who makes me well when I am ill?
Who makes me rest and take my pill?

ALL: *Your mother.*

MISS JENNIE JONES:
  Who holds my hand when I am scared?
  Who takes my shoes to be repaired?
ALL: *Your mother.*
MISS JENNIE JONES:
  Who's always smiling when I'm glad?
  Who loves me when I'm good or bad?
ALL: *Your mother.*
MISS JENNIE JONES:
  My mother does all this for me,
  And also does much more.
  So I want *her* to have some fun
  To even up the score.
  This May Queen stuff is out of style.
  It's time we change our ways,
  And celebrate the month of May
  With thirty Mother's Days.
ALL: Thirty Mother's Day! What an idea!
MISS JENNIE JONES:
  I'll *not* be Queen! Go get another!
  But first—I nominate—*my mother!*
ALL: Mrs. Jones for May Queen! Mrs. Jones for May Queen! (*The* EMCEE *exits.*)
INTERVIEWER: Mrs. Jones, please. Is Mrs. Jones in the audience?
MRS. JONES (*Standing in audience*): I am Mrs. Jones.
INTERVIEWER: Will you please come to the platform, Mrs. Jones? (*Speaking into mike as* MRS. JONES *comes to the platform*) Ladies and gentlemen, this is all very exciting. Miss Jennie Jones, who up until a few min-

utes ago was to be our May Queen, has just nominated her mother for the honor. Ah, here is Mrs. Jones herself. Mrs. Jones, do you have any comment?

MRS. JONES: Comment! Indeed I have a comment! But it is not for the microphone. It is for my daughter. Jennie Jones, what do you mean by acting like this?

MISS JENNIE JONES: But, Mother, I thought you'd be pleased!

MRS. JONES: Pleased! To see you coming out in front of all these people in your housecoat, with your hair in pin curls and in your bedroom slippers! Aren't you ashamed?

MISS JENNIE JONES: But, Mother!

MRS. JONES: Now you listen to me! You go right back to that dressing room and take off that housecoat and get into that pretty new dress I made for you! And let this nice lady brush your hair, or I'll use that hairbrush myself!

MISS JENNIE JONES: But, Mother! I wanted to make you happy! I thought you'd like to be the Queen!

MRS. JONES: Oh, Jennie, you don't understand about mothers.

MISS JENNIE JONES: No, I guess not.

MRS. JONES: Every mother is a queen, Jennie, as long as her children love and respect her.

MISS JENNIE JONES: But I wanted you to wear a pretty dress and a golden crown.

MRS. JONES: That was sweet of you, dear, and I appreciate it. But look out there in the audience. What do you see?

MISS JENNIE JONES: A lot of people.
MRS. JONES: And most of them are mothers (*Pointing to herself*), like me, with children (*Pointing to* JENNIE) like you. Now don't you think that every child up here on the stage would like his mother to be the queen?
MISS JENNIE JONES: I suppose so. But you're the best.
MRS. JONES (*Hugging* JENNIE): Thank you, dear. But that is what every child thinks about his own mother, and that is why every mother is a queen. Not just for one day—but every day.
MISS JENNIE JONES: I think I understand.
MRS. JONES: Now run along and put on your pretty dress. I will be the proudest and happiest mother here if you are a good and beautiful queen.
MISS JENNIE JONES: I will be, if you say so, Mother. (JENNIE *exits, followed by* HAIRDRESSER, *two* MAIDS, FLOWER GIRL, LADIES-IN-WAITING, *and* TRAIN-BEARER.)
DANCERS (*Singing*):
Miss Jennie Jones is smiling, is smiling, is smiling,
Miss Jennie Jones is smiling,
For she's the Queen of the May.
ALL THE OTHERS (*Singing*):
We are glad to hear it, to hear it, to hear it,
We are glad to hear it, she'll get her crown today.
EMCEE (*Re-entering with bouquet of roses and wide ribbon with the words* "Queen Mother" *on it*): Mrs. Jones, I have a suggestion. In every royal procession and at every coronation, there is a place of honor for

the Queen Mother. As the mother of our beautiful and gracious Queen, will you wear these and take your place in the Court of Honor?

MRS. JONES (*As she puts ribbon on and accepts flowers*): I will be delighted. (*Crosses to throne platform and takes her place on lower step to the right of the throne chair.*)

EMCEE:
And now our May Day will begin.
It's just like all the others,
Except that this one will be done
Especially for mothers.
We wish to welcome every Mom
Who's here with us today,
And greet her with a joyous song
And happy roundelay.

ALL OTHERS (*Singing to the tune of "Did You Ever See a Lassie?"*):
Sing a welcome to our mothers, our mothers, our mothers,
Sing a welcome to our mothers, on this happy day.
To you we are bringing our dancing and singing,
So welcome to our mothers on this happy day!

EMCEE: Miss Jennie Jones—
The Queen of the May!
(*To recorded processional music, the May Day Procession enters.* JENNIE, *now in her queen's dress, approaches. The* QUEEN MOTHER *steps forward, offers her hand and helps her daughter ascend the throne.* CAMERAMEN *are busy taking pictures. The* CROWN-

BEARER *steps forward with the crown on the royal cushion. The* PAGE *takes the crown and places it on the* QUEEN's *head.*)
PAGE: I crown you now the Queen of the May!
May you justly rule and hold full sway!
And may your subjects give a cheer
For the loveliest Queen of all the year. (*All cheer as* FLOWER GIRL *hands* QUEEN *her bouquet.*)
QUEEN: As Queen of the May and youth and beauty,
My very first official duty
Must be to thank you all and say—
Let the fun begin—without delay! (*Curtain closes on Maypole dance.*)

THE END

Note: This play may be used as a prologue to a complete May Day program of songs and dances, ending with the traditional Maypole Dance.

THREE LITTLE KITTENS

Characters

MOTHER KITTY-CAT
HAPPY ⎫
NAPPY ⎬ *kittens*
SCRAPPY ⎭
BETTY, *the girl next door*

BOBBY, *the boy next door*
SPORT, *the dog next door*
SPEAKER
CHORAL SPEAKING GROUP

SETTING: *No furnishings are required.*
AT RISE: *The* CHORAL SPEAKING GROUP *is on the apron of the stage. The* SPEAKER *is in the center of the group.* MOTHER KITTY-CAT *stands at one side of the stage with the three kittens.*

SPEAKER: We are going to tell you the story of "The Three Little Kittens." It begins like this.

ALL (*The group should sound like the kittens and the mothers in the appropriate places*):
Three little kittens they lost their mittens
And they began to cry:
"Oh, Mother dear, we sadly fear
Our mittens we have lost!"
"What! Lost your mittens,
You naughty kittens,
Then you shall have no pie."

THREE LITTLE KITTENS

"Meow! Meow! Meow!"
Now they shall have no pie!

SPEAKER: Now aren't you curious about those kittens? What were their names? How did they lose their mittens? Where did they find them? You'll find the answers to all your questions, as you watch Mother Kitty-Cat sending her three little kittens out to play.

MOTHER (*Holding three pairs of mittens behind her back*): You've been such good little kittens lately that I have a surprise for you. I'll give you three guesses.

KITTENS: Candy?

MOTHER: No, not candy. It's bad for your whiskers.

KITTENS: Ice cream?

MOTHER: No, not ice cream. Ice cream is not for pussy cats.

KITTENS: A new toy?

MOTHER: No, you have too many toys already. (*Holds up mittens*) Look, I have a pair of mittens for each of you. (*Giving mittens to kittens*) A blue pair for Happy, a white pair for Nappy, and a red pair for Scrappy.

KITTENS: Thank you, Mother. Thank you. (*Putting them on*) They're beautiful.

HAPPY: May we wear them when we go out to play?

MOTHER: Oh, no. These mittens are just for Sunday!

NAPPY: Please, Mother. Let us wear them.

MOTHER: I'm afraid you'll lose them.

KITTENS: No, we won't. We'll be careful.

MOTHER: That's what you always say. But sometimes I think you are the most careless kittens in the world.

SCRAPPY: Please, Mother. Please let us wear them out to play.

MOTHER: Oh, very well. But remember, they're your Sunday best, so don't lose them.

KITTENS: We won't! We won't. (*Kittens skip around the stage as* MOTHER *exits. After circling the stage, they return to center.*)

HAPPY: Now what shall we play?

NAPPY: Let's play "Pussy Wants a Corner."

SCRAPPY: I'd rather make mud pies.

HAPPY *and* NAPPY (*Shocked*): We'd ruin our pretty new mittens.

SCRAPPY: Then let's climb a tree in the park.

HAPPY: Don't be silly. We can't climb trees when we wear mittens. Our claws won't hold.

SCRAPPY: Then let's go mouse hunting.

NAPPY: We could never catch a mouse with mittens on our paws.

SCRAPPY: These mittens are a bother. They're spoiling our fun.

HAPPY (*Admiring mittens*): But they are so beautiful!

SCRAPPY: What shall we do? We can't play any of our games. (*Offstage voice calls:* "*Kitty, kitty, kitty! Here, kitty, kitty, kitty.*")

HAPPY: The children next door are calling us. They want us to play with them.

NAPPY: That will be fun.

SCRAPPY: If that puppy of theirs is with them, I'll scratch his nose!
HAPPY: Now, Scrappy, be a good kitty and stay out of fights. Let's answer the children and tell them where we are.
KITTENS: Meow! Meow! Meow! (*Enter* BETTY *and* BOBBY. BETTY *has a rubber ball on a string.* BOBBY *has a small, wind-up toy mouse.*)
BOBBY: Oh, there you are! We've been calling and calling.
BETTY: Aren't they the cutest kittens, Bobby? I wish we could take them home with us. (*Kittens purr with pleasure.*)
BOBBY: We'd have to ask Mother.
BETTY: Maybe we would have to ask *their* mother, too.
BOBBY: Besides, they wouldn't get along with Sport. Only yesterday he chased them up a tree.
KITTENS: Meow! Meow! Meow!
BETTY (*Laughing*): See, they know you are talking about Sport. But, never mind, Kittens. Sport won't chase you today. He's in the dog house. Look what I have for you. (*Shows kittens the rubber ball on the string. She tosses it back and forth, but none of the kittens can catch it.*)
BOBBY: What's the matter with you clumsy kittens? Can't you catch a ball?
BETTY: Look, Bobby, look! No wonder they can't catch the ball. They're wearing mittens.
BOBBY: Who ever heard of a kitten wearing mittens!

BETTY: Kittens don't need mittens. They have their own little fur mittens right on their feet.

BOBBY (*Petting* NAPPY): This little fellow used to be so good at catching a ball. Now see how clumsy he is! (NAPPY *tries again to catch the ball, but misses.*) If only they'd get rid of those mittens! (NAPPY, *after several more tries at the ball, removes mittens and throws them on the ground. Then he catches the ball and tosses it back and forth in imitation of a kitten at play.*)

BETTY: Good! Good for you, Kitty. Bobby, you'll have to use this little catcher on your baseball team.

BOBBY: Wait till I show them this. (*Puts wind-up mouse on floor and sets it going. Kittens chase it wildly.*)

BOBBY *and* BETTY: Catch it! Catch it! Take off those mittens. (HAPPY *removes mittens and catches toy mouse.*)

BETTY: That was a lot of fun. (*Offstage voice calls:* "Bobby! Betty! Time for supper!")

BOBBY: Do you hear that? Mother's calling us for supper. Come on, let's go. (*Runs offstage, calling*) We're coming, Mother.

BETTY (*As she runs offstage*): 'Bye, kittens. See you tomorrow.

HAPPY: I love to play with Betty and Bobby.

NAPPY: So do I. They always think of good games.

HAPPY: I'm glad I took off my mittens.

NAPPY: Why don't you take yours off, Scrappy?

SCRAPPY: Because Mother said *be careful*. (*Sound of dog barking*)

NAPPY: Look out! That's Sport.
HAPPY (*Looking offstage*): He's out of the dog house!
SCRAPPY (*As barking gets louder*): He's coming into our yard.
HAPPY *and* NAPPY: Let's run. Let's run.
SCRAPPY (*Standing his ground in fighting position*): I'm not running away any more. That dog has chased me up a tree for the last time.
NAPPY: What are you going to do?
SCRAPPY: Scratch his nose good and proper, so he will leave me alone.
HAPPY: But you can't scratch his nose. You're wearing your mittens. (SPORT *rushes in with wild barking and much jumping.*)
HAPPY: Run, Scrappy, run!
NAPPY: Hurry! Hurry! Hurry!
SCRAPPY (*Removing mittens and advancing on* SPORT): This time I'm ready for you. (SPORT *and* SCRAPPY *play in cat and dog manner.* SPORT *barks and rushes at* SCRAPPY. SCRAPPY *hisses and spits, and makes passes at* SPORT. *The other two kittens meow in fright. Finally* SCRAPPY *strikes out toward* SPORT *and there is a dreadful howl.* SPORT *holds his nose and runs off.*)
HAPPY *and* NAPPY: You got him! You got him!
SCRAPPY (*Dusting off his paws*): I guess I showed him who's boss in this yard. He'll never come back here again.
MOTHER (*Entering*): Happy! Nappy! Scrappy! Time for supper.

KITTENS: We're coming, Mother. We're coming. (*They run to* MOTHER.)
HAPPY: Mother, Mother, Scrappy chased Sport right out of our yard.
NAPPY: He was very brave.
SCRAPPY: I scratched his nose and he ran and ran. (*As kittens and* MOTHER *talk,* SPORT *steals back on stage. He picks up mittens, shakes them in puppy fashion and runs off with them.*)
MOTHER: That's fine. But where are your mittens?
KITTENS: We took them off.
HAPPY: I couldn't catch a ball with those mittens.
NAPPY: I couldn't catch a toy mouse with those mittens.
SCRAPPY: I couldn't scratch Sport's nose with those mittens.
MOTHER: Just as I told you! They were for Sunday and not for everyday! Now go find them at once. (KITTENS *run to look for mittens and discover they are gone. They return to* MOTHER, *heads hanging.*)
KITTENS: Oh, Mother dear, we *sadly* fear our mittens we have lost!
MOTHER: What! Lost your mittens! You naughty kittens! Then you shall have no pie!
KITTENS: Meow! Meow! Meow! (BOBBY *and* BETTY *run in with mittens.*)
BETTY: That naughty Sport! I know these mittens belong to those poor little kittens.
BETTY *and* BOBBY: Here, kitty, kitty, kitty.
BETTY: Come get your mittens! Come get your mittens!

KITTENS: Look, Mother, look! They've found our mittens! (KITTENS *run to* BETTY *and* BOBBY *and get their mittens.*)
BETTY: There, you have your mittens back again!
BOBBY: And don't ever leave them where Sport can get hold of them!
KITTENS: Meow! Meow! Meow!
BETTY: I think the kittens are saying thank you.
BOBBY: You're welcome, kittens. Goodbye.
BETTY: We'll be over to play with you tomorrow. (*Exit children*)
KITTENS (*Running to* MOTHER): See, Mother! We've found our mittens. Now, may we please have some pie?
MOTHER: I'll think it over. But remember, from now on, you keep your mittens for Sunday best!
KITTENS: Meow! Meow! Meow!
MOTHER: And now let's see about that pie.
KITTENS: Purr! Purr! Purr! (*The curtain closes. The* CHORAL SPEAKING GROUP *resumes the story, again sounding like the mother and the kittens.*)
SPEAKER: So that's the end of our story, just as it says in the poem.
ALL:
Three little kittens they found their mittens,
And they began to cry:
"Oh, Mother dear, see here, see here,
Our mittens we have found."
"Put on your mittens, you silly kittens,

And you shall have some pie!"
Purr-r, purr-r, purr-r!
Now they shall have their pie!
Purr-r, purr-r, purr-r. (*Curtain*)

THE END

THE TEDDY BEAR HERO

Characters

BRUCE	TEDDY THE TOUGHY
TOMMY	TEDDY THE TEASE
BEN	TEDDY THE TOMBOY
CINDY	TEDDY THE TEARFUL
BEVERLY	TAGALONG TEDDY
PEGGY	SCOUT LEADER
TEDDY THE TERROR	THE SCOUT PATROL

SETTING: *A picnic grove with a long table center stage. The table bears a sign,* FOR TEDDY BEARS ONLY. *At either side of the stage are clumps of bushes or trees large enough to conceal several children.*

AT RISE: *Six children enter with picnic baskets, thermos jugs, a beach ball and any other picnic equipment.*

TOMMY: This looks like a good place for a picnic.
BRUCE: I hope there's a swimming pool.
BEVERLY: It's cool and dark in here and sort of spooky. I don't know if I like it.
BEN: It's always cool and dark in the woods. This looks like a good place for Indians or bears.
CINDY: You're just trying to scare us. Come on, let's put our things on this table.

PEGGY: Oh, look! There's a sign. I wonder what it means. (*All gather around table and put down picnic baskets.*)

BEN (*Reading*): FOR TEDDY BEARS ONLY! That must be some sort of joke.

BRUCE: If this table is for Teddy Bears only, I guess that makes us Teddy Bears.

TOMMY: I'm as hungry as a bear right now. Let's eat.

BEVERLY: Funny there aren't any people around. Picnic places are always crowded on Memorial Day.

BEN: So much more room for us. Where's the lemonade?

PEGGY: Right here . . . only. . . .

BEN: Only what?

PEGGY: Only I wonder if we should put our things on this table when it says, FOR TEDDY BEARS ONLY.

BRUCE: There isn't any other table. And besides, what would Teddy Bears want with a picnic table?

CINDY: Maybe they're having a picnic the same as we are.

TOMMY: Who ever heard of Teddy Bears having a picnic? (SCOUT PATROL *enters singing.*)

SCOUT PATROL (*To tune of "Pop Goes the Weasel"*):
All around and through the woods,
The Teddy Bears will picnic.
All the other folks beware!
Bears on a picnic!

SCOUT LEADER (*To squad*): Halt! (*To children*) What are you doing here? Don't you see that sign, FOR TEDDY BEARS ONLY?

BRUCE: Yes, sir, we saw it, but we didn't understand it.
CINDY: Are the Teddy Bears really having a picnic?
SCOUT LEADER: They certainly are. And if you know what's good for you, you'll leave at once.
TOMMY: But why should we be afraid of Teddy Bears? They never hurt anyone.
SCOUT LEADER: They just don't like anyone around when they're having a picnic. My Scout Patrol is making sure the woods are cleared.
CINDY: Thanks for warning us.
SCOUT LEADER: You're welcome. And now we must go up to the road and warn everyone else to stay away from the woods today. (*To squad*) Squad, attention! Forward march! (SCOUT PATROL *marches out, repeating song.*)
PEGGY: Let's hurry and get out of here fast.
BRUCE: Oh, don't get so excited. I still don't believe a Teddy Bear would hurt anyone.
BEVERLY: How do you know?
BRUCE: Haven't you ever had a Teddy Bear?
BEVERLY: Oh, sure, lots of them.
BRUCE: Then you know they are too soft and cuddly to hurt anyone.
TOMMY: Bruce is right. Let's stay to see the fun.
BEN: Do you suppose they play games and run races and maybe have a peanut scramble? (*Off-stage rumble, a sound similar to thunder.*)
ALL (*Startled*): What's that?
BEN: Sounds like thunder to me!
BEVERLY: It's the Teddy Bears! They're growling! Let's

hide! Let's hide! (*Another off-stage rumble, even louder.*)

PEGGY: Hurry! Hurry! I'm afraid!

CINDY: Here they come! Here they come! (*Children run for cover behind the bushes, taking their picnic things—all but a box of sandwiches. The* TEDDY BEARS *march in, single file, each one carrying a basket.*)

TEDDY BEARS (*Singing to the tune of "Heigh-Ho," from "Snow White and the Seven Dwarfs"*):
Heigh-ho, heigh-ho,
It's picnic time, you know,
We'll romp and play the whole long day,
Heigh-ho, heigh-ho,
Heigh-ho, heigh-ho,
We'll have a jolly show,
We Teddy Bears will all be gay,
With a heigh, heigh-ho!

TAGALONG TEDDY (*Running in after the others have marched around the stage*): Wait for me! Wait for me!

ALL (*In disgust*): It's Tagalong Teddy!

TEDDY THE TERROR: What are you doing here? We told you not to come along.

TAGALONG: But this is a picnic, and I love picnics!

TEDDY THE TOUGHY: You can't come. We won't let you!

TAGALONG: But I belong here! This is a picnic for Teddy Bears!

TEDDY THE TEASE: But you're not a regular Teddy Bear. You don't look like the rest of us.

TEDDY THE TOMBOY: You're a sissy Teddy Bear! All dressed up in a red, white and blue suit.
TEDDY THE TEARFUL: Go away! We don't want you to play with us.
TAGALONG: I won't go away! I won't! I won't!
TEDDY THE TOUGHY: Then keep right on tagging along with us! But we won't let you play in any of our games.
TEDDY THE TEASE: Let's not bother with him. Come on! Here's our table. Let's eat. (*As they approach the table, they see the sandwich box.*)
ALL: Sniff and snarl! Growl and roar! Someone's used this spot before.
TEDDY THE TOMBOY: Growl and growl and mutter, mutter!
I smell ham and peanut butter!
TEDDY THE TERROR: Search the woods! Drag them out! We'll have no one else about.
(TEDDY BEARS *scatter and make a search of the stage. They soon discover the hidden children and drag them out, shouting, "Here they are! Here they are!"*)
TEDDY THE TERROR: Line them up in front of the table. They are our prisoners. (*The* TEDDY BEARS *line children up.*) Now, explain what you are doing here at the Teddy Bears' picnic.
BRUCE: We always have a picnic on Memorial Day.
TEDDY THE TOUGHY: Didn't you see that sign: FOR TEDDY BEARS ONLY?
TOMMY: Yes, we saw it, but we didn't think you'd mind.

TEDDY THE TOMBOY: Well, we *do* mind. We mind very, very much.

TEDDY THE TEASE: We don't allow strangers at our picnics. They're just for Teddy Bears.

BEN: Then what about him? (*Pointing to* TAGALONG) He's a Teddy Bear, and you don't even want him at your picnic.

TEDDY THE TEARFUL: Oh, him! He's not a *real* Teddy Bear at all.

PEGGY: How do you know he's not a real Teddy Bear?

BEVERLY: He looks like a Teddy Bear, and he acts like a Teddy Bear.

TEDDY THE TERROR: But he's red, white and blue.

TOMMY: What's the matter with red, white and blue?

BRUCE: They're the best colors in the whole, wide world.

TAGALONG: That's what the Major said.

CINDY: They're the colors of the American flag.

PEGGY (*To* TAGALONG): You should be very proud of those colors.

TAGALONG: That's what the Major said.

BEVERLY: Who is the Major?

TAGALONG: The Major is my friend. He gave me these colors.

TEDDY THE TERROR: What are you talking about?

TEDDY THE TOUGHY: We never heard of any Major.

TAGALONG: That's because you never listen to me. You never let me talk.

TEDDY THE TERROR: Go ahead. You may talk now. We're listening.

TEDDY THE TEASE: I'll bet he's only making this up. I'll bet he doesn't even know a major.

TAGALONG: I do so. The Major was my friend. He and I were in the war together.

TEDDY BEARS (*Holding their sides with laughter*): Ho! Ho! Ho! That's a good one! Imagine a Teddy Bear in the war!

TEDDY THE TEASE: What did you do in the war, Tagalong? Did you tag along ten miles behind the soldiers so you wouldn't get hurt?

TAGALONG: Now you're making fun of me, but I don't care. It's true. I *was* in the war with the Major, and I saved his life. (*More laughter from* TEDDY BEARS)

BRUCE: Won't you please let him tell his story? Maybe he did save the Major's life.

CINDY: Please go on with your story.

TAGALONG: Well, I met the Major in England. I wasn't a red, white and blue Teddy Bear then. I was golden brown like the rest of you, and when the Major came into the toy shop, he thought I was the prettiest Teddy Bear there.

TEDDY THE TOMBOY: What was the Major doing in a toy shop?

TAGALONG: He was looking for a toy for his little boy, and he found me. His little boy and I had the same name—Teddy. He knew Teddy would like me as much as he did, so he took good care of me. The other men in the crew of the Major's plane liked me, too. They called me their . . . I forget the word. It began with an "M."

BEN: Mascot? Is that the word?

TAGALONG: Yes. It meant that I would bring them luck as long as I rode in the plane.

BRUCE: And did you bring them luck?

TAGALONG: I guess so, because we went on a lot of missions. But one night we ran into trouble.

TEDDY THE TERROR: What happened?

TAGALONG: The enemy chased us. One wing was on fire and one of the engines was out. I was in the pilot's seat with the Major. Suddenly he picked me up and stuffed me inside his jacket. It was dark in there, but I could hear terrible noises. Then I felt a sharp pain in my side and the next thing I knew we were back at the base. I was on the Major's bed, and some of my sawdust was running out of a big hole in my middle.

TEDDY THE TEARFUL: Oh, dear. This is a very sad story. I don't like stories with unhappy endings.

TAGALONG: This story has a good ending. The Major cut a piece out of his jacket and sewed me up. I was as good as new, only I didn't look very nice. I was afraid the Major would buy a new toy for Teddy.

BEVERLY: But he didn't buy a new toy, did he?

TAGALONG: No, indeed. He said I had saved his life and helped him bring the plane back safely. He and the co-pilot got some red, white and blue paint and gave me a brand-new coat to hide the patches. The Major said they might be funny colors for a Teddy Bear, but if they were good enough for the American flag, they were good enough for me!

BRUCE: Tagalong, you're a real hero. You saved a soldier's life.

TOMMY: You Teddy Bears should be ashamed of yourselves! Don't you know that Memorial Day is a day for honoring our country's heroes? And you won't even let Tagalong come to your picnic!

TEDDY THE TERROR: I guess we are ashamed, Tagalong. We just didn't understand.

TEDDY THE TOUGHY: But we'll make it up to you, Tagalong. Honest, we will.

TEDDY THE TOMBOY: You can be the captain of all our teams.

TEDDY THE TEASE: And we'll never tease you again.

TEDDY THE TEARFUL: I'm sorry we called you Tagalong. We'll call you the Teddy Bear hero, if you'll just be friends.

TAGALONG: Sure, I'll be friends. But I like my name. Tagalong is a good name for a Teddy Bear. I like it fine.

TEDDY THE TERROR: Then what do you say we make our picnic in honor of Tagalong, our own Teddy Bear hero?

TEDDY BEARS: Hooray! Hooray for the Teddy Bear hero!

TAGALONG: Thanks, everybody. But I'd like to invite my new friends to stay, too. How about it?

TEDDY THE TERROR: How about it, boys and girls? Will you join us in our picnic and show us how to honor our Teddy Bear hero in true Memorial Day style?

CHILDREN: Thank you. We'll be glad to stay.
BRUCE: And the best way to honor our Teddy Bear hero and all of America's heroes is to give three big cheers for the red, white, and blue. (*All help* TAGALONG *to jump up on the table. Then the* TEDDY BEARS *and the children unite in singing the third chorus of "Columbia, the Gem of the Ocean."*)
ALL: Three cheers for the red, white, and blue!
Three cheers for the red, white, and blue!
The army and navy forever,
Three cheers for the red, white, and blue!
(*While they repeat this chorus, the* SCOUT PATROL *enters. The* PATROL *performs a short flag drill, ending with a tableau as the curtains close.*)

THE END

PRODUCTION NOTES

The Busy Barbers
Characters: 14 male; 23 female.
Playing Time: 15 minutes.
Costumes: Children wear everyday school clothes. Barbers wear white uniforms. Presto wears a long-tailed coat and a fierce mustache. His helper may wear a yellow or gold uniform. Barber Pole wears a cylinder of paper painted the traditional red and white, and a tall red-and-white-striped hat.
Properties: Three pairs of large silver cardboard scissors, three combs, and three large towels or bibs, for Barbers; one pair of large gold cardboard scissors and a folding canvas chair, for Presto; folding screen with sign "Tricky Haircuts," for Presto's Helper and Barber Pole; name signs, for children; name signs and umbrellas, for mothers.
Setting: A barber shop. There are three large chairs at center stage, and chairs or benches upstage for customers.
Lighting: No special effects.

The Half-Pint Cowboy
Characters: 23 male.
Playing Time: 15 minutes.
Costumes: Traditional cowboy clothes and hats, for Cowboys. Rustlers wear black cowboy suits and masks. Indians wear war outfits and feathered headdresses. Little Red Dog wears Indian suit and blanket.
Properties: Broomstick horses, guns, tomahawks, peace pipe, bundle containing a bandanna and sandwich, tied in another bandanna, and guns.
Setting: The Bar-X Ranch. Along the back of the stage is a rail fence. Near center stage is a small campfire, over which hangs a big cooking kettle with a spoon in it. Beside the fire is a wooden bench, with a water bucket, dipper, some tin plates and spoons on it.
Lighting: No special effects.

The Broken Broomstick
Characters: 5 male; 3 female; 3 Small Skeletons and 3 Jack-o-Lanterns may be male or female; there may be as many children as desired, male or female.
Playing Time: 15 minutes.
Costumes: Little Witch wears a long black robe and a pointed

hat. Skeletons wear black leotards with white "bones" sewn on. Black Cat is dressed in black and has whiskers and a bushy tail. The Ghosts wear sheets. Jack-o-Lanterns wear orange tissue paper over a frame; faces are drawn on the paper, and each carries a flashlight inside the frame. Mr. Goblin is dressed in all green. Mr. Owl is dressed in brown, has wings, and wears a graduation cap and spectacles. Old Woman wears a long dress and apron. Children are dressed in everyday clothes.

Properties: Broken broomstick, for Witch; hand mirror, for Goblin; broom, for Old Woman.

Setting: A clearing in the woods. There should be at least one tree stump. There may be as many other trees, stumps, bushes, etc. as desired.

Lighting: No special effects.

Spunky Punky

Characters: 4 female, 5 male; 11 male or female; 2 or more male or female for Sunbeams.

Playing Time: 15 minutes.

Costumes: The pumpkins wear orange cardboard circles concealing their bodies. Each circle is covered with green crepe paper. Spunky's cardboard has been cut in the form of a jack-o'-lantern. Scarecrow, Blue Jay, and Sunbeams wear typical costumes. The Witches are in traditional witch costumes. Farmer Boys, Jack and Jill wear appropriate attire.

Properties: Watering can, 3 hoes, 3 brooms.

Setting: A garden. Stage is bare, but backdrop of a field may be used if desired.

Lighting: No special effects.

The Wishing Stream

Characters: 4 male; 4 female; as many male and female extras as desired to be members of the Chorus and the Orchestra.

Playing Time: 15 minutes.

Costumes: All of the characters are in Chinese costumes and wear coolie hats. The Old Woman wears a long cloak with a hood, and carries a cane. Under her cloak she wears a beautiful costume.

Properties: Kazoos, combs and other rhythm band instruments for the Orchestra; scroll for Property Man; lunch basket containing cookies and cakes for Small Sister; tray with teakettle and cups for the Maids; bait (small magnets) for children; cane, firewood for Old Woman. In the Property Chest are the following items: roll of blue cloth for stream; cardboard or metal fish; three fishing rods; Chinese umbrella; basket; net. (If the fish for the stream are cut out of thin sheet metal, it will be easy for the children to "catch" the fish with the magnets on the fishing lines. If cardboard fish are used, a piece of metal should be attached to each fish.)

Setting: The stage is bare except for two rows of chairs, one at right and one at left, a large chest upstage center, and a Chinese gong beside the chest.

Lighting: No special effects.

THE LIBRARY CIRCUS

Characters: 9 male; 16 male or female; any number of children.

Playing Time: 15 minutes.

Costumes: The Barker wears a derby hat and a bright tie. The Ringmaster and Animal Trainer are dressed in jodhpurs, cutaway coats and tall silk hats. The clowns are dressed appropriately. The animals should all wear overall clown costumes: gray for the elephants, brown for the bears, spotted brown and white or black and white for the dogs, etc. They should have ruffs around their necks, and wear the appropriate animal masks, if possible. Mr. Mouse has a top hat and cane. The children wear school clothes.

Properties: Megaphone; pair of cardboard eyeglasses; whip; small chair; two skipping ropes; wire hoop.

Setting: The stage represents the inside of a circus tent. Along the back is a row of bleachers or benches on a raised platform. On stage right are stools for the performing animals. Downstage left is the Barker's booth.

Lighting: No special effects.

Sound: Circus music and musical fanfare should be played off-stage as indicated.

THE MOTHER GOOSE BAKESHOP

Characters: 8 male; 6 female; 1 male or female; as many extras as desired.

Playing Time: 10 minutes.

Costumes: The bakers wear long white aprons and tall chefs' hats. Mr. Frosting wears a chef's hat decorated to simulate frosted ornaments. The Mother Goose characters are dressed in traditional costumes. Teacher and birthday boy or girl and other children wear everyday school clothes.

Properties: 3 large wooden spoons; 3 large sugar shakers; 3 hand egg beaters; large mixing bowl; 3 cake pans; sheets of paper for "orders"; small sugar cake; doughnuts; small pie; cinnamon bun; loaves of bread; notebook and pencil; cardboard boxes; large birthday cake on a cake stand; large shopping bag.

Setting: A bakeshop. There is a counter slightly left of center stage with a few cake stands, loaves of bread, and a jar of

doughnuts. There is also a tray of paper bags presumably filled with cakes, cookies, pies, etc. Slightly right of center is a small work table on which are a huge mixing bowl and the cake pans, sugar shakers, and egg beaters.
Lighting: No special effects.

THANKFUL'S RED BEADS

Characters: 7 male; 3 female.
Playing Time: 15 minutes.
Costumes: Puritan dress. The Mother and the girls wear long, dark dresses and white aprons. Thankful's dress has a large white fichu or collar. The boys and the Father are dressed in dark breeches and jackets. The Indians wear brightly colored blankets, and war paint.
Properties: Silver buckles sewn on elastic bands; bright-colored shawl; long blue scarf; small box containing string of large red beads (wooden ones will do), strung on lightweight thread that will tear with a sharp yank; small pile of wood; pail of water; tomahawks; tin trays of bread or rolls.
Setting: The stage represents a colonial cabin. There is a fireplace, center, flanked by a large dower chest and a bench for water buckets. There are several stools, a spinning wheel, and a rough table. Characters entering from another room in the cabin enter right; those coming from the outside enter left.
Lighting: No special effects.

A THANKSGIVING RIDDLE

Characters: 5 male; 6 female.
Playing Time: 15 minutes.
Costumes: Everyday school clothes, for children. Tailored suit or dress, for Miss Harper. Five Puritan caps and aprons, for girls; five Puritan hats, for boys.
Properties: Three card tables, and white paper to cover them. Large, bright-colored cardboard turkey gobbler, its tail spread out like a fan. In the tail there are eleven feathers, which can be pulled out of their cardboard slots. Toy broom, for Mabel; rulers or other wood, for Billy; sewing basket and stool, for Rose; toy hoe, paper fish, and scissors, for Mike; book, for Molly; yardstick, for Ralph and Sam; basket, for Cindy; pointer, string, and paper fish, for Johnny; wooden bowl and block of wood, for Penny.
Setting: An ordinary classroom.
Lighting: No special effects.

A VISIT TO GOLDILOCKS

Characters: 2 male; 3 female; 4 male or female.
Playing Time: 12 minutes.
Costumes: The Three Bears are dressed as bears. The owls

wear owl costumes. Goldilocks wears a pretty dress. Her mother wears a cotton dress and an apron. Goldilocks' father wears a sport shirt and slacks.

Properties: Newspaper, sewing, doll, milk, cookies.

Setting: SCENE 1: A clearing in the woods. The stage may be bare, or may be set with trees, flowers, etc., as desired. SCENE 2: A room in the home of Goldilocks. There are two chairs for her parents and three empty chairs of different sizes. A screen may serve as a door.

Lighting: No special effects.

THE LOST CHRISTMAS CARDS

Characters: 7 male; 6 female; 8 male or female.

Playing Time: 15 minutes.

Costumes: Winter wraps for Children in Scene 1. School clothes for all Children. Uniform for Postman. Large placards, addressed like Christmas cards, for Season's Greeting Quartet.

Properties: Christmas cards, for Children; mail pouch, for Postman; prepared address and return address stickers, for Trudy and Bill.

Setting: Scene 1, before curtain, is a street corner with a mailbox in center. Scene 2 is a schoolroom. There are two tables on stage, and a white flannel board upstage center. At one table are 4 trays of Christmas cards. At the other is a big box, overturned to show piles of Christmas cards spilling out.

Lighting: No special effects.

WAKE UP, SANTA CLAUS!

Characters: 6 male; 3 female; 7 male or female; several male or female extras.

Playing Time: 15 minutes.

Costumes: Santa wears traditional costume, but does not wear his jacket and hat while sleeping; Mrs. Santa wears traditional costume; Roly, Poly and the Elves wear leotards which may have Christmas decorations; Mr. Tick-Tock wears coveralls; Reindeer Master wears work clothes; the animal costumes may be as simple or elaborate as desired; Oopah and See-Gloo wear snowsuits, with fur-trimmed hoods, if possible.

Properties: Knitting and feather duster, for Mrs. Santa; tool kit containing tools, wires, springs, wheels, etc., for Mr. Tick-Tock; sleigh bells, for Reindeer Master; fur mittens, for Oopah and See-Gloo.

Setting: Santa's bedroom. There is a small cot for Santa. Hanging on a nearby clothes tree are his red coat and cap. On a bed table are his spectacles and a big alarm clock. Near Santa's bed is a rocking chair

for Mrs. Santa. Piled at the foot of the bed are several green bags, filled with drums, wood blocks, triangles, sand blocks, Indian headdresses, cowboy hats, etc.
Lighting: No special effects.

THE REAL PRINCESS

Characters: 10 male; 8 female.
Playing Time: 15 minutes.
Costumes: The King, Queen, and Prince wear royal robes and crowns. The Wise Men are bearded and wear long black robes. The Page and Servants are dressed in tights and tunics. The Princesses, except for Princess Sunday, should each wear a long dress or robe of one of the six colors of the rainbow. Princess Sunday wears dirty and ragged clothes.
Properties: Six placards with the days of the week printed plainly on them.
Setting: The stage represents a room in the palace. There is a long table at center, with nine chairs. Thrones may be placed at back center, if desired.
Lighting: No special effects.

THE SAFETY CLINIC

Characters: 8 male; 11 female.
Playing Time: 15 minutes.
Costumes: Modern dress. The nurse wears a white uniform, and the doctors may wear white coats. The patients are appropriately bandaged.
Properties: Thermometer; large bottle of "pills"; cane or crutch; placards bearing large red, green, and yellow circles; large syringe, of the type used for basting meat; cotton swab; throat stick; small red pincushion on a ribbon; three boxes of facial tissue; three empty glasses; placard with words to Safe Skating song; jar of "Sticky Salve"; small notebook and pencil.
Setting: The stage represents the waiting room of a clinic. The chairs and benches for patients are at back center. The doctor's desk, with a chair beside it, is at right. At left is an easel on which the placards may be displayed.
Lighting: No special effects.

TEN PENNIES FOR LINCOLN

Characters: 3 male; 3 female; 15 or more male or female.
Playing Time: 10 minutes.
Costumes: Modern dress for all.
Properties: Bowl or bank and pennies.
Setting: A club meeting. Stage is decorated with Lincoln theme, including a picture of Lincoln and an American flag. A table with three chairs is on one side and chairs for members on the other.
Lighting: No special effects.

The Country Store Cat

Characters: 15 male; 6 female; 6 or more male or female. (Children may double in the roles of storekeepers and mice, if desired.)
Playing Time: 12 minutes.
Costumes: The storekeepers all wear large white aprons and shirts with cardboard cuffs. Each of the pantomiming storekeepers carries an article appropriate to his own shop. The clerk is in shirtsleeves, with a pencil behind his ear. Billy, wearing everyday clothing, puts on a long white apron, cardboard cuffs, eyeglasses and a mustache, as indicated. The customers are dressed as grown-ups. The cat and mice may wear simple or elaborate animal costumes, as desired.
Properties: Jars of candy; scales; paper bags; ball of string; round cheese container; broom; bowl of milk.
Setting: The stage represents a country store with a long counter across the back. On the counter are the jars of candy, scales, paper bags, string, and container of cheese. In front of the counter, at one side of the stage, is a cracker barrel, plainly labeled. On stage right and left, backdrops painted to simulate shelves of goods may be used to increase the effect.

Wait and See

Characters: 4 male; 9 female.
Playing Time: 10 minutes.
Costumes: Modern, everyday dress. The children may wear party clothes, if desired. The fairies wear ballet costumes.
Properties: Cups and saucers, for Mr. and Mrs. Button; six gift-wrapped packages, for the children; paper and crayons, for Betsy; birthday cake with candles; cardboard box containing two cupcakes with small candles; two "birthday cards."
Setting: The stage represents a dining room, with a table downstage right. There are sufficient chairs, cabinets, bookcases, etc., to provide hiding places for the children. (This furniture can be simulated of cardboard.)
Lighting: No special effects.

The Shower of Hearts

Characters: 12 male; 8 female; any number, male or female, for Vendors and Children.
Playing Time: 15 minutes.
Costumes: All costumes are decorated with hearts. The King and Queen wear royal robes and crowns. The Jack of Hearts may wear royal robes, but he does not wear a crown. The Pages, Ladies-in-Waiting, Guards and Herald may wear the traditional costumes of royal attendants. The

Kitchen Maid wears a white cap and apron. The Weatherman is bearded, and wears a long, gray robe trimmed with hearts, and carries two black umbrellas trimmed with hearts. The Children wear everyday dress; the Vendors, red and white costumes.

Properties: Black umbrellas for the Weatherman; hand-bells and decorated tea wagons loaded with valentines for Vendors; umbrellas for Children, Queen, and Ladies-in-Waiting; poem for King; basket containing tarts for Jack.

Setting: The throne room of the King and Queen of Hearts. Two thrones decorated with hearts are in the center of the stage.

Lighting: No special effects.

Sound: Off-stage thunder, as indicated.

The Weatherman on Trial

Characters: 5 male; 2 female; 6 male or female, to be Raindrops; any number, male or female, to be Jury.

Playing Time: 15 minutes.

Costumes: The Judge wears black robes. Babe Booth wears a baseball uniform. The Raindrops wear blue plastic raincoats and hats. All the other characters wear everyday modern dress.

Properties: Gavel for Judge; hatbox containing bedraggled bonnet for District Attorney; sheet of tin for Weatherman.

Setting: A court room. The Jury is seated in two rows of chairs at right. The Judge sits in a chair mounted on a small platform at center. The witness stand is beside the Judge's chair. There is a table, downstage left, for the District Attorney and the Weatherman. Extra chairs should be placed at this table for the Raindrops.

Lighting: No special effects.

Old Glory Grows Up

Characters: 5 male; 4 female; 10 male or female.

Playing Time: 10 minutes.

Costumes: George Washington and Betsy Ross wear traditional Colonial attire. Washington has a white wig tied with a black ribbon. The five speakers wear red, white, and blue paper caps. Vermont is a girl in Colonial costume; Kentucky is a boy in pioneer outfit. Francis Scott Key wears the appropriate dress of the period. Uncle Sam and Columbia wear traditional costumes. The Confederate boy and girl are in Civil War costume; New Mexico and Arizona wear cowboy or pioneer outfits. Alaska is dressed as an Eskimo, and Hawaii, in South Seas costume. The government officials and Narrator may wear modern dress, or period costumes.

Properties: Six large cards bearing the dates 1777, 1795, 1818, 1861-1865, 1912, and 1960; red and white stripes for flannel board flag; notebook, for Francis Scott Key; document; fields of fifteen, twenty, thirty-four, forty-six, and fifty stars, for flag; two Confederate flags; stars, for New Mexico and Arizona.
Setting: The stage is bare. On the apron of stage is an easel bearing a large placard labeled "Old Glory." Under the placard are six date cards, arranged in order. At upstage center is a large cardboard Colonial flag, with a flannel board field. Beside the flag is a table or small sewing stand on which the other fields are placed so they will be available as needed.
Lighting: No special effects.

Garden Hold-up

Characters: 18 or more, male and female. Cast may be all-boy or all-girl, if desired.
Playing Time: 15 minutes.
Costumes: Gardeners and Farmers wear overalls and straw hats. Robins, Rabbits, and Squirrels wear typical animal or bird costumes. Jack Frost wears elf costume. Weatherman wears coat and hat.
Properties: Each Gardener has a red bandanna and a cardboard carton containing a toy shovel, toy rake, pack of seeds, and small watering can.
Setting: A garden. Stage is bare, but backdrop of trees may be used if desired.
Lighting: No special effects.

The Rabbits Who Changed Their Minds

Characters: 3 male; 1 female; 15 male or female.
Playing Time: 15 minutes.
Costumes: Rabbits wear rabbit costumes. Easter Elves wear bright-colored costumes representing pieces of candy. Peppermint Stick Guards wear red-and-white-striped uniforms. Chefs wear white coats and caps. Candy King wears a red robe and a candy crown.
Properties: Easter baskets, eggs, 3 toy wheelbarrows, washtub, large pitcher and big brush.
Setting: A forest glade. At right is a worktable and at left is a large toadstool. A backdrop of trees, flowers, etc., may be used.
Lighting: No special effects.
Sound: Sound of thunder and recorded march music.

Trouble in Tick-Tock Town

Characters: 7 male; 6 female; 12 male or female.
Playing Time: 12 minutes.
Costumes: Each "clock" is dressed in a costume suitable for the type of clock he represents. The twelve members of the Council of the Hours

wear long black robes and tall peaked hats. The gowns and hats are decorated with silver numbers and other suitable time symbols. The Time Fairies are dressed in ballet costumes: black for Night and white for Day. Tick and Tock wear the uniforms of guides. Tommy Tucker wears school clothes.

Properties: Rhythm sticks; wood blocks; gongs and chimes; bells; long sheet of paper; wrist watch.

Setting: The stage represents the Town Hall of Tick-Tock Town. A large cardboard clock face with movable hands is in center of stage, with the various clocks lined up, four on each side. At one side of the stage is a long table for the Council of the Hours. The chimes, bells, and other sound effects are on the table.

Lighting: No special effects.

May Day for Mother

Characters: 10 male; 10 female; any number of girls to be dancers.

Playing Time: 15 minutes.

Costumes: The Dancers wear pastel dresses. The May Queen's attendants may wear costumes suggesting the clothing of fairy tale royal attendants. Miss Jennie Jones first enters in a housecoat and bedroom slippers, her hair in pin curls. For the procession, Jennie wears her queen's dress and shoes, and her hair is combed out. (Jennie is wearing her queen's dress under her housecoat when she first enters, so that she does not have to change while the play is in progress. The dress carried onstage by the Maid should be similar to the dress Jennie is actually wearing.) All the other characters wear everyday modern clothing.

Properties: Cameras for Photographer and TV Cameraman; mike for Radio Interviewer; notebook for Reporter; golden crown on pillow for Crown-Bearer; bouquet for Flower Girl; trumpets for Heralds; brush and comb for Hairdresser; dress and shoes for Maids; bouquet of roses and wide ribbon with words "Queen Mother" for Emcee.

Setting: A traditional May Day scene. At center is the throne on a small platform. At left is the Maypole, hung with colorful streamers. The stage may be decorated with flowers, and the backdrop may depict an outdoor scene.

Lighting: No special effects.

Three Little Kittens

Characters: 5 male; 3 female; as many male and female extras as desired to be in the Choral Speaking Group.

Playing Time: 10 minutes.

Costumes: The children in the

Choral Speaking Group wear brightly colored bows tied under their chins, pussy-cat style. Betty and Bobby wear everyday clothing. Sport and the kittens may be dressed in animal costumes, or may wear only a few touches suggesting animals—tails, whiskers, etc.
Properties: Three pairs of mittens (one red, one white, and one blue); rubber ball on a string for Betty; toy mouse for Bobby.
Setting: No furnishings are required.
Lighting: No special effects.

THE TEDDY BEAR HERO

Characters: 4 male; 3 female; 6 male or female, to be bears; male extras for Scout Patrol.
Playing Time: 15 minutes.
Costumes: Everyday clothing for the children, uniforms for the Scout Patrol. The bears may wear animal masks and everyday clothing. Tagalong has a red, white, and blue costume on.
Properties: Picnic baskets, thermos jugs, ball, box of sandwiches.
Setting: A picnic grove. A long table is at center. On the table is a sign: FOR TEDDY BEARS ONLY. At either side of the stage are clumps of bushes or trees large enough to conceal several children.
Lighting: No special effects.

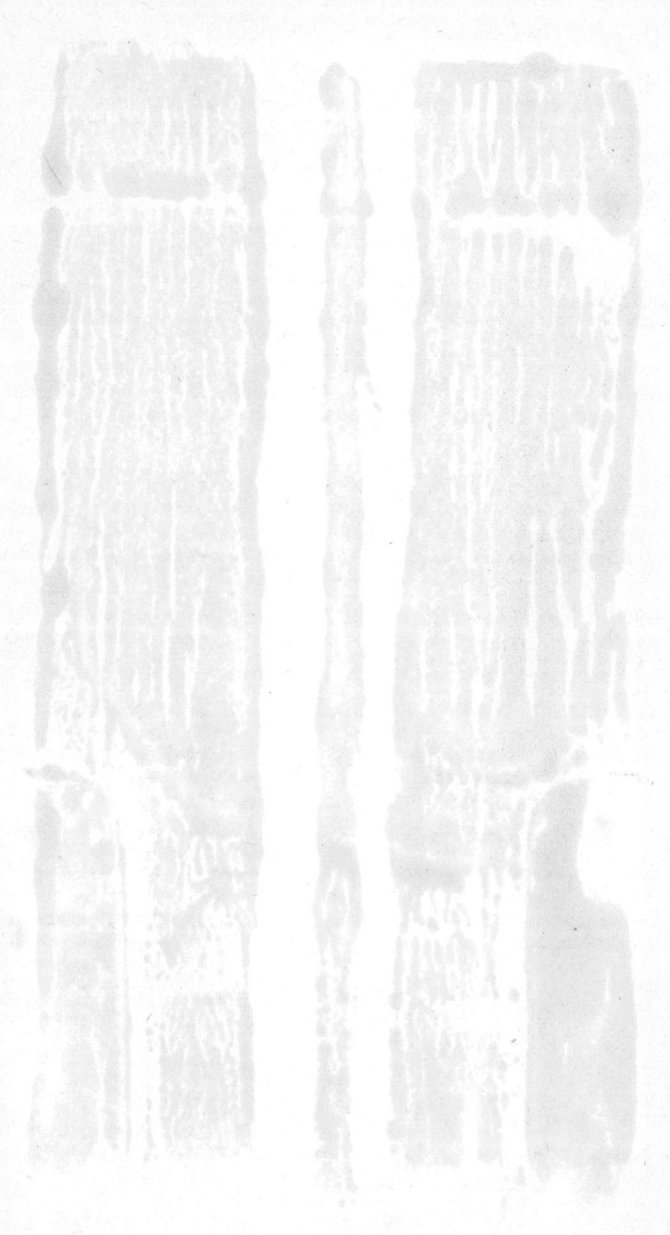

```
j812    Miller, H.L.
 Mil     1st plays for
         children


c.1
```

Clark Public Library
Clark, N. J.
388-5999